Marriage Matters
Extraordinary Change through Ordinary Moments

Winston T. Smith

New
Growth
Press

www.newgrowthpress.com

New Growth Press, Greensboro, NC 27404

Cover Design: faceoutbooks, Nate Salciccioli and Jeff Miller, www.faceoutbooks.com

Typesetting: Lisa Parnell, Thompson's Station, TN

ISBN-13: 978-1-935273-61-5
ISBN-10: 1-935273-61-2

Library of Congress Cataloging-in-Publication Data

Smith, Winston T., 1966–
    Marriage matters : extraordinary change through ordinary moments / Winston T. Smith.
        p. cm.
    Includes bibliographical references and index.
    ISBN-13: 978-1-935273-61-5 (alk. paper)
    ISBN-10: 1-935273-61-2 (alk. paper)
    1. Marriage—Religious aspects—Christianity. I. Title.
    BV835.S73 2010
    248.8'44—dc22

                                                              2010002966

Printed in the United States of America

24 23 22 21 20 19 18 17   8 9 10 11 12

TO MY KIM
*Your childlike delight in the most ordinary things,
your revelry in the good and your angry tears over the bad,
your humility and faithfulness—
in these and a thousand other ways
you show me the love of Christ every day.*

Contents

Preface   ix

Acknowledgments   xiii

Section 1: God Is in the Ordinary Moments

1   Marriages Change in Ordinary Moments   3

2   Ordinary Moments Reveal Our Problems with God   15

3   Worship: Extraordinary Love for God   25

4   Living in Jesus' Extraordinary Love   39

5   God's Dream for Your Marriage   57

Section 2: Extraordinary Love in the Details of Marriage

6   Person or Object, Honor or Manipulation?   75

7   Honesty Is Important   93

8   Being Honest about Yourself   107

9   Speaking the Truth to Your Spouse   121

10   God Is Up to Good in Conflict   137

11   Moving Forward in Conflict   151

12   Foundations of Forgiveness   163

13   Forgiveness in Marriage   181

14   Understanding Your Role   193

15   Intimacy and Sex   217

Section 3: Staying on the Path

16	Growing in Grace	239
17	Your Actions Make a Difference	253
18	Knowing Your Story	267

Notes	283
Scripture Index	287

Preface

IF YOU'VE VISITED the love/relationships section of a bookstore lately, you might well ask whether the world really needs another book on marriage. Though you're obviously holding my answer to that question, let me offer a brief explanation of how this book came to be.

Usually, unhappy couples want change and they want it fast. Who can blame them? When the source of your suffering is the relationship that stands at the center of your life, the suffering can be intense. In their unhappiness they look for solutions that offer the fastest, most dramatic change possible. But couples who experience the most significant, lasting change aren't the ones who have a dramatic "aha" moment or locate some forgotten secret to marriage. Rather, they're the couples who begin to see their day-to-day interactions from a different perspective, take simple steps to love one another more effectively, and take those steps over and over again. What used to devolve into pointless annoyances and fights become steps in a journey in which God's activity and love become increasingly evident and powerful.

The title communicates well what I hope you'll learn about marriage. First, marriage matters, not only because it's important to us, but also because it's important to God and he intends to use it in ways that you may not have imagined. Second, moments that seem the most ordinary—moments of annoyance, conflict, pain, or cold indifference—can become moments in which you're able to understand God's incredible agenda for love and begin to do something new. Ordinary moments are steps that take your marriage to extraordinary places and lead you into a deeper relationship with an extraordinary God.

I am especially hopeful that this book will be useful to those who find marriage a daily battle. I ask those couples to read this book thoughtfully and prayerfully, and with hope. During a difficult time in my own life, a wise friend and counselor reminded me of Jacob's wrestling match with God in Genesis 32. After wrestling all night, God asked Jacob to let him go and "touched the socket of Jacob's hip so that his hip was wrenched" (Genesis 32:25). But Jacob refused to give up and let go. Instead Jacob replied, "I will not let you go unless you bless me" (Genesis 32:26). And so God blessed him. "Winston," my friend said, "don't just wish things were different. Don't just look for the easy way out. Don't let go until you get every blessing that God is trying to give you through this." I pray that you'll hold on and wrestle well and that God will bless you with more than you've dared to ask for.

But I want you to understand, as well, that while a marriage book can be a tremendous help, if misused it can do as much harm as good. Therefore, let me offer a few precautions to keep you on track:

Don't read this book simply because you think your spouse *needs to read it.* No doubt, as you read it your spouse's failings will come to mind. But your real focus must be on how *you* can change. Resist the temptation to meditate on your spouse's shortcomings. Instead, concentrate on learning how to live a life of love and trust God with the results.

Don't allow any marriage book to become a substitute for personal support and counsel. God designed life and marriage to be community enterprises. A book may help, but the complexities of life and marriage will always require more than a good book. Strive to include trusted friends, godly ministers, and wise counselors on your journey, *especially if your spouse is battling addictions or is abusive.*

I hope that this book, in addition to being useful to individuals and couples, will be useful in other settings: small group Bible studies, Sunday school electives, perhaps even seminary classrooms.

One final note: Some of the examples in the book are fictionalized for the purposes of illustration. Others are composites of many different couples I've seen over the years who embody similar dynamics. Illustrations and examples aren't meant to foster gender stereotypes or give license to prejudice and are but an honest reflection on my own experience. They aren't intended to be prescriptive in any way.

Acknowledgments

I HAD NEVER given much thought to acknowledgment pages, but now that I've written a book I understand their absolute necessity. Without them, there would be no escaping a nagging sense of unworthiness as I consider the contributions others have made to this book. I sincerely want to thank the many people who have made this book possible:

Of course, thanks to my wife, Kim, for whom none of what follows is simply theoretical. Thanks for allowing me to think, teach, and write about such things when I've got so far to go myself. (If you ever regret letting me write it, just keep rereading the dedication page.)

A special thanks to John Bettler. After teaching a marriage counseling course for many years, John entrusted his course and many of his ideas to me. It would be impossible to separate his foundational wisdom from that which has developed over the past fifteen years, but I've tried to document in the notes the portions that I most clearly inherited from him. A wise and humble man, he has always been content to work in the background, while promoting the efforts of others. For all of these reasons, John, I admire and thank you. If you ever decide to write a marriage book, feel free to take back any ideas you entrusted to me—and freely refute any of mine!

Thanks to my friends and colleagues at CCEF, past and present: Ed Welch, David Powlison, Paul Tripp, Tim Lane, Mike Emlet, Jayne Clark, and Bill Smith, all of whom have deepened my understanding of Christ and the importance of living out his love in the details of life. Thanks to everyone at CCEF, counselors and staff who labor diligently to make it a ministry where Jesus is known.

Thanks to the many couples who I've worked with over the years. Thank you for honoring me by opening your lives to me. Thank you for your patience and kindness as we've learned together how to walk down difficult paths through dark moments. You have all been a blessing, and I thank God for you all.

Thanks to dear friends who over the years have lived out their marriages with openness and authenticity that have encouraged Kim and me in our own marriage: Tuck and Stacy, Arlin and Cathy, John and Joanna, David and Wendy, Kris and Dave, Bob and Seanne. Your friendship is a treasure.

Finally, many thanks to New Growth Press. Thanks, Mark and Karen, for taking risks with untried authors like me. Thanks to my editor, Jonathan Rogers, for reading, editing, and crafting my ramblings. Thanks, Barbara Juliani, for your instincts as a writer and editor and for staying on top of this project.

SECTION ONE

God Is in the Ordinary Moments

In chapter 1 we learn that change requires seeing from a new perspective. We must realize that the hurts and frustrations in marriage that are common to the point of seeming ordinary are, in fact, opportunities to know and share God's extraordinary love.

Chapter 2 shows how God uses ordinary moments to help us see ourselves more clearly and recognize what obstacles to knowing and sharing his love lurk in our hearts.

In chapter 3 we see how all struggles to love stem from problems of worship. We are transformed by God's love as we learn to build not just our marriages but our lives around him.

Chapter 4 reintroduces us to love itself—to Jesus. By learning love from him we are freed from distortions and misunderstandings and are empowered to love in new and surprising ways.

Finally, in chapter 5 we see that God's vision for marriage has always been grander than our own. All along he intended it to be nothing less than a celebration and a showcase of his love.

one

Marriages Change in Ordinary Moments

What You'll Learn in This Chapter:

- Our marriages are made up of ordinary moments, recurring irritations and disappointments. God doesn't seem involved in them, and we don't really expect them to change.
- Ordinary moments become extraordinary opportunities for change when we realize that:
  - ~ God is love and is involved in every moment in which we struggle to love.
  - ~ Jesus empowers us and teaches us how to love in practical, concrete ways.
  - ~ Change involves making daily choices to love consistently, over time.

An Ordinary Moment

I COULD FEEL my blood pressure rising. With every passing moment I was getting more and more angry. It was 2:30. My son's baseball practice was at 3:00, my daughter had a birthday party at 4:00, and I had to lead a Bible study at 5:00. What's more, my wife was not answering her cell phone. I'd been calling her every few minutes since 1:00, and now it was almost 2:30. She should have been home long ago. She knew what was on the schedule, and she'd assured me she'd be home on time.

How was I going to prepare my Bible study with all this taxiing to do? Did she not care that I was juggling this all by myself? My anger mounted as I pictured her chatting with friends, while her cell phone, set to vibrate, hummed away unnoticed in her handbag.

I resigned myself to plan B: all three kids would come to baseball practice, and the girls would play in an empty part of the field, while I sat in the van and worked on the Bible study. There would be distractions. I would want to watch practice, and the girls would need to be watched. They would get bored and start asking for things. It was not ideal, but it would have to do.

I barked orders at the kids to get ready to go. There were a hundred questions:

"Where's mommy?" "Why do *we* have to go to baseball practice?" "Am I going to miss my party?" "Where are my shoes?" "Can we stop at the store and get a snack?"

Every question was a frustrating reminder that I shouldn't have to be dealing with this.

Just then the phone rang, "Win, have you been trying to call me?"

"Yeeeeees," I replied, injecting as much sarcasm as possible into that one word. "I have to get Gresham to practice and Charlotte to her birthday party, and I'm not prepared for Bible study. Why haven't you answered your phone?"

"I didn't hear it ringing in my bag. I'm so sorry. I'll be home in a few minutes. I just couldn't get away as soon as I thought I could."

Instead of waiting for Kim to return and let her deliver our son to practice, I loaded the kids into the car and took them myself. When I returned home, fifteen minutes later, Kim was there wondering why I hadn't waited for her.

She retreated to a safe distance. I sat alone staring at the kitchen table. I was more than just annoyed; I was fuming. Beneath the anger I also felt embarrassed and ashamed. Part of me felt justified in my anger, while another part of me wondered why I'd gotten so worked up. Irritation would be understandable, but anger? My response was out of proportion, and I knew it.

I soon realized that part of my frustration stemmed from the fact that this feeling was familiar, even *ordinary*. How often have I been angry with Kim because I felt that she hasn't stopped to think about me? And how often have I had the same pouty reaction and witnessed the same destructive result?

I was tired of reliving this moment, tired of having the same old argument and getting the same old result.

What Makes Ordinary Moments Ordinary?

Every marriage has these moments—moments marked by frustration, disappointment, anger, or sadness—when you want things to be better but you've no idea what to do next or how to do things differently. We aren't perfect, and we don't marry perfect people.

Moments like these are ordinary in several other important ways.

Ordinary Moments Happen Over and Over Again

Maybe the exact thing happens over and over again. Maybe the same familiar thoughts, feelings, actions, and reactions haunt every difficult situation. For me, there have been many times when I felt that my wants or needs weren't showing up on Kim's radar (though on many of those occasions that was not actually the case). The situations aren't always the same: it isn't always baseball practice or errands or

Bible study. It can be the way money has been spent, or the status of the laundry, or how long it has been since we've slowed down enough to connect. But there's a familiar pattern in it all. There's my sense of being forgotten, followed by her surprise, then my smoldering anger, then her retreat. It's just too ordinary.

In Ordinary Moments God Seems Uninvolved

Because these moments happen again and again, it may be difficult to detect God's involvement. Perhaps you've never even thought to ask God for help precisely because these moments are so ordinary. Why bother God?

No matter how spiritual we think we are, it's easy to find ourselves living as if God were far, far away.

Maybe you're afraid to ask God to get involved because you're ashamed. You should be able to do better. God must be disappointed in you.

Or maybe you asked God for help, but there was no answer. God's apparent silence after prayer is especially hard. He seems more than uninvolved; he seems to have abandoned or forgotten you.

Whether or not you've sought God's help, these moments feel ordinary because they aren't accompanied by miracles or dramatic changes; they're God-*less* moments. If you don't see—or can't see—how God fits into the picture, it doesn't really matter whether you consider yourself a religious person or not.

Recall my own frustration with Kim when I was being denied time that I deemed necessary to prepare a Bible study. My mind was engaged in trying to know God's Word so that I could help others, and yet my heart was far from him. In the moment, it didn't occur to me to turn to God for help or to believe that he was concerned or involved. No matter how spiritual we think we are, it's easy to find ourselves living as if God were far, far away.

We Don't Expect Ordinary Moments to Change

If you've experienced enough of these ordinary moments without sensing any change, you either become accustomed to the annoyance and indifferent to it or, worse, you abandon any hope for change. Indifference and hopelessness are both dangerous. The danger isn't simply that you're unhappy or that your marriage is less than it could be; it's that God becomes increasingly irrelevant to your marriage, the relationship that defines your life more than any other.

God, in his mercy, has prevented Kim and me from ever reaching that point. As I sat fuming at the kitchen table, God, as always, began to work in my heart, reminding me of important truths, softening me so that we could move forward. Knowing God makes ordinary moments extraordinary.

How Ordinary Moments Become Extraordinary

In marriage, the biggest obstacle to change is our attitude toward it. Often we expect change to be ushered in by a dramatic turning point that can forever be remembered as the moment things got better.

We wish this turning point—this momentous change—would happen for our spouse rather than for us, right? They're the ones who need an experience like Ebenezer Scrooge had. Your spouse goes to bed dour and embittered, three spirits (or a marriage counselor) visit in the night, and the next morning he or she wakes up generous and joyful.

Sometimes lasting change happens quickly and dramatically, but usually this kind of change requires deliberate, careful steps over a long period of time. People who insist on quick fixes and dramatic turning points often miss the path to real, lasting change. What's more, the longer path to change is what the Bible holds out to us as the more typical way that God works in our lives. Usually, change is more like the Israelites' long trek to the Promised Land than like the apostle Paul's dramatic conversion on the road to Damascus.

Staying on the long path to change requires understanding how God operates in the ordinary moments. The path to change in your marriage is built on this truth: God is involved in every moment of your marriage. In that sense, there are no ordinary moments, only moments filled with God's activity, of which you may or may not be aware and in which you may or may not choose to participate. God is the ruler of the entire universe, and yet, he has a special concern for you, and he wants you to see him act in the ordinary details of your marriage. More than that, he wants you to be a part of that work.

Active Ingredients

In his first letter, the apostle John explains how God wants to make a difference in our relationships:

> Dear friends, let us love one another, for love comes from God. Everyone who loves has been born of God and knows God. Whoever does not love does not know God, because God is love. This is how God showed his love among us: He sent his one and only Son into the world that we might live through him. This is love: not that we loved God, but that he loved us and sent his Son as an atoning sacrifice for our sins. Dear friends, since God so loved us, we also ought to love one another. No one has ever seen God; but if we love one another, God lives in us and his love is made complete in us. (1 John 4:7–12)

This passage identifies three ingredients necessary for the ordinary moments of marriage to become extraordinary moments of change. These are the three critical ingredients that this book will build upon.

1. Marriages change when we recognize God's agenda for so-called ordinary moments

"Dear friends, let us love one another, for love comes from God. Everyone who loves has been born of God and knows God. Whoever does not love does not know God, because *God is love*" (1 John 4:7–8, italics mine).

"God is love." We all want more love in our marriages. Who doesn't love love? For the most part, we marry because of love—or at least because we hope for love. But in the most difficult moments we don't feel loved, and we find it hard to love. God may not seem to make much difference in these moments; however, his involvement is crucial because God is love. When we find it hard to love, we need him all the more. A lack of love should prompt us to not just look more closely at our marriage but at our relationship with God.

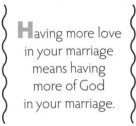

Having more love in your marriage means having more of God in your marriage.

The bad news: your love problems are bigger than you think because love problems are God problems. The good news: the solution is bigger than you think because God cares and is involved. Having more love in your marriage means having more of God in your marriage. Having trouble loving is evidence either that you don't know God or that something is interfering in your relationship with God.[1]

As a little girl my daughter, Sydney, earned a reputation for being a picky eater. We even found it hard to entice her with fast-food burgers and fries! Once when my mother-in-law learned that we'd eaten at a McDonald's, she asked, "Sydney, what did you eat at McDonald's?"

"I ate a cheeseburger," she replied proudly.

"You ate a cheeseburger!" my mother-in-law said with surprise. "I thought you didn't like cheeseburgers."

"I just take off all the stuff I don't like," Sydney explained. "First, I take off the pickles and the onions, and then the cheese, and then the ketchup and the mustard, and finally the *big round brown thing in the middle.*" My daughter had discovered the secret to liking cheeseburgers: remove the hamburger itself and just eat the bread!

We can all be like Sydney. We may pay lip service to the notion that God is love and that we want to be more loving, but then we remove God from the discussion. If we believe that God is love, then he must be part of the solution. In fact, he must be the most important part—the "big thing in the middle," if you will.

2. Marriages change when we're willing to love in practical, Christlike ways, especially in the difficult moments

"This is how God showed his love among us: He sent his one and only Son into the world that we might live through him. This is love: not that we loved God, but that he loved us and sent his Son as an atoning sacrifice for our sins" (1 John 4:9–10).

Ask ten different people what love is, and chances are you'll get ten different answers. Love isn't quite the mystery it seems. Based on what we hear on the radio, see on television, or read in magazines, we might get the idea that love is a wonderfully indescribable something that happens *to* us, an uncontrollable and unpredictable thing that comes and goes. That makes for great romance novels, but it doesn't offer much hope for our marriages.

The Bible tells us specific things about love. In the passage above, we learn that love became a human being named Jesus who lived among us. While love can be exciting and feel wonderful, ultimately, love is a person, not an experience. When you need help loving your spouse, you don't have to wait to feel loving or yearn for lost romance or guess what love is; you can look to Jesus and learn from him. Jesus, as love, took action. He spoke and acted in ways that made a difference, ways that made love visible among us. As we trust him and learn from him, we can *do* love too.

There are two critical ingredients to loving in a Christlike way. The first ingredient is connecting with and depending on Christ, not as a religious man who lived two thousand years ago, but as God's own

Son who's with you and able to help you in the most difficult moments of your marriage. The second ingredient is knowing what love looks like in the details of the moment. Jesus doesn't just motivate us to love; he teaches *how* to love in the moment—what it looks like and how to do it.

Jesus isn't just an encouraging coach or an example to follow but our champion who's able to defeat giants we'd never be able to tackle on our own.

As a four-year-old, my son was enthralled with the Bible story of how the shepherd boy David courageously kills the giant Goliath, by striking him with a single stone flung from his sling. (Though David carried five rocks with him, he only needed one.) Pretending to be David, my son would run through the house with one of my socks wadded up and stuffed inside of the other, swinging it madly over his head looking for giants to slay. Hoping to help him reflect on the deeper meaning of the story, I commented to him once as he stalked giants, "David sure had a lot of faith to go up against that giant, didn't he?" Without a moment's hesitation, my son replied, "He had a lot of faith *and* a lot of rocks!"

Maybe you're facing giants in your marriage, and being asked to look to Jesus feels like being offered faith without rocks! Remember that faith is only a prelude to action. You need faith that Jesus will help you every step of the way, but you also need to take concrete action. In every area of marriage we examine, we will explore both the whys and the hows of love.

When the Bible tells us that Jesus is "an atoning sacrifice for our sins," that means that Jesus is able to remove from your heart all obstacles to loving others. Sin isn't a very popular topic, but we must take it into account. Some of the biggest giants in our marriages reside in our own hearts. As much as we say we want to love, sin squashes our best efforts. Jesus isn't just an encouraging coach or an example to follow but our champion who's able to defeat giants we'd never be able to tackle on our own. We will explore these giants in the next few chapters, but for now understand that for love to make a difference it must be more than an emotional boost. It can only be found in Jesus and it has to show up in the details of your marriage.

3. Marriages change when we're willing to love consistently, over time, not because our spouses change but because we're in a growing relationship with God

"Dear friends, since God so loved us, we also ought to love one another. No one has ever seen God; but if we love one another, God lives in us and his love is made complete in us" (1 John 4:11–12).

If you aren't seeing miracles, it might be that you don't know how to recognize them. The apostle John tells us that learning to love each other involves at least two miracles: first, God lives in us, and, second, God becomes visible. "God lives in us and his love is made complete." The invisible becomes visible. That is a miracle.

At some point in marriage, you have to realize that you can't make your spouse change. If your happiness hinges on your ability to control your spouse, you doom yourself to the frustration and hopelessness of trying to do the impossible.

God offers something much better than a changed spouse; he promises to change *you*. He gives himself to you. When you're tempted to believe that your spouse stands between you and all the joy you hoped to find in marriage, hear God's invitation to something far better. This doesn't mean that your spouse won't change; it means that whether your spouse changes or not, you're invited to become part of the most important program in history—the program of letting God live inside of you so that his love becomes visible in our broken world.

It may be that your spouse does begin to change once you stop trying to change him or her and focus instead on being all that you can be. Or maybe not. But your *marriage* will change when you make different choices and keep making those choices in light of your relationship with God—a relationship that's bigger than your marriage.

But how can my marriage change if my spouse doesn't change? Think of your marriage as a dance. Dancing is most enjoyable and beautiful when both dancers are hearing the same music and are in step with one another. When the dancers are hearing different music and don't know the steps, it becomes an awkward and painful ordeal. The dancers step on each other's toes as they stumble along. You can't make your *spouse* a better dancer, but *you* can become a better dancer. Even if only one partner improves, the dance improves. Your toes are safer, spills are less frequent, and you may enjoy the dance even though your spouse is never quite in rhythm with you. On the other hand, your spouse may begin to notice that you're becoming a better dancer and want to improve as well. When you're living for more than mere marital happiness, you have staying power. Rather than looking for a gimmick, you're willing to embark on a journey that lasts a lifetime but is lived one day at a time.

Where Are We Going?

The book is built around these three central ideas:

Section 1: God Is in the Ordinary Moments

This section makes the connections between the details of your marriage relationship and the reality of your relationship with God, so that you see a bigger purpose and new possibilities in the ordinary moments of your marriage. You'll be challenged to examine yourself to recognize how you make ordinary moments difficult. You'll learn how knowing and worshipping God transforms the details of marriage, and you'll learn how Jesus makes all the difference.

Section 2: Extraordinary Love in the Details of Marriage

This section gets practical. You need to know what love looks like in the details of the moment. You'll learn how honesty, conflict, confessing wrongs, and forgiving can be expressions of love and a critical part of God's activity in your marriage.

Section 3: Staying on the Path

Whether your spouse changes or not, there are many joys and riches to encounter on your journey with God. In this section you'll be invited to understand how your story fits into the story of your marriage and your story with God. You'll be challenged to pursue the highest manifestation of love there is: loving when you're being wronged. You'll also learn how to cultivate hope.

Sometimes ordinary moments never become much more than regular irritations; sometimes they explode into angry tirades, shouting matches, or worse. But as ordinary as these moments may seem, they have the potential to radically change your marriage.

Think about It

- What are some of the ordinary moments in your marriage? What are some of the aggravations, conflicts, or disappointments that happen over and over again? Are there thoughts and feelings that are common to all of them?
- Have you asked God for help? If so, have you seen any change? If you haven't seen any change, how do you make sense of that? Do you wrestle with feelings of abandonment, anger, hopelessness?
- Think of one of the ordinary moments in your marriage. How might you change just one thought, attitude, word, or action to make God's love more visible? How might this ordinary moment be different if you realized in that moment that God was loving and supporting you as you worked to make his love visible?

two

Ordinary Moments Reveal Our Problems with God

What You'll Learn in This Chapter:

- Because God is love, the problems we have loving our spouse are often a reflection of problems in our relationship with God.
- Sometimes we discover areas of blindness, ways that we need to love our spouse that we haven't seen before.
- Sometimes we discover areas of stubbornness, ways that we know we should love but simply don't want to because we value something else more than love, more than God.
- Because God is love, improving our relationship with him will improve our relationship with our spouse. He is love, and we can count on his help when we want to learn to love.

An Ordinary Moment, Part 2

AS I SAT staring at the kitchen table, a couple of questions occurred to me. When I couldn't reach Kim, why had I been angry with her rather than worried? Why was I so ready to assume she was being selfish rather than wondering if her car had broken down or, worse, if she'd been in an accident? What if she'd been lying in a hospital bed attached to a ventilator, while I stewed about the inconvenience of taking the kids on a few errands?

I began to see my selfishness. Then as I thought about resuming my Bible study preparation, an even more troubling question hit me: How could I teach about a loving God and be so unloving? I hadn't just experienced a breakdown in my relationship with Kim; this was a breakdown in my relationship with God. I realized that my problem with Kim pointed me to a much deeper problem that I had with God. I was going to have to face the brokenness in my relationship with him before I could do anything about the brokenness of my marriage.

Jesus Shows Up in an Ordinary Moment

In the gospel of Matthew, Jesus meets a young man not unlike us— someone who has blind spots when it comes to love. As Jesus instructs him, we begin to get a sense of why showing love to our spouses is difficult, and how we can begin to change.

> Now a man came up to Jesus and asked, "Teacher, what good thing must I do to get eternal life?"
>
> "Why do you ask me about what is good?" Jesus replied. "There is only One who is good. If you want to enter life, obey the commandments."
>
> "Which ones?" the man inquired.

Jesus replied, "'Do not murder, do not commit adultery, do not steal, do not give false testimony, honor your father and mother,' and 'love your neighbor as yourself.'"

"All these I have kept," the young man said. "What do I still lack?"

Jesus answered, "If you want to be perfect, go, sell your possessions and give to the poor, and you will have treasure in heaven. Then come, follow me."

When the young man heard this, he went away sad, because he had great wealth. (Matthew 19:16–22)

At first Jesus seems a bit sarcastic, even testy. "Why do you ask me about what is good? There's only One who is good." But why shouldn't the young man ask Jesus about what is good? Jesus is God's Son, after all—the Messiah.

> Jesus often doesn't answer questions the way we expect him to because his answers are designed to tell us as much about ourselves as they do about God.

When Jesus' words surprise or shock you, pay special attention. Jesus often doesn't answer questions the way we expect him to because his answers are designed to tell us as much about ourselves as they do about God. Jesus isn't being snippy; rather he is inviting the young man to see that his own question suggests that there's a problem. Jesus is essentially saying, "What an odd question. You already have a 'good' teacher—God himself. He's given you his commands, so go do them. Why are you asking me for a second opinion?"

"Which commandments should I obey?" the young man continues. Another peculiar question. Does he not understand that by definition commands aren't optional? Jesus could have simply answered, "All of them," but instead he highlights certain commandments: "'Do not murder, do not commit adultery, do not steal, do not give false testimony, honor your father and mother,' and 'love your neighbor as yourself.'" Jesus' answer can be summarized as "love people." His answer provides a clue to the kinds of commands the young man wants to avoid thinking about or just doesn't understand: "'All these I have kept,' the young man said. 'What do I still lack?'"

Jesus tells the young man to sell all his possessions, give to the poor, and follow him. Because the young man won't do it, Jesus makes the point that if he wants eternal life he will have to learn to love as God has commanded, even with his wealth. Jesus asks the young man to love in a way he's never considered.

For a moment resist the temptation to get stuck on the issue of how much money Christians should have and instead appreciate that Jesus has put his finger on a major area of the young man's life in which he is blind to the needs of others—an area in which he is unwilling to love. This is a *rich* man surrounded by *poor* people. For all of his concern about how to please God and achieve eternal life, the rich man is blind to God's most clearly stated concerns and to the need of those right in front of him. Jesus clarifies, for this particular man, what loving should look like: "sell your possessions and give to the poor." No doubt the young man never expected the conversation to take the turn that it does.

Your Relationship with Your Spouse Is a Window into Your Relationship with God

The rich young man seemed to have heavenly issues on his mind— just as I did when I fumed because I couldn't prepare my Bible study. He wanted to know how to obtain eternal life. This doesn't sound as if he was looking for advice about his relationships, but that's exactly where Jesus directed him—to the details of his relationships.

"God is love" is much more than a nice thought. Your ability or willingness to love your spouse says as much about your relation-ship with God as about your relationship with your spouse. This may surprise you, especially if you don't think of marriage in spiritual terms. Maybe you've always thought about marriage in romantic terms. Or maybe marriage is a practical reality—just the way you live your life.

Even when we're willing to look to God for marital advice, we don't usually think of the way we treat our spouses as a measure of our relationship with God. Like the rich young man, we limit God's concerns to religion. We suspect that God cares about our prayers, going to church, and reading the Bible, but our marriages don't really seem religious or spiritual.

God's command to "Love your neighbor as yourself" reminds us, however, that every human interaction, including every marital interaction, is a spiritual matter. Think about it: your spouse is your most immediate neighbor. You don't just live next door; you live in the same house! The way you treat your spouse, then, reveals how seriously you take God and his command. Your obedience or disobedience is a window into your relationship with him.

When You Look through the Window, What Do You See?

When you peer *through* your marriage into your relationship with God, what do you see? Do you love your spouse well? Do you love God well? As we begin to think about those questions, let's notice a few more things about Jesus' interaction with the rich young man.

Blindness

Notice the rich young man's distorted view of himself. He likely sees himself as spiritually minded. There's no reason to think that his question to Jesus is insincere, as were the questions of many of the religious leaders. In fact, in the gospel of Mark we're told that in the middle of their conversation "Jesus looked at him and loved him" (Mark 10:21). Not only does he seek Jesus out, but he knows God's law and is familiar with its commands. His problem is that when he examines his life in light of God's commands, he thinks he's okay. He knows God's Word, he lives among God's people, but he is blind to his true condition.

Let's make sure that we don't suffer from the same blindness. Knowing God's Word or what he says about marriage isn't enough; we must be willing to see ourselves accurately, in action, as we interact with our spouses.

Being religious can sometimes contribute to spiritual blindness. After Jesus' conversation with the rich young man, he has a similar conversation with some religious leaders, who aren't honest seekers but men determined to trip Jesus up and destroy his plans. When quizzed about which of God's commands is the greatest, Jesus tells them, too, that they must obey God's command to love their neighbor. But he roots that command in an even more fundamental one. Jesus puts it this way:

"Love the Lord your God with all your heart and with all your soul and with all your mind." This is the first and greatest commandment. And the second is like it: "Love your neighbor as yourself." All the Law and Prophets hang on these two commandments. (Matthew 22:37–40)

In other words, the command to love your neighbor as yourself is rooted in or based upon the command to love God with all of your heart, soul, and mind.

Jesus links the two commands here to make the same point to the religious leaders that he made with the wealthy young man. If God is love, then our duty in loving others should be obvious. But that connection is often lost on us. In this passage, Jesus is speaking to Pharisees and teachers of the law. Because they consider themselves experts in worship, Jesus is especially troubled by their blindness and lack of love. Of *all* people, they should understand that the only way to love God is to love others! But they'll not make the connection, so in this same passage Jesus says to them,

Woe to you, teachers of the law and Pharisees, you hypocrites! You give a tenth of your spices—mint, dill, and cummin. But you have neglected the more important matters of the law—justice, mercy, and faithfulness. You should have practiced the latter, without neglecting the former. You blind guides! You strain out a gnat but swallow a camel. (Matthew 23:23–24)

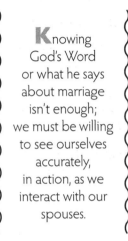

Knowing God's Word or what he says about marriage isn't enough; we must be willing to see ourselves accurately, in action, as we interact with our spouses.

On the one hand, the Pharisees appear to be ultra-religious, diligently following every detail of the law. One of the requirements of the law was that a tenth, or *tithe*, of one's possessions be given to God. Jesus points out that the Pharisees are scrupulous in keeping this demand. In fact, they're so careful to uphold their religious duty that they even tithe their "mint, dill, and cummin"—the herbs and spices that grow in their gardens! They seem to love God with all their hearts and with all their souls and with all their minds. They seem not to hold anything back from God.

But Jesus calls them hypocrites: they claim to be one thing but, in reality, are something different. The Pharisees claim to love God but have, in fact, neglected the heart of God's commands—justice, mercy, and faithfulness.

The Pharisees show the same disconnect that many of us suffer from. They only know worship as religious ritual. Their definition of worship doesn't include relationships, and Jesus can see that their relationships aren't shaped by the God they claim to worship, the God who says that he is love.

In my case, I was preparing a Bible study fully convinced that I was loving God and others, but the real litmus test of how I was relating to God was in my attitude and actions toward my wife. My heart and mind were filled with concern for myself rather than for her. My actions didn't say love; they said selfishness.

In what ways are you blind to God's command to love your spouse?

Turning Away from God

Jesus clarifies the young man's problem for him and tells him what he must do, but the young man's response is to turn away. Jesus tells him to sell his possessions, give to the poor, and follow him, but the young man can't do it. He *won't* do it. He literally looks into the face of love and chooses something else. The details of the young man's relationships reveal that his wealth is the love of his life, more important to him than people or God.

Are there things in your life that keep you from loving your spouse—from loving God? Reading this Matthew passage might be like going to the doctor for a nagging cough, expecting to get some antibiotics and receiving, instead, a diagnosis of cancer. But a diagnosis is easier to take when you know there's a cure. I thought I was having trouble loving my neighbor and my wife, Doc. You're telling me that it's just a symptom of a failure to love God?

Your Relationship with God
Can Powerfully Transform Your Marriage

If you're going to grow in love, then you're going to need God's help. Jesus described our duty to love God with all of our heart, soul, and mind as the "first and greatest commandment." It's essentially a command to turn to God as *the* source of love. God doesn't simply command us to love one another and then leave us to accomplish that on our own. Like the wealthy young man, we're blind to what's really going on in our relationships and our hearts. Without help we've no reason to believe we will be any more successful than he was.

Jesus doesn't just expect us to connect our marriages to the second great commandment, but to realize that the command to love our neighbor is inextricable from the command to love God. If you love God with all of your heart, soul, and mind, would you not expect to grow in your ability to love? Would you not expect to know *how* to love and to have the *power* to love?

You need not be afraid to take an honest look at yourself. You won't find anything that there's no solution for. The God who commands you to love will show you what genuine love looks like, and he will empower you to exercise that kind of love as you love him. In the following chapters we will look more closely at what it means to love God this way and how Jesus fits into the picture. In the next chapter we will take a closer look at how we can begin to identify the things that keep us from accepting God and turning to him.

Think about It

- If Jesus were to evaluate your relationship with God based on the way you treat your spouse, how would you score? In what ways would you score well? In what ways do you think you need to improve?
- Name some blind spots that exist in the way you love your spouse? Take some time to think about ways that your spouse may need to be loved that you've missed or neglected. Ask your husband or wife if there are ways they'd like you to love them more.
- What things in your life do you value more than loving your spouse (or even God himself)? When are you tempted to turn away, as the rich young man did? When do you feel that loving your spouse or God costs too much?

three

Worship:
Extraordinary Love
for God

What You'll Learn in This Chapter:

- God teaches that all of our problems with him can be understood as worship problems. Whatever we depend on, seek out, or organize our lives around other than God is what we worship instead of God.
- Our marriages suffer when we worship something other than God. Our desires to be liked, to be comfortable, or to have power and control can become idols that break our relationship with God and our spouses. Even good things can become idols when we make them too important.
- Idolatry is always selfish. We serve idols that we think will benefit us.
- Worship changes us. Worshipping idols changes us and our marriages for the worst. Worshipping God changes us for the better.

A Closer Look at the First Great Commandment

WHAT MAKES ORDINARY moments hard is that they're rooted in a problem that's bigger than our marriages. A lack of love means that whatever problems you may have with your spouse, you have a bigger problem with God. In the last chapter we saw that, according to Jesus, our ability to love others is based on our love for God. He told the religious leaders,

> "Love the Lord your God with all your heart and with all your soul and with all your mind and with all your strength." The second is this: "Love your neighbor as yourself." There is no commandment greater than these. (Mark 12:30–31)

Jesus gave two commandments instead of one to show that loving your neighbor is a necessary way of expressing love for God. Learning to love God is *the* pathway for loving your spouse or anyone else.

How do we learn to love God? How do we deal with the things that interfere with our love for God? The first great commandment provides the answer to these questions: in a word, the answer is *worship*.

Think for a moment about what the first great commandment requires. To love God with all of your heart, soul, mind, and strength is a far-reaching task covering every area of your life. The terms *heart, mind, soul,* and *strength* obviously overlap. God uses these overlapping terms so that there can be no mistaking that he requires from us an all-consuming love. Is there any part of life that falls outside of your heart, mind, soul, and strength?

We're accustomed to dividing life into the spiritual and nonspiritual, handing the spiritual things over to God and managing the rest by ourselves. There are certain areas that we like to consider outside God's control, and marriage is one of them. But this command makes clear that God should be at the center of it all. All barriers between the spiritual and nonspiritual are broken down.

The Bible has a word for this kind of all-consuming love, a devotion that shapes and directs every area of life: *Worship.* That may surprise you since we often use the word worship in a very limited sense. We think of worship as a set of specific activities that we perform on one day of the week. We go to a special place, sing songs, pray, listen to a message, stand, kneel, and so on. We think of all of these things as worship. We then leave that special place, and worship is over. It's true that God tells us to worship him that way, but the command to love God with our whole being teaches that every aspect of our lives is an act of worship. *Everything* we do is guided by our love of God, our every act one of devotion to him.

> The command to love God with our whole being teaches that every aspect of our lives is an act of worship.

To appreciate the connection between worship and a wholehearted love of God recall that Jesus was quoting from the Old Testament, from Deuteronomy 6:4–5, when he spoke of the first great commandment. In Deuteronomy 6, Moses reviews the Ten Commandments (and other laws) with the Israelites before they enter the Promised Land. The book of Deuteronomy reviews what Israel learned during their forty years wandering in the desert.

The first great commandment is a summary of the summary reminding us what God commands in the first four of the Ten Commandments. These are the commandments that prohibit worshipping God in the wrong way: Don't worship any other god, don't make an image or idol of God, don't misuse his name, and keep the Sabbath holy (do no labor on that day). Notice that these commandments are largely *prohibitions.* They tell us how *not* to worship God. But what does it mean *to* worship God? The first great commandment is basically that instruction. Where the Ten Commandments tell us what we *must not do,* the first great commandment tells us what we *must do.*

To worship God, then, is to have your entire life and being oriented around love for him. You could say, then, that the foundation of loving your spouse is truly *worshipping* God. Understanding the connection between loving and worshipping God is an important one. As you'll see, worshipping God always leads to transformation and change. The first great commandment isn't just an obligation that God lays upon us, but a pathway to change.

What Do You Worship?

Psalm 71 offers a beautiful picture of what it means to worship God with your whole being. "In you, O Lord, I have taken refuge . . . . For you have been my hope, O Sovereign Lord, my confidence since my youth. . . . My mouth is filled with your praise" (Psalm 71:1, 5, 8). Look at some of the words the psalmist uses to describe God: his refuge, his hope, his confidence, the object of his delight and praise. Now ask yourself: Where do you take refuge? Who is *your* rescuer and deliverer? Into whose ear do *you* speak when you need help? Where do you turn? A best friend? A neighbor? Your spouse? Do any of these substitute for seeking help from God himself?

Or maybe your refuge isn't a *who* but a *what*. Do you look for refuge in "harmless" distractions—books, TV shows, work, and so forth? These things aren't bad in themselves, but they become bad when they function as gods in your life, preventing you from knowing and loving God.

Where do you place your hope and confidence? In God or in your job skills and career, for example? In your happy, well-adjusted family? Or maybe you trust most in your own strength and ability to do it all on your own. The person or thing in which you place your confidence is your god.

What fills you with excitement and joy so that you burn to tell others about it? Your latest purchase? New hobby? Favorite sports team? Where do you go for wisdom and knowledge? If you honestly examine yourself, can you say that God fills all of those roles? Are you loving him with your entire being?

This understanding of worship exposes us all as worshippers who have gone astray. Even the atheist places faith in something. Everyone has answers to the questions that Psalm 71 raises. The question isn't whether you'll worship; the question is who or what you'll worship.

Idolatry

The first of the Ten Commandments forbids idolatry—substituting something else for God. You may think of an idol as a revered statue or image. And, yes, God forbids us to fashion an image of him or any other supposed god and worship it. But idolatry encompasses worshipping *anything* other than God. Our most natural inclinations—for example, seeking comfort, refuge, hoping, relying—are the behaviors of worship. The most insidious idols are the ones that we erect in our own hearts.

If you're willing to see yourself as a worshipper gone astray, then ask yourself, "What are my idols?" If you examine your life and your relationships, you may identify one or more of the following popular candidates:

Approval: For some of us, nothing feels as good as the affirmation of others. We do whatever it takes to make sure others like us. We agree to others' demands, no matter how unreasonable they may be. We keep our opinions to ourselves and swallow anger and disappointment because being different and disagreeable aren't good ways of getting people to like you.

Comfort: Others of us prefer to submerge ourselves in ease and pleasure. We don't like hassles, and we hate conflict. We like things the easy way. People may or may not fit into our plans, depending on whether or not they make things comfortable for us. Sure, we will fight if we have to but only to protect our comfort zone.

Power: Others of us crave the feeling of being in charge and making things happen. We can't stand being controlled by other people, and, in fact, sometimes conflict feels good because it proves we aren't living at the mercy of someone else. We tend to be critical, competitive, sharp-tongued, and good at arguing our point of view.

Add to these a multitude of other idols, such as intimacy, belonging, security, safety, success, and admiration. Notice that none of these things is *bad* in and of itself. It isn't wrong to want approval or enjoy comfort or be in control. Often, we aren't aware of how idolatry is affecting us because what we're pursuing isn't a bad thing. It becomes a bad thing when we attach too much importance to it—when it eclipses love for God and your spouse. Of course, idols can be things that are inherently bad, such as an adulterous relationship, but the ones that often bedevil us the most are the ones that we've convinced ourselves are good, but become bad when they become too important to us and are driven by selfishness.

Notice that the things that control your life may not be the things that you pursue but the things you avoid. For instance, rejection can be an idol in the same way as approval. The fear of being rejected is the flip side of the desire to be accepted. In this case, however, you're more motivated to avoid rejection than to secure approval. What's the difference? The person seeking approval is going to pursue relationships with others to find that approval, but the person who fears rejection may choose complete isolation from others. Other things that people tend to avoid to the point of idolatry are isolation, shame, hassles, chaos, being controlled, failure, humiliation, and weakness.

How Idols Affect Marriage

Back to My Story

Recall how I fumed because Kim was late getting home on a Saturday afternoon and I had to scramble to do errands so I could finish preparing for a Bible study. More angry than concerned at Kim's absence, I realized that I was being selfish. How could I sit with the Bible in my hands and be filled with anger at my wife? Suddenly

I realized that I had a problem with God that was bigger than my problem with Kim.

I was being selfish toward Kim. But relationship problems are worship problems. I was loving something more than I was loving God. What had displaced my love for God? What was the idol? Convenience would be an obvious culprit. I didn't like being inconvenienced. Or maybe doing a good job at Bible study was just too important to me. It could have been about performance or perfection. But digging deeper I recognized another culprit that's been my companion since I was a boy: a *desperate craving for approval and fear of rejection.*

The things that control your life may not be the things that you pursue but the things you avoid.

How does the desire for approval translate into angry pouting? To serve my idol of approval, I work hard to perform for others. I wanted to do a good job with the Bible study, but I also work hard to be liked by Kim. After all, I was taking care of the kids on a Saturday so she could enjoy her friends. Did I not deserve some credit for that? When I perceive myself as overlooked and ignored, it feels as if none of my hard work and efforts are going to pay off. Usually I'm good at getting others to like me. When Kim doesn't fall in line, I get angry. In my anger I want to punish her for not noticing how hard I'm working for her affirmation, approval, and affection.

Am I being too hard on myself? Reacting with anger is normal when you perceive your needs are being ignored. Again, the problem was not the anger itself. It was the intensity of the anger; the pouting, snipping, withdrawing that resulted from the anger; and how the anger eclipsed love for God and for Kim. Sometimes an idol is a good thing that's become too big—a desire that's become a demand or a normal fear or concern that rules us. These are the idols that often operate unnoticed in the background of our marriages. But sometimes these good-things-gone-bad become idols that you trumpet as your just cause! You demand them openly and, full of righteous indignation, hold them over your spouse's head. Meanwhile, love for God and for spouse grows cold.

Round and Round

As I've already mentioned, focusing on our spouse's faults can be a real trap. But you do need to realize that you didn't marry a perfect person. Your spouse is as prone to weaknesses and sin as you are. To give you a sense of how our sins interact, Kim is willing for you to know that there's more than one idolater in my marriage. Kim loves comfort.

> The Bible's understanding of worship makes it obvious that every area of life is touched and changed by worship.

It isn't that Kim doesn't love people, or me; it's just that sometimes Kim's enjoyment and pleasure of the moment eclipses her love for others. In this instance, it's easy to understand why she didn't answer my phone calls. She couldn't hear her phone. But for the sake of this example, let's assume that there's more to the story. Let's pretend that Kim had this nagging sense that she should check in on things at home but dismissed the thought because she was having fun with her friends.

There's a sense in which love requires her to be aware of the needs of others even when she's tempted to be absorbed by what's happening in front of her. If she's committed to being somewhere by 1:00, she may need to make a special effort to keep track of time, even though it breaks the flow of the moment. She may need to excuse herself at an uncomfortable moment to meet her obligation to another.

My idol of acceptance and Kim's idol of comfort can interact in diabolical ways. As I sat at the kitchen table, punishing Kim because my efforts to please her seemed fruitless, Kim was feeling increasingly uncomfortable. When Kim feels uncomfortable she wants to withdraw. She moves toward comfort and away from discomfort. Of course, as she withdraws, I feel increasingly ignored and rejected. The more she withdraws the more I scowl, pout, and direct verbal barbs her way.

And the more I pout, the more she withdraws. Our idols reinforce and amplify each other. Round and round we go.

Idolatry Is about Self

In one sense, idolatry is the way sinners look *outside* of themselves to find salvation, salvation being rescue from hardship and a path to fulfillment. We hope that acceptance, comfort, control, power, success, or something else will make our lives okay. Our idols may seem to focus and depend upon others. Regardless, idolatry is always rooted in self. Though our idols may require the participation of others, idolatry is a strategy to benefit self. So, for example, I want to please others so that I'll feel better about myself. Making others happy is only a means to an end, not an end in itself. As a strategy for gratifying myself, it's inherently *self*-ish.

But more than selfishness, at its root, idolatry is the way we play God. When we refuse to worship the true God and choose to build our lives around something or someone else, we're exalting ourselves above God. As idolaters we, in effect, survey the universe, including God, and decide what's best for us. God created all things to worship and serve him, but as idolaters we play God by devising strategies to make the world serve us. But even our efforts to rid ourselves of God take on the expression of worship. This is because we were made for worship, and even in our rebellion against God we can't stop worshipping; we just find a "worshipful" way to serve ourselves. We find someone or something else to organize our lives around and to love with all we've got.

Worship Always Changes You

The Bible's understanding of worship makes it obvious that every area of life is touched and changed by worship. That which you serve with all of your heart, mind, soul, and strength shapes every area of your life. But in addition to changing the worshipper's world, worship changes the worshipper too.

If You Make Them You'll Be Like Them

Psalm 115 paints a picture of idolatry and how it changes us. First, the psalmist contrasts the true God with idols,

> Our God is in heaven; he does whatever pleases him.
> But their idols are silver and gold, made by the hands of
> men. They have mouths, but cannot speak, eyes, but they
> cannot see; they have ears, but cannot hear, noses, but they
> cannot smell; they have hands, but cannot feel, feet, but
> they cannot walk; nor can they utter a sound with their
> throats. (Psalm 115:3–7)

The psalmist is describing the idols that were common in the ancient Near East, little statues or figures of what the worshipper imagined his or her god to look like. The psalmist's argument is obvious. Although made in the image of a living, breathing being, the idol isn't alive and can do nothing to rescue or deliver the worshipper. The idol is dead.

But the punch line comes in verse 8: "Those who make them will be like them, and so will all who trust in them." In other words, idols are lifeless, and those who make and trust in them will become lifeless. While the imagery is that of figurines and statues, the principle holds true for the idols that we serve in our marriages as well.

Consider how this holds true for the idol of approval. When I chose this as my god, I did so believing it would bring me life: joy, peace, and happiness. It seemed to work, at least for a while. But over time, just as Psalm 115 predicts, I found it less and less effective. As I sat at the kitchen table that Saturday afternoon, I didn't feel alive and free; I felt paralyzed. I didn't know what to say or do. I was trapped by my own strategy. Approval doesn't offer any solutions for anger. Idols bring death in exactly the way the psalmist describes. As I trained my eye to look for approval, I began to lose my ability to notice anything but its presence or absence. As I trained my ear to listen for the sounds of affirmation and praise, I became tone deaf to other important sounds, and even the most helpful and well-meaning criticism became unbearable. I chose an idol that I thought would bring me life, but instead I found that my life became flatter and flatter, reduced to the harsh monochrome reality of experiencing only acceptance and rejection.

Everyone Who Has This Hope in Him Purifies Himself

Mercifully, true worship is life giving. Psalm 115 points us to this truth. "The LORD remembers us and will bless us: He will bless the house of Israel, he will bless the house of Aaron, he will bless those who fear the LORD—small and great alike" (Psalm 115:12–13). In other words, if we worship God, he will bless us.

If you aren't used to the language of worship, it can feel awkward and unnatural. But the Bible uses other images to illustrate the kind of relationship we're intended to have with God. One prominent image is that of a father's relationship with his child. He's devoted to us as a loving father, and we're to be devoted to him as loving children. Notice how the apostle John uses this image of relationship to describe how it changes us.

> How great is the love the Father has lavished on us, that we should be called children of God! And that is what we are! . . . Dear friends, now we are children of God, and what we will be has not yet been made known. But we know that when he appears, we shall be like him, for we shall see him as he is. Everyone who has this hope in him purifies himself, just as he is pure. (1 John 3:1–3)

As a little boy, I often stood beside my father at the sink as he shaved in the morning before work. He used a razor with a removable blade, and as little boys often do, I wanted to imitate my father, so I'd stand beside him with my face lathered up and use an empty razor to scrape the shaving cream off of my face.

One morning I asked him, "Papa, will I *really* be able to shave one day?" "Of course you will," he replied. "How do you know?" I asked. "Because you're my son," he answered.

Like it or not, children often end up being like their parents to some degree. Looking at my father I could, in a fashion, see my own future. Because he shaved in the morning, one day I could expect to need a shave in the morning.

John is making a similar argument. Those who trust Jesus have the privilege of being considered God's children. That alone is an amazing fact, but it gets better. God's children, like natural children, grow and mature to become more and more like him. As we learn how to love and worship God, we're changed—we become like him.

Make a Change

In an ordinary moment, objective self-criticism is difficult. Spotting another person's (especially a spouse's) faults first and using them to explain your own unhappiness is only natural. But for things to be different you have to try something different. You must begin the process of change by examining yourself. Your spouse has his or her own faults, but you can begin changing your marriage this instant by taking an honest look at yourself. Are there desires and fears that you've made into idols? (Remember, that even good things can become idols when our felt needs become demands.) Ask God's forgiveness for trying to make life work on your own. Tell him that you want to learn to love him with your all.

If your marriage is going to change, you need to change. It's easy to waste time waiting, hoping, perhaps insisting that your spouse change. Sadly, you have no power to make another person change. When you begin your quest for change by looking at yourself and your own need for change, then you can have hope. You have a responsibility and also the ability to change. But you can only do that in a lasting, meaningful way as you turn from your own idols and learn to live a life of true worship.

Think about It

- Spotting the activity of idols in our lives can be difficult. One sure sign of idolatry is when we overreact to something. Try to think of a recent incident in your marriage when you overreacted. If you were angry, how did you feel you were being wronged? What were you fighting to get? If afraid, what were you afraid of?
- Think of five good things that are important to you in marriage. Try to imagine what it looks like when any one of those things becomes most important to you, an idol. What would you do to have that thing or to avoid losing it?
- Worshipping God changes us. Think of one or two of God's attributes that you appreciate and admire. Take some time to meditate on them, look for them in the Bible, thank God for them, and ask him to help you become more like him.

four

Living in Jesus' Extraordinary Love

What You'll Learn in This Chapter:

- We all have certain ways of thinking about love that may not be true. Jesus often provides us with a surprising picture of love.
- Jesus highlights some common misconceptions about love. It isn't about making others happy. It isn't about finding someone who makes you comfortable. It isn't something that can be earned. Jesus shows us by his life that a most important quality of love is a willingness to give love to those who aren't giving it back.
- Learning to love involves more than trying hard to follow Jesus' example. It involves living in an intimate relationship with him, trusting him, and asking him to give us the ability to love.
- Learning to love can be hard. Often you'll learn to *do* it before you ever *feel* it. Loving requires taking action even when you don't feel like it.

What Is Love?

MY MOTHER-IN-LAW LAUGHS when she tells the story of how, years ago, she gave my father-in-law a beautiful brass wastebasket for Father's Day. The funny part isn't that my father-in-law wanted an ornamental wastebasket. He didn't. The funny part is how my mother-in-law had convinced herself that he would like what she really wanted for herself!

> While there's a great deal that's mysterious about love, we can know a lot about it because God has shown us love.

The desires, especially the idols, of our hearts often pollute our efforts to love. We dare not trust ourselves to understand love on our own.

While there's a great deal that's mysterious about love, we can know a lot about it because God has shown us love. In chapter 1 we looked at verse 9 in 1 John 4: "This is how God showed his love among us: He sent his one and only Son into the world that we might live through him." God is love, and because he sent his Son to us, love has lived and walked among us. We're accustomed to thinking about love as an emotion or an experience that happens to us, but the Bible teaches us that love isn't a *what* but a *who*. In Jesus, love has walked, talked, and touched us. Although we can't physically see him now, we can see him as he shows himself to us in the Bible.

Sometimes our idols make it difficult for us to see Jesus or to love clearly. We're tempted to recast both Jesus and love in the image of our personal desires. If our understanding of love is going to grow we need to be willing to learn the lesson of the rich young man (recall chap. 2) and recognize that we don't know that much about love. We also have to know that once we understand it, we might not like it. This is going to require humility. We have to be willing to learn something new, to be surprised by what love really is.

Jesus Loves in Surprising Ways

Love Sick

I was twenty-one years old, driving home from work on a perfect spring afternoon, windows down, radio on. Suddenly, a paralyzing sense of dread gripped my body, first squeezing my chest and my throat and then seizing my mind. With my heart pounding, my skin tingling, and struggling to breathe, I wondered, "Am I having a heart attack? Am I losing my mind?" The feeling lasted no longer than a minute, though it felt like an eternity to me. I didn't have a label for it then, but in the coming weeks I'd learn that I'd experienced my first panic attack.

A few weeks later I sat with a Christian counselor. As we talked, my life story was laid out like a mural before us. I told him about my childhood in a semirural area. I told him about my large extended family, about weekends on my grandparents' farm, and about the strong sense of belonging I'd experienced. We examined my pride in academic success, my desire to help others, and my fears about letting people down. We talked about my faith.

During one of our sessions my counselor said, "Winston, as you tell your story I can't help but notice how important it is to you to please others." Looking back this must have been obvious; I'd broken down in sobs several times as we explored the mere possibility that I'd failed someone. "But could you help me understand something?" he added. "What's the connection between pleasing others and loving them?" To me nothing could be more obvious. "Doesn't everybody want to make the people he loves happy?" I answered.

"I don't know," he said thoughtfully. "Yesterday I told my daughter she couldn't ride her bike to the park by herself and she got pretty angry." He waited to let the idea sink in, then added, "Do you think I should feel bad about that?" I didn't know what to say. As I considered his question, I began to get his point, but I was not ready for it to be true for me.

The sessions continued, and he helped me to consider Jesus and his love for people. "Have you ever noticed how angry and disappointed people were with Jesus?" he asked. "We know Jesus loved people, and yet they were always getting angry with him. What do you think about that?" Intrigued, I began to meditate on this paradox: Jesus loves people, and yet they're disappointed in him. I began to realize that I'd had it all wrong. My definition of love—my identity as a person—had been rooted in the belief that it was my duty to please others and make them happy. As I became an adult and my world grew, as I moved from college life to a new career, new friends, and new responsibilities, I was finding it impossible to please everybody. The occasional highs of making another person happy were quickly outweighed by the number of people I thought I was disappointing. The reality that I could no longer please everyone began to sink in and my anxiety grew.

My soul began to burn with hope. It was as if the locked door of a dungeon of panic and dread had suddenly opened and I was walking out into the light. Could it be true that God doesn't expect me to please everyone? Do you mean to tell me that love and making others happy aren't the same thing?

Love Isn't about Making Others Happy

Think about it: Jesus loved people and yet, more often than not, people were disappointed, even angry, with him. Jesus came to his people with the good news of the gospel and with the authority to support his claim. He cast out evil spirits, healed lepers, and made the lame to walk. What was the response? The religious leaders accused him of being demon-possessed (Matthew 12:24; Mark 3:22; Luke 11:15), in league with Satan. His own mother and brothers came to take him home thinking that he was out of his mind (Mark 3:21). These aren't just moments of feeling unappreciated; these are moments of utter rejection.

Even more amazing is Jesus' response in continuing to love them. He didn't shrink back from those he loved but pressed forward heroically. Could your love survive such a withering blast of rejection? As you've seen, mine usually doesn't. I withdraw or pout or panic if I don't get sufficient approval—never mind being rejected!

The gospel of John relates a story about Jesus' surprising love. Jesus receives an urgent message from his dear friends Mary and Martha saying, "Lord, the one you love is sick" (John 11:3). Their brother, Lazarus, is gravely ill, and the message is clear; they want Jesus to come and heal their brother. What would anyone with the power to heal do but go immediately and heal a friend? Jesus' response surprises us: "Jesus *loved* Martha and her sister and Lazarus. *Yet* when he heard that Lazarus was sick, *he stayed where he was two more days*" (John 11:5–6, italics mine). Jesus loves

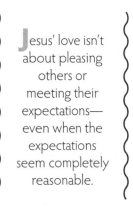

Jesus' love isn't about pleasing others or meeting their expectations— even when the expectations seem completely reasonable.

Lazarus and his sisters, yet he waits two more days fully realizing that his delay will result in Lazarus's death (John 11:11–13).

Jesus arrives to a heartbreaking scene. Lazarus has been in the tomb four days. When the sisters meet Jesus they both have the same burning question. When Mary reaches Jesus outside the village she falls at his feet weeping and says, "Lord, if you had been here, my brother would not have died" (John 11:32b). How could Jesus face her? Can you imagine Mary, broken and grieving at Jesus' feet, as she looks up at him and wants to know why he didn't save her brother? How could Jesus' behavior square with any definition of love?

Jesus' love isn't about pleasing others or meeting their expectations—even when the expectations seem completely reasonable. Listen to the critical factors that make up Jesus' decision to let Lazarus die. "This sickness will not end in death. No, it is for God's glory so that God's Son may be glorified through it" (John 11:4). Later, before arriving at Mary and Martha's village, Jesus says to his disciples, "Lazarus is dead, and for your sake I am glad I was not there, so that you may believe" (John 11:14b–15). Jesus' concerns outpace any expectations. He wants his friends and his disciples to know him in his fullness as Son of God and Redeemer, the one who overcomes spiritual and physical death. Jesus answers Martha's disappointment: "I am the resurrection and the life. He who believes in me will live, even though he dies; and whoever lives and believes in me will never die" (John 11:25–26). Thus, Jesus isn't focused on how Mary and Martha feel about him in the short term and is willing to let the awful drama play out. Lazarus dies and his sisters are heartbroken, wondering how Jesus could have failed to save their brother's life.

> It's a common mistake to believe that loving others is the same thing as making them happy.

You may already know the story's magnificent conclusion. Over the protests about how the body will stink, Jesus commands that the tomb be unsealed. Still focused on the greater purposes of God's love, Jesus reminds them, "Did I not tell you that if you believed, you would see the glory of God?" (John 11:40). Jesus prays and then issues a command to the dead, "Lazarus, come out!" No stench, no zombie, only a living man wrapped in grave cloths steps out into the sunlight. That day everyone received more love than they asked for. They got more than a teacher and a healer, they got "the Son of God who was to come into the world" (John 11:27).

As I wrestled with my own fears about disappointing others, I fed on stories like these. I burned with admiration for Jesus who had the courage to love with boldness, not backing down at the disappointment and rejection of others. I wanted the freedom to love with that kind of power. Thus, I began to speak with Jesus and pursue him with a new zeal. I came to learn that at the root of my anxiety was ignorance about the true nature of love.

Just prior to my first anxiety attack I began dating my wife-to-be, Kim. As we grew closer, I began to experience increasing anxiety, the cause of which mystified me. I really liked her and she seemed right for me; nevertheless, I was filled with doubts. Once I learned about Jesus' love, it all made sense; I was terrified that I might make a mistake, let her down, say something I'm not ready to say yet and have to retract it. If I hurt her feelings or disappointed her it would be *horrible*. But now a new reality was emerging in my mind. Would it be horrible if I made a mistake? No. My duty is to love her, not to be perfect. In fact, sometimes loving her may well disappoint her. My flawed understanding of love had placed me in an impossible situation: How could I possibly avoid disappointing others?

Sometimes we suffer in our marriages because we labor under false understandings of love built upon the foundations of our own desires and fears. It's a common mistake to believe that loving others is the same thing as making them happy. And, of course, your gentle, patient, kind, generous moments will undoubtedly contribute to his or her happiness. But, still, you married someone who has the same capacity as you to be unreasonable, selfish, and blinded by the idols of the heart. Truly to love another sinner as Jesus has loved you will mean having difficult conversations, disagreeing, and even saying no to sinful and destructive behavior. If you truly love your spouse as Jesus has loved you, you'll sometimes get the same response Jesus got—conflict and rejection.

Love Isn't about Getting Comfortable

Over the past few years there has been an explosion of matchmaking services. "Compatibility" figures in many of these services. From "patented systems of compatibility" to those who claim to be experts in "love engineering," the idea seems to be that a happy marriage is based on compatibility. Obviously, there's wisdom in marrying someone who you like and enjoy being around. That's why the Bible advises us to avoid marrying a quarrelsome person. "Better to live on a corner of the roof than share a house with a quarrelsome wife" (Proverbs 21:9). (We can safely assume that quarrelsome husbands are just as unbearable and to be avoided as well.) What exactly is compatibility? Does it mean that you should marry someone who's as much *like* you as possible? Is the goal to marry someone so much like yourself that differences won't show up, that you won't be challenged, that you won't have to grow or change? Is compatibility the critical ingredient of marital love?

If anyone understands compatibility, Jesus does. He knows what it's like to live in complete harmony with another. Consider the absolute bliss and harmony that he's always enjoyed with the Father and the Holy Spirit. We can't delve into the mysteries of the Trinity here, but if you understand that God exists as three persons—Father, Son, and Holy Spirit—then you can imagine the perfect bliss that God has enjoyed within himself for all eternity. Father, Son, and Holy Spirit have always lived in perfect harmony, without argument, jealousy, hurt, or sin. There's no compatibility that surpasses *the* love that the three "persons" of love share within God. That's a harmony we can't fully grasp.

> Jesus has loved us by moving away from what was comfortable and easy to be with us in our problems for our sakes.

Out of love for us, Jesus chose to leave that harmony. Jesus left that place and position of relational bliss to be with us, people who aren't compatible with him at all. He left compatibility and harmony to be married to his bride, the church. We can't fully appreciate the bliss Jesus has known with the Father and Holy Spirit; likewise, we can't grasp how painful it would be to leave that bliss to live in a fallen, broken mess with us; to leave paradise to be born in the stench of a barn; to leave absolute comfort to live in poverty; to leave perfect love and join himself to those who'd betray and murder him. It doesn't sound like anything we'd choose for ourselves. It doesn't even seem rational. But it is love.

You may or may not have ever used a dating service, but how often have you lived as if the purpose of love is to maximize your relational comfort? How often do you view your spouse's problems as simply a violation of your marital rights? "Hey, I got married to find compatibility, not problems!" But Jesus has loved us by moving away from what was comfortable and easy to be with us in our problems for our sakes.

Love Isn't about Giving to Get

Another idea that seems to have gained traction in recent years is the idea of the "love bank."[2] Your love bank is your reservoir of positive sentiment toward your spouse. The basic idea is this: Couples fall in love and stay in love because, on balance, they make each other feel good. Every time you make your spouse feel good, a deposit is made in his or her love bank and vice versa. The bigger the balance in a person's love bank, the more positive you feel about him or her. When a spouse acts in a way that makes the other unhappy, however, a withdrawal is made. A smaller balance in the account means less affection and less love in the marriage. Learning how to identify and meet each other's needs is the key to making deposits, maintaining a positive balance, and remaining in love.

True, we tend to want to be in relationship with people who give us what we want, especially when what we want feels very like something we need. Thousands of years ago Jesus commented on our tendency to be nice to people who are nice to us. Jesus, however, doesn't consider this a worthy definition of love. Instead, he said,

> If you love those who love you, what reward will you get?
> Are not even the tax collectors doing that? And if you greet
> only your brothers, what are you doing more than others? Do
> not even pagans do that? (Matthew 5:46–47)

In other words, being nice to those who are nice to you is ordinary; there's no particular virtue in it. It's self-interest cloaked in kindness.

Do you feel loved when you've had to earn it? We all have to work to accomplish things. I have to teach and counsel to earn a paycheck, but when I receive it I don't feel loved by my employer. If my boss refused to pay me, I wouldn't charge into his office and demand to know why he doesn't love me anymore; I'd demand my pay as something I'd earned. The attitude of earning love is disastrous in marriages and leads to anger and insecurity. Spouses who believe they've earned or deserve love angrily demand it or toil anxiously to avoid losing it.

Jesus contrasts "giving to get" with God's love.

> You have heard that it was said, "Love your neighbor and
> hate your enemy." But I tell you: Love your enemies and pray
> for those who persecute you, that you may be sons of your
> Father in heaven. He causes his sun to rise on the evil and the
> good, and sends rain on the righteous and the unrighteous.
> (Matthew 5:43–45)

God bestows his love on those who have neither deserved it nor earned it. Jesus invites you to consider how God gives gifts of sun and rain to both the good, those who "deserve it," and the evil, those who don't "deserve it."

Here Jesus points us to the most surprising and powerful aspect of God's love: it is given, not earned. This is good news for several reasons. First, it means that God's love is more powerful than our shortcomings and sins. Hopefully our exploration of worship and idolatry has convinced you that none of us really knows or worships God as we ought; rather, we serve ourselves and our own desires. God's goodness and love aren't restrained by our bad behavior. If they were, our sin would be more powerful than God's love. Because God meets our sinfulness with his powerful love, we have hope that he can change us.

Secondly, God's unconditional love means that he can give us that kind of love for our spouses. We aren't left to generate positive emotions for our spouses when they happen to be giving us what we want. We can give them the love that we've received from God—powerful, unconditional love that doesn't change when disappointed or sinned against.

The Bible calls this grace. We will be looking more closely at the concept of grace throughout this book, but for now know that the simplest meaning of grace is love that's undeserved. This is the kind of love God gives us, and it's the kind of love he enables us to give our spouses.

Playing Love in Every Key

Over the past few years my daughters have started taking piano lessons. I think we've made it through the most painful stage—the maddening repetitious plinking of the same six or eight notes as they've learned the very basics. Now they're playing real songs, the left hand playing the bass line or chords and the right hand laying down the melody. It's nice to hear them play, even though they're a long way from playing Beethoven's *Moonlight Sonata* or a Chopin nocturne. They're still at the stage where their hands don't stray far from middle C, and most of the songs have a similar tempo and style.

But pianos are capable of a tremendous range of expression. The keyboard has eighty-eight keys, from the deep sonorous notes on the far left to the light and airy notes on the far right. In addition to the range of notes, the volume can be controlled by the amount of pressure on the keys: press keys gently to produce soft tones and more forcefully to produce louder ones.

Most of us love our spouses the same way my daughters play the piano. Not necessarily painful to listen to, it's far from the full capability and range that love offers. We stay safely within the ten to fifteen keystrokes we're comfortable with. Some of us prefer the softer lighter notes; others seem to major on the deeper challenging ones. Maybe a few of us even play with both hands!

Jesus has mastered every scale, can play in every key, and is capable of playing whatever tune best meets the need of the moment. From the sweetest lullaby to the most challenging fugue, Jesus has mastered the keyboard. Likewise, we shouldn't get comfortable in our amateurish range but strive to play the tune that the moment calls for. As you grow in your understanding of Jesus' love, experiencing it firsthand, listen for the unexpected notes—the ones you yourself would never have chosen to play—and be willing to be stretched. Like the piano, you'll learn that you'll never completely master love; there will always be more depths to explore and appreciate.

Jesus Fulfills the Law

This understanding of God's love is life giving. But Jesus' final comment on the subject in this passage can be daunting: "Be perfect, therefore, as your heavenly Father is perfect" (Matthew 5:48). Be perfect? Am I supposed to match the perfection of God's love?

Jesus himself addresses that question earlier in Matthew 5: "Do not think that I have come to abolish the Law or the Prophets; I have not come to abolish them but to fulfill them" (Matthew 5:17). Jesus' purpose in helping us to understand God's law isn't to urge us to try harder. He knows we're *incapable* of keeping the law. That's why he explains that he's come to fulfill "the Law and the Prophets." Jesus has come to keep the law on our behalf, meeting all of its requirements, so that we wouldn't be condemned by God's justice.

This is hard to grasp, but while God's law gives wisdom and guidance on how to live our lives, its purpose is also to show our inability to keep it—so we look to God for help. On the one hand, we rejoice that we can't earn God's love; but on the other hand, we *want* to earn it. Our sinful hearts yearn for the satisfaction and control of knowing that we deserve God's love. In Matthew 5, Jesus connects God's law with sins of the heart. He says that if you've ever lusted, you're guilty of adultery; if you've ever hated, you're guilty of murder (see vv. 21–22, 27–28). Jesus insists on reminding us that we don't have what it takes to earn God's love: "Be perfect as God is perfect."

In the end, we have no hope but in God's grace. When we insist on earning God's approval, we end up living as angrily and anxiously with

God as we do our spouses. Only when we accept God's love as something we can't earn can we begin to give unearned love to our spouses. It's critical to know this grace as the foundation of love for your spouse. Without knowing God's gracious love for you in Christ, you can't *give* gracious love. Your best efforts will be driven by a giving-to-get love that falls short of what God intended for marriage.

If you're willing to acknowledge your inability to keep God's law of love and your desire to serve yourself, and ask God's forgiveness because of who Jesus is and what he's done, then you can receive God's gracious love. It's the only way to have a right relationship with God, which is the only secure foundation for marriage.

Worship Is More Than Knowing

Worship Is a Relationship

Why is simply following Jesus' example not enough to live a life of love? Listen to the way Jesus describes his relationship to his disciples:

> Remain in me, and I will remain in you. No branch can bear fruit by itself; it must remain in the vine. Neither can you bear fruit unless you remain in me. I am the vine; you are the branches. If a man remains in me and I in him, he will bear much fruit; apart from me you can do nothing. (John 15:4–5)

Jesus describes himself as a vine and his followers as branches that live and grow attached to the vine. Jesus asks us to do more than think as he thinks and do as he does. He tells us to remain in him as he desires to remain in us. It's the language of two lives joined as one—the language of an *intimate relationship*.

In what sense can you have a relationship with Christ when you can't see him, touch him, or hear his voice? Sight, touch, and hearing are the basic ways that people relate, but they aren't the most important. Perhaps the most critical ingredient of an intimate relationship is *trust*. You have to know that the other person means what he or she says, won't let you down, and wants what's best for you and not just what's convenient for them. Jesus is eminently trustworthy, and a relationship with him requires trust in who he is. The Bible's word for that trust is *faith*.

Being in relationship with Jesus has everything to do with how you act in the ordinary, difficult moments of marriage. If Jesus is nothing more than a dead philosopher, then his words won't have much force when your spouse is standing in front of you pushing your buttons. How will the ideas of a man who died two thousand years ago help you in this real-life moment? To live in love in the moment, you need more than Jesus' ideas; you need a relationship with him. He is the *living* God, not a *dead* philosopher, and not a *lifeless* idol. You need to be able to draw near to him, share your heart with him, ask for his help, and know that he will give you wisdom, power, and love as you need it.

Worship Means Learning by Doing

Jesus speaks about bearing fruit. What does this mean and how do we do it? Ultimately we bear fruit by depending on Jesus, the Vine. But we aren't passive in that process. Living in trust and faith isn't about emotions; we aren't called to feel something before we do it. We can be certain that in marriage we will often do the right thing before we realize there's any benefit to it.

Think back to Jesus' interaction with the rich young man (chap. 2). Did you notice that the young man didn't see himself clearly until he was challenged to *do* something in his relationships? Marriages can get stuck because of misunderstandings about how learning and change happen.

Some of us learn by first studying a set of ideas or concepts and, next, by applying what we read. In this case understanding precedes action. Sometimes, however, you don't *really* understand something until you *try* to do it. Like the wealthy young man, sometimes we don't understand until we act.

My son has developed a love for baseball, a sport that, unfortunately, I have no experience playing. At first, I tried to help him by reading books about the sport, and I was pleased with how quickly I could get a handle on hits, runs, base stealing, and so on, just by a little reading. I even found that I was able to offer a few tips from behind the batter's box when my son was at the plate (to the coaches' chagrin, I'm sure).

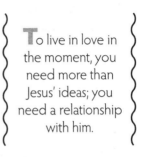

To live in love in the moment, you need more than Jesus' ideas; you need a relationship with him.

My most valuable lesson came one afternoon when I took my son to an automated batting cage to practice. As my son swung at the balls pitched out of the machine, I couldn't help but notice things that might help. I thought it would be easier to demonstrate my helpful pointers so I stepped into the cage prepared to crush the ball. I hoped I wouldn't embarrass him by hitting it *too* far. To my surprise, not only did I whiff the first pitch; I completely missed the next three balls. I slunk out of the batting cage avoiding eye contact with my son. (Adding further insult to my pride, I noticed later that I had sorely aggravated my tennis elbow.)

I learned then that knowing and doing aren't the same thing. No number of baseball books would make me a good baseball player. There's no substitute for swinging the bat. In fact, until you swing the bat you probably won't even know what you need to learn. But after swinging the bat, I read the batting chapters more attentively and got much more out of them. I've even connected with a few balls.

Growing in your marriage and in your relationship with God works the same way. You shouldn't assume that reading this book or even the Bible will, in itself, change you. You need to take action in order to change, or even to understand what you need to learn.

You may be thinking that trying something that you don't understand or feel like doing is hypocritical. To do something that doesn't feel good isn't phony. If only the wealthy young man had asked for Jesus' help, a whole new life would have opened up for him. He would have found that Jesus was more than a "good teacher."

C. S. Lewis explains the difference between being a phony and learning by doing.

> What is the good of pretending to be what you are not? Well, even on the human level, you know, there are two kinds of pretending. There is a bad kind, where the pretence is there instead of the real thing; as when a man pretends he is going to help you instead of really helping you. But there is also a good kind, where the pretence leads up to the real thing. When you are not feeling particularly friendly but know you ought to be, the best thing you can do often, is to put on a friendly manner and behave as if you were a nicer person than you actually are. And in a few minutes, as we have all noticed, you will be really feeling friendlier than you were. Often the only way to get a quality in reality is to start behaving as if you had it already. That is why children's games are so important. They are always pretending to be grown-ups—playing soldiers, playing shop. But all the time, they are hardening their muscles and sharpening their wits, so that the pretence of being grown-up helps them to grow up in earnest.[3]

Thinking about your marriage, and even thinking about what God says about your marriage probably won't be enough. You must be willing to *do*, even before you feel like it or understand it. In fact, sometimes in the act of doing, the lights go on. As we look at communication and problem solving and other important ways to love your spouse, you'll be challenged to do things in new ways—ways that will be difficult for you and may even feel impossible. Don't wait until you feel different. Try these things as you reflect on Jesus' words, and trust that he's helping you. In trying you'll learn more about how you need to grow. You'll learn what you need from God. Most important, you'll experience his faithfulness.

My Story, Part 3

As I sat at the kitchen table, it was obvious that I had failed to love God and Kim. But that moment of realization was a moment of hope, not hopelessness. I was not alone; Jesus was with me. As I sat frustrated and confused, his Spirit opened my eyes. He didn't come to condemn me for my law-breaking but to fulfill his law. I asked for his forgiveness and help. I had, for a season, returned to an old lover, an old idol, that had failed me again. I wanted to walk in freedom and love. With Jesus' help and forgiveness I knew I needed to approach Kim in love and in an entirely different way.

Think about It

- Has anyone ever surprised you in showing you love? How?
- God loves in surprising ways. Based on what you know about him from the Bible, how has he acted in surprising ways in your own experience? Since he is love, can you see how his actions can be understood as loving?
- What are some ways that you find it easy to love? What are some ways that you find it difficult?
- How easy or hard is it for you to believe that God loves you even when you fail? What would it look like to trust more in Jesus and his love for you? How might you think or act differently?

five

God's Dream
for Your Marriage

What You'll Learn in This Chapter:

- Though we might marry to avoid loneliness, God has greater purposes in mind. Marriage and relationships are an important way that we resemble God.
- We image God in relationship because God is relationship. He exists as three persons in perfect unity. Marriage teaches us to love as God loves. Marriage teaches us to live in commitment and grace as God lives with us in commitment and grace.
- Jesus is the perfect image of God, and so marriage is designed to make us more like Jesus.

Reading with New Lenses

WE NOW TURN to the Bible to see what God says about marriage. Connections between relationships, worship, and love give us a new lens for reading passages that may be familiar. Expect to see Jesus play a central role in the way the Bible describes God's purposes for marriage.

The Problem of Aloneness

The Bible introduces us to marriage with a simple observation. "The LORD God said, 'It is not good for the man to be alone. I will make a helper suitable for him'" (Genesis 2:18). If you've spent much time alone, God's observation may seem obvious and hardly worth mentioning. But the *way* God delivers that line grabs our attention.

A predictable rhythm is established in the creation story through the first chapter of Genesis. Each day God creates—light, darkness, land, sea, plants, animals—and at the end of each day, God speaks his pleasure in his creation: "And God saw that it was good" (Genesis 1:4, 10, 12, 18, 21, 25). But on the sixth day, in Genesis 2:18, it all comes to a screeching halt. God makes Adam, notes that he is alone, and says, "It is not good."

There used to be a series of check card commercials in which everyone is moving through a cafeteria line or retail store picking up their goods and swiping debit cards on the way out. The fabulous check card keeps everything moving along like a beautifully orchestrated ballet until somebody tries to pay with cash (requiring the cashier to make change), and the whole production comes to a crashing halt. People bump into each other, dishes crash to the floor, and everyone turns to stare at the clueless troublemaker who pays with cash. Genesis 2:18 is a bit like that. The comfortable, impressive rhythm of creation followed by the proclamation, "it was good," is broken by the jarring clang of "it is *not* good." Surely God could have made it "good" on the first attempt.

Pay close attention: God is creating drama to underscore something important about marriage.

Having observed that it isn't good for the man to be alone, God has Adam initiate a search for a helper. He parades all of the animals before Adam so that the man can name them. This isn't a silly exercise for Adam. He's on a quest to find that "suitable helper," the one who'll rescue him from aloneness. The act of naming something in Hebrew culture was about more than coming up with something catchy or memorable. To name something was to recognize its role, to give someone or something its job description. In naming the creatures Adam was really discovering and describing what these animals would do. But none of them could be named as his true companion or helper.

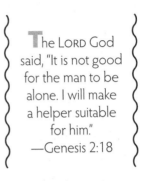

The LORD God said, "It is not good for the man to be alone. I will make a helper suitable for him."
—Genesis 2:18

This passage reminds me of the dating process, which felt like a painful parade of unsuitable prospects. (To be fair, I'm sure I was a painful part of their parades too.) Perhaps you've been painfully aware of that aloneness as you searched for the one you could name as companion and helper. What was it like for Adam to examine and name animal after animal waiting to discover the one that was created for relationship with him?

Finally, God puts Adam into a deep sleep and creates Eve:

> So the LORD God caused the man to fall into a deep sleep; and while he was sleeping, he took one of the man's ribs and closed up the place with flesh. Then the LORD God made a woman from the rib he had taken out of the man, and he brought her to the man. (Genesis 2:21–22)

When Adam finally meets *the one*, he grows suddenly poetic: "This is now bone of my bones and flesh of my flesh; she shall be called 'woman,' for she was taken out of man" (Genesis 2:23). In other words, "Yes! This is the right one! She's like me because she was made out of me!"[4]

The punch line of the story comes in the following verse. "For this reason a man will leave his father and mother and be united to his wife, and they will become one flesh" (Genesis 2:24). This story explains what marriage is all about. A man and a woman come together to form a new oneness because people were never intended to be alone. Marriage solves the problem of aloneness.

> God has something in mind for our marriages that's much better than delivering on our natural desires.

Note again how God draws attention to the creation of marriage. Remember, he could have done it some other way. He could have created Adam and Eve at the same time and simply explained their roles. Instead, he orchestrated an object lesson that will never be forgotten.

I've assumed that the problem of Adam's *aloneness* is the problem of his *loneliness*, and that God created marriage as a response to this loneliness. If I'm alone for long, I become lonely. I long to find acceptance, comfort, and safety in others. When I'm alone all of my dreams for marriage come to the foreground. Put more starkly, when I'm alone all of the desires and fears most likely to become my idols begin to rage. But as we've learned, marriage and relationships weren't created as substitutes for God. Just the opposite, marriage and relationships are expressions of the perfect love and relationship we find in God.

Our personal dreams for marriage seem so beautiful and convincing that we don't stop to consider that God's dreams for us may be different. There's nothing wrong with wanting to be accepted, comfortable, and safe; but those natural desires can quickly grow into idolatrous demands. God has something in mind for our marriages that's much better than delivering on these natural desires.

When God intentionally and dramatically highlights the problem of and the solution to Adam's aloneness, he's not just saying that loneliness is bad, and marriage is designed to remedy loneliness. The Bible has much more to teach about marriage, and those teachings should shape the way we understand the foundation of marriage in Genesis.

Created to Look Like Jesus

We sometimes refer to our spouses as our other or better half. The expression suggests that our spouses complete us. Although a sweet idea, it isn't God's view. Jesus is the One who completes you as a person created for a life of love. As you explore the following passages about marriage, notice how they make Jesus the focus of marriage.

About Husbands

The fifth chapter of Ephesians may be the most well-known marriage passage in the Bible, offering a powerful image of God's dreams for marriage. Here are the apostle Paul's instructions to husbands:

> Husbands, love your wives, just as Christ loved the church
> and gave himself up for her to make her holy, cleansing her
> by the washing with water through the word, and to present
> her to himself as a radiant church, without stain or wrinkle
> or any other blemish, but holy and blameless. (Ephesians
> 5:25–27)

In other words, if you want to know how to be a husband, Jesus' love for us is the perfect starting point. Jesus' goal and motivation for his bride, the church, is only what makes her more beautiful. He's not after some shallow Hollywood version of beauty but an inner beauty of purity and goodness that never fades or wrinkles. Jesus wants his bride to be beautiful and good through and through, to the core of her being. To accomplish his goal he lays down his life for her; he dies on the cross for her.

How wonderful to be loved by someone motivated to give you the best, committed to seeing you become all you were created to be, and willing to give everything to accomplish it.

About Wives

In his first epistle, the apostle Peter writes to us as people who'll sometimes suffer because we live under the authority or control of someone who'll treat us harshly and unfairly.

> But if you suffer for doing good and you endure it, this is commendable before God. To this you were called, because Christ suffered for you, leaving you an example, that you should follow in his steps. "He committed no sin, and no deceit was found in his mouth." When they hurled their insults at him, he did not retaliate; when he suffered, he made no threats. Instead, he entrusted himself to him who judges justly. He himself bore our sins in his body on the tree, so that we might die to sins and live for righteousness; by his wounds you have been healed. For you were like sheep going astray, but now you have returned to the Shepherd and Overseer of your souls. (1 Peter 2:20b–25)

Peter's encouragement is this: Sometimes we will suffer, even be punished, for doing good. But that suffering shouldn't stop us from doing good, because it was through suffering that Jesus accomplished his purposes for us. He suffered for doing good and through that experience God was able to redeem and save us.

You may be thinking, "I'll keep that in mind if I'm ever tortured for being a Christian or imprisoned for smuggling Bibles." But you might be surprised at how Peter applies this truth in the next verses where he says,

Wives, in the same way be submissive to your husbands so that, if any of them do not believe the word, they may be won over without words by the behavior of their wives, when they see the purity and reverence of your lives. (1 Peter 3:1–2)

A few verses later he writes,

Husbands, in the same way be considerate as you live with your wives, and treat them with respect as the weaker partner and as heirs with you of the gracious gift of life, so that nothing will hinder your prayers. (1 Peter 3:7)

Husbands and wives are "in the same way" to look to Christ's example as they live with one another in marriage. Peter portrays Jesus' suffering as an encouragement and guide for your marriage. The notion of submission and the description of the wife as the "weaker partner" may be so objectionable to you that you miss the bigger picture. Let's explore that concept later; for now let me simply ask you to see that wives, like husbands, are to be motivated by a vision of Christ and his love. When Jesus' disciples teach us about marriage, they point husbands and wives to nothing less than Jesus' amazing love—love that's willing to suffer, that submits to God's purposes, and that accomplishes our salvation.

What's the Problem with Aloneness?

The problem of aloneness and Christ as the center of married love: How do these two ideas connect? In Ephesians 5 Paul quotes Genesis 2:24:

"For this reason a man will leave his father and mother and be united to his wife, and the two will become one flesh."

This is a profound mystery—*but I am talking about Christ and the church.* (Ephesians 5:31–32, italics mine)

In other words, from its creation, marriage was designed to be an expression of Jesus' love for us.

Created in His Image

Genesis 2, which we considered at the beginning of this chapter, is an expanded account of the creation of man as described at the end of Genesis 1:

> Then God said, "Let us make man in our image, in our likeness, and let them rule over the fish of the sea and the birds of the air, over the livestock, over all the earth, and over all the creatures that move along the ground." So God created man in his own image, in the image of God he created him; male and female he created them. God blessed them and said to them, "Be fruitful and increase in number; fill the earth and subdue it. Rule over the fish of the sea and the birds of the air and over every living creature that moves on the ground." (Genesis 1:26–28)

In Genesis 1 God's focus in creating human beings is to create them in his image. What it means to be made in God's image has been the subject of much debate, but we can say with certainty that, at the very least, it means that God wants us to be like him. We can see this from the tasks that he assigns mankind. In the same way that God rules over creation, he wants us to rule over creation. In the same way that God creates and multiplies life, he wants us to create and multiply life. He wants us to act as his representatives on earth, running things the way he would.

64

God Is Relationship

Why does God create multiple people to bear his image? Why not just one person? Subduing the earth would be a big task for just one person, so Adam needed a helper in that sense. And given the way human beings enter the world, via sexual intercourse, Adam also needed help creating more helpers. God could have given Adam the ability to reproduce himself—sprouting off-spring like a potato or dividing like a para-mecium. He could have, but the Bible shows that imaging God well requires us to exist as people, male and female, rather than as individuals.

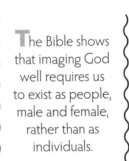

The Bible shows that imaging God well requires us to exist as people, male and female, rather than as individuals.

Scripture portrays God not only as an individual but also as a group of persons. In Genesis 1, for instance, God says "Let *us* make man in *our* image" (italics mine).[5] You may have heard the term *Trinity*. The Trinity is a way of describing God as he exists in three persons: Father, Son, and Holy Spirit. These three persons are all completely God, equal in their power, equal in their majesty and dazzling glory, and yet truly three persons who are essentially one God. Christians of all ages have known this as a mystery. It's difficult to comprehend how God can describe himself as one God and as three persons at the same time, but knowing God will always involve mystery. After all, he is the Creator; we are not; and although we are made in his image, he will always be, in some ways, different from us and beyond our understanding.

Hold on to this idea: Because God exists in relationship, it makes sense that he would want his image bearers to exist in relationship. Just as God mysteriously exists as persons who form a unity, God created us to mirror that reality. Remember how God created Eve in Genesis 2? Out of one he formed two and brought them together to form one again, two persons acting in such intimate concert that they could be described as one flesh.

God Is Love

As we imagine God in relationship, other important qualities come into view. How would we describe God as he acts in relationships? The Bible is the story of God in relationship with his people. The more familiar we are with that story, the more readily words describing God's character will come to mind. We can get a quick window into God's character by looking at how David describes God in Psalm 103. He "forgives all your sins and heals all your diseases" (v. 3); is "compassionate and gracious" (v. 8); is "slow to anger" (v. 8); is "abounding in love" (v. 8); and "does not treat us as our sins deserve" (v. 10).

From the psalmist we get the sense that God is wonderful, someone we'd want to be in relationship with. Elsewhere in the Bible God is described as merciful, gentle, kind, patient, understanding, and humble. We could properly summarize all of these character traits with one word: love. God is love.

All of these wonderful aspects of God's love would be hard to recognize or express outside of relationship. What does it look like to be kind or merciful or gentle when you're all alone? You might be a loving person, but apart from relationship it would be difficult for anyone, including yourself, to see it. God intends to be known and seen on this planet, and his image is to be visible through us, the people he created. For the image to be clear, we need to be seen in relationship.

Commitment and Grace

One feature of love that stands out in Genesis 2 is commitment. Although the word doesn't appear in the passage, it's one of the critical ingredients of being one flesh. Look again at Genesis 2:24: "For this reason a man will leave his father and mother and be united to his wife, and they will become one flesh." God creates two people out of one flesh (Eve is created from Adam's rib) and then reunites the two to become "one flesh" again in marriage. The image of one flesh communicates companionship, intimacy, belonging, and mutual influence. It's a picture of commitment.

Jesus' perfect life and death in our place is the foundation of his love for us.

The only way flesh can be separated from flesh is by painful, even fatal, tearing or cutting. Marriage joins a man and woman at such a level of profound intimacy that separating them should be as unthinkable and painful as cutting someone in two. If you've ever lost a spouse to divorce or death, you know how excruciating that pain can be. To safely become one flesh, we need to know that the union will last, that we aren't going to get torn in two. That's why marriage requires commitment, the promise to remain one for life.

Because we're all broken and sinful, commitment can be difficult to keep. Sin has destroyed our oneness with God and our oneness with our spouses. Our sins and shortcomings, big and small, tear at our oneness. No matter how committed we are to our spouses, we are going to create tears in oneness. What then is the solution?

Here is where we can deepen our understanding of grace. We've already learned that grace means getting love that we don't deserve and haven't earned. How does God give that love, and how can we give it even when we feel our spouse is tearing us apart? When flesh is torn or cut in two, it can be fatal. Actually, whenever our sin creates a tear in our relationship with God, it is *always* fatal. These tears are the result of our sin, and God can't be one with sin. The penalty for sin is always death. (See Romans 6:16, 21, 23.)

God doesn't want to be separated from us; he wants to remain one. Jesus made the repair in our relationship with God by allowing himself to be torn apart, separated from God on the cross, so that we'd not be torn apart and separated from God. Jesus' perfect life and death in our place is the foundation of his love for us. Grace doesn't mean that God has chosen to overlook our sin. Just the opposite, he has seen our sin and dealt with it. The punishment has been meted out so that we can be one with God.

God will work for our good in whatever challenges we face.

Since we've received God's mercy and love as those who have torn our oneness with him, we can extend that same mercy and love to our spouses when they tear at our oneness in marriage. There's real power, the power to change your heart, thoughts, and attitudes as you turn to Jesus and ask for the ability to love when you're being wounded by your spouse. We will look at this in more detail when we explore the issues of conflict and forgiveness. For now simply understand that the one flesh relationship of marriage requires commitment as well as grace, the solution to our unfaithfulness to that commitment.

Jesus, the Perfect Image of God

We've already explored how Jesus as God's Son is the perfect expression of God's love—the perfect image of God. God created us in his own image as his representatives on earth to create, cultivate, and care for the creation and each other as God does. Because of sin we are now distorted images of our Creator. Jesus is what we were all intended to be as descendants of Adam—what we are no longer able to be because of our sin. In the book of Hebrews, Jesus is described as "the radiance of God's glory and the exact representation of his being" (Hebrews 1:3). Jesus is the perfect image of God, the perfect picture of what we were created to be.

One way to think about how Jesus fulfills the law and rescues us is that he restores the image of God in us. By removing our sin and restoring our relationship with God he begins to change us, causing us to grow. We become the people we were created to be, more and more like Jesus. As Paul and Peter write about marriage they can't help but write about Jesus as God's perfect image. We are to image Jesus in our marriages, just as we are to bear his image in every area of life.

Jesus Is the Answer

It may seem peculiar to think about Jesus being the focus of marriage and the solution to every marriage problem. The reason the Bible makes that connection quickly and easily is because the Bible offers the same answer to every question it addresses.

When a person has one solution to every problem, we're tempted to write him or her off as simplistic or shallow. We aren't interested in pat answers. But Jesus isn't a pat answer. Knowing Jesus and understanding that he's your Savior and the solution to life's problems doesn't make working through life's problems easy. As you grow in understanding his rich and varied love and wisdom, you'll know that there's nothing simplistic about this answer. As we look at different areas of marriage and how we're to follow him, you'll see the richness and power of Jesus and his love.

For now, let me just give you one example of how the Bible offers Jesus as the solution to another problem, the problem of suffering. In chapter 8 of the apostle Paul's letter to the Romans he offers encouragement in suffering. He reminds them that it isn't just Christians who suffer, but that the whole creation suffers as we wait for Christ to return and complete the work he's already started—the work of removing sin and suffering from our lives and from the entire world. Paul reminds the Romans that Jesus' Spirit in them groans on their behalf as they pray, asking for things that they don't even realize they need.

In verse 28, he continues: "And we know that in all things God works for the good of those who love him, who have been called according to his purpose." It's good news to know that in whatever we suffer, God is going to work for our "good." As we think about marriage, we need to know that God will work for our good in whatever challenges we face, whether it's being mired in conflict, living with an indifferent spouse, recovering from adultery, or even abuse.

How do we know what good God is promising to accomplish? We would all define good differently depending on our personal preferences. Obviously, the good I'd prefer is that everyone would like me and be happy with me. Kim might prefer that conflicts disappear and all relationships be harmonious. How does God define good?

The word *purpose* gives us a clue as to what comes next. What is God's purpose? Paul writes in the next verse: "For those God foreknew he also predestined to be conformed to the likeness of his Son" (Romans 8:29). When we suffer we can find hope as we begin to understand how God will use that suffering to help us grow to become more like Jesus. Don't let the words *foreknew* and *predestined* trouble you. This means that if you're in a relationship with Christ it's no mistake; it's part of God's plan for you and always has been. That just gives you all the more reason to trust in his love for you.

Too Easily Pleased

Most of us didn't marry because we had a grand vision of becoming more like Jesus. But for now, if you don't find this motivating at least accept that this is what God's Word clearly teaches. At least then you can set goals for yourself. For one, you're going to need to spend time getting to know Jesus better. After all, how can you be motivated to grow closer to him and become like him if you don't know him? Remember, you're being invited into relationship with him, not only to imitate him or think like him. Second, expect your love for him to grow as you grow in your relationship with him. Even if you don't find him attractive now, if he is love incarnate, do you not want to learn to love him? C. S. Lewis wrote:

Indeed, if we consider the unblushing promises of reward and the staggering nature of the rewards promised in the Gospels, it would seem that Our Lord finds our desires, not too strong, but too weak. We are half-hearted creatures, fooling about with drink and sex and ambition when infinite joy is offered us, like an ignorant child who wants to go on making mud pies in a slum because he cannot imagine what is meant by the offer of a holiday at the sea. We are far too easily pleased.[6]

You may feel that Jesus is no match for the dreams and desires you brought to marriage, that to live without those dreams and desires would be unbearable. To think that Jesus himself is the grandest prize of all, the purpose of marriage and every other human endeavor may seem silly to you. You're too easily satisfied. Whatever pleasure you may have set your sights on pales in comparison with what God offers us in his son. Jesus isn't a consolation prize for the unhappily married. He's the grand prize for the married and unmarried alike.

If your marriage is going to be transformed, it must start with you. You need a new way of understanding the ordinary moments of your marriage. You need to learn to see the extraordinary in what you've taken for granted. Let that start with Jesus. If you don't know him, then begin now. If you've taken him for granted, pray that God would help you to see and value him as God, the Father, values and delights in him.

Think about It

- What are you like when you're alone? How are you different when you're around others? Why is there a difference? Do you think marriage and relationships make us better or worse as people?

- What do you think it means to become more like Jesus? Does that sound good or bad to you? Do you think it would mean that your personality disappears?
- Which statement more accurately describes your attitude: "I want my marriage to serve God's purposes" or "I want my marriage to serve my purposes"? If you believed that God's greatest good for you in marriage is to make you more like Christ, how would it change your attitude?

SECTION TWO

Extraordinary Love in the Details of Marriage

God intends his love to shape our marriages and, indeed, every area of life. The chapters in this section help you learn to love your spouse in the details of the moment, no matter how difficult.

Chapter 6 helps you transform your most basic attitude toward your spouse from manipulation to honor. You'll learn to spot these fundamental attitudes in the details of marriage and how to identify which one governs your interactions.

Chapters 7 through 9 discuss how love requires honesty, and why honesty can seem difficult and dangerous—learning to be honest in a way that builds up your marriage rather than destroys it takes wisdom and practice. These chapters help you to spot the ways emotions, desires, and fears distort the messages that we need to share with our spouses. You also learn to speak the truth in love.

Chapters 10 through 13 walk you through the difficult territory of conflict with the goal of learning how God uses it to strengthen our marriages. You also learn how to confess your wrongs to your spouse and offer forgiveness.

Chapter 14 helps you understand how problems can

crop up in the way we think about our marital roles and how love can deliver us from cultural confusion over gender differences. It addresses what it means to be a husband or a wife and how to decide who does what.

Finally, chapter 15 shows you how to build sexual intimacy on a foundation of love.

Person or Object, Honor or Manipulation?

What You'll Learn in This Chapter:

- Sometimes even when we think we're loving our spouses, we're manipulating them. We treat them like objects whose sole purpose is to give us what we want. We reward them if they give us what we want and punish them if they don't.
- Loving your neighbor as yourself means not evaluating, judging, or responding to people based on whether they can give you what you want or help you avoid what you fear.
- An attitude of honor is a critical ingredient of love. Honoring your spouse means:
  - ~ Understanding that your spouse belongs to God.
  - ~ Being willing to work to help your spouse grow.
  - ~ Being willing to learn from him or her.
- Larger patterns of manipulation can help us identify the desires and fears that prevent us from loving our spouses. To get what we want or avoid what we fear, we might move toward others, away from others, or against others.

Attitude Evaluation

THE LAW OF love, as we've seen, is to love your neighbor as yourself. The first step in applying the law of love to your marriage is to examine your most basic attitude toward your spouse. When you look at your spouse what do you see, a *person* or an *object*? It seems like an insulting question. Even if you did see your spouse as an object, would you admit it? Before you answer "person" too quickly, let's see how easy it is to slip into seeing others as objects and how difficult it can be to spot.

A Random Act of Manipulation

Howard, a counselee, stood in the checkout line of a grocery store. In front of him an elderly woman dug through her change purse.

"You're short seventy-three cents," the cashier informed the woman.

"I'm sure I have it in here somewhere," the woman explained as she began dropping pennies onto the countertop. She looked apologetically at the line behind her and continued digging through her purse in search of anything bigger than a nickel.

A few moments later Howard leaned forward, handed her a dollar bill, and said quietly, "Take this. It's okay." The woman looked up with a sheepish grin, uttered a quiet thank-you, and quickly paid the cashier.

As Howard shared his story I wondered if something had clicked. I'd been challenging him on his attitude toward his wife and was not sure if anything was making sense. "That's encouraging, Howard," I remarked. "It sounds like you saw an opportunity to love someone in a simple, concrete way, and acted on it."

"No," Howard answered. "I saw an old woman in my way, and I realized that the quickest way to get rid of her was to give her a dollar."

"Oh," I responded, suddenly not at all sure where this was going.

"I know that woman walked away thinking that I did a nice thing for her, but I didn't. I didn't love her. I just wanted her out of the way."

"So, what does that mean?" I asked.

"It means I'm a selfish jerk," he said.

Howard didn't see a *person* in front of him at the grocery store; he saw an *object*, an obstacle to his goals. The difference between people and things is that love requires us to treat people with an honor and respect that we don't give to things. Unlike things, all people share three characteristics: (1) they have a unique identity and purpose, (2) they are free to make responsible choices, and (3) they have worth.

> **P**eople bear God's image and deserve honor as existing uniquely for God's purposes.

Being a person means more than these three things, but at the very least, person-hood involves these things. When we speak of God as a person, we mean that these three things are true of him. God has a unique identity and his own purposes, God makes responsible choices, and God has infinite worth.

Made in God's image, every person ultimately belongs to God. God has the final say on who people are, what purposes they serve, what choices they make, and what they are worth. People bear God's image and deserve honor as existing uniquely for God's purposes. Honoring them doesn't mean we approve of everything they do. It doesn't even mean that we like them. It means we view them and treat them as belonging to God, not to us.

An object is a thing that may or may not be unique, makes no choices, and may or may not belong to anyone or have value. In everyday life, we value objects that are useful. An object can lose its value suddenly if we no longer want it or can use it. By definition, we manipulate objects; they exist for our use. We may use objects wisely or foolishly, but using them isn't bad in itself.

When we use people—when we treat people like objects—we violate the law of love, degrade the image of God, and destroy relationships.

Manipulation in Marriage

Howard hadn't taken the step of love that I had hoped, but he had made a critical first step. He realized that he could, in the guise of being thoughtful and caring, be selfish and manipulative. He didn't become a loving person that day, but he was no longer blind to his own self-ishness. He realized that he was manipulative, that he was willing to use other people to get what he wanted. It would no longer be as easy for him to point to all the nice things he had done for his wife, while brushing off her complaints that he didn't care about her. In reality, many of those so-called nice things were part of a strategy for silencing her, getting her out of the way, and keeping her from coming between him and the things he really loved.

Howard isn't a monster or even that unusual. Howard is much like all of us. He was simply "giving to get." Recall how we saw that Jesus observed our tendency to be nice to the people who are nice to us. We give to get and we give only when we get. It's so common that, as Jesus says, even those who seem to have no conscience at all (the "pagans" and "tax collectors" of his day) live that way (Matthew 5:43–48).

A formal agreement to give to get is called a contract. If you do your part then I'll do my part. We all live with contracts. Contracts are often put into place to prevent people from manipulating one another. We use contracts to enforce rules of fair play. In that sense, even the pagans and tax collectors observe a crude form of love. But that isn't the fullness of love that we're called to in marriage.

On our wedding days most of us promised something to the effect, "I take you to be my lawfully wedded wife [or husband] . . . for better or for worse, for richer or poorer, in sickness and in health, as long as we both shall live." That's a poetic way of promising, "You have my love forever, no matter what." But when you bring to marriage the agenda of giving to get, you break your commitment to love. The "no matter what" quality of the wedding vow is replaced with "give me *this* or *else*." Rather than acting out of genuine concern for your spouse, you treat him or her as a means to an end, as a way to get what you want. Instead of serving your spouse, you're using him or her to serve yourself. You're treating a person like an object.

Manipulation by Punishing

Sometimes manipulation is easy to spot. The most obvious forms involve punishing our spouses for failing to do what we want. It's as simple as me wanting Kim to be home on time to run errands so that I can finish my Bible study. Focused only on what I wanted and needed, I saw nothing else. For that hour, Kim existed only to make my schedule work. I lost sight of her as another person who needed my care and concern. That's why it didn't occur to me to worry about her. When she came home I punished her through sullen withdrawal, removing myself from the relationship. My message was, "If you don't care enough to be available when I need you, then you can feel what it's like for me to be unavailable to you!" In a small but significant way I treated Kim as if she were an object, even threatening to discard her like a possession that's beyond repair.

Manipulation as Favoritism

As Howard realized, a more subtle and attractive form of manipulation is a strategy of offering rewards instead of punishment. The Bible calls this kind of manipulation, favoritism. Cloaked in the guise of love, favoritism can be nearly unrecognizable as manipulation.

In the second chapter of James, the Bible describes how the wealthy were getting special treatment in church. A poor man is asked to sit on the floor or to stand so that a wealthy man can have a good seat. Notice how James diagnoses the problem of favoritism. He writes, "have you not discriminated among yourselves and become judges with evil thoughts?" (James 2:4). By playing favorites, the church leaders have elevated themselves above others, judging and evaluating who's more likely to give them what they want. Hoping that the wealthy man will bless them with money and power, they give him what they can—

a good seat—and take it away from the man who has nothing. The leaders have treated both the wealthy and the poor man as objects, things to be valued by their degree of usefulness. The rich man is chosen, and the poor man cast aside.

> For our marriages to grow in love, they must be built on a foundation of honoring our spouses as people who have value regardless of whether we're getting what we want.

James notes that these judges don't seem concerned about the law. In fact, by practicing favoritism they violate the essence of the law, love. James writes, "If you really keep the royal law found in Scripture, 'Love your neighbor as yourself,' you are doing right. But if you show favoritism, you sin and are convicted by the law as lawbreakers" (James 2:8–9). When we elevate ourselves above others, judging and evaluating them, we aren't loving them.

In many ways, Howard was not an angry or difficult husband. In fact, he could be warm and charming, planning surprise getaway weekends, bestowing lavish gifts, and telling his wife how wonderful she was. For many years his wife loved this about Howard. But over time Howard's attentions made her feel manipulated. Often, they followed angry arguments or preceded upsetting news. She began to realize that she was being paid off. Howard needed to see beyond the acts, which seemed loving, to his self-serving heart.

For our marriages to grow in love, they must be built on a foundation of honoring our spouses as people who have value regardless of whether we're getting what we want. If we show them favor only to get what we want, even if the things we want are good things, we become manipulators who suck love out of our marriages.

Loving Your Neighbor as Yourself

The way James applies the law of love helps us to understand what it means to "love your neighbor as yourself." As simple as this command seems, there's been much confusion about what it means, especially in recent years.

Some have taken it as a command to love yourself as well as a command to love others. Some have even argued that the command to love others—even your ability to love others—is founded on the love that you have for yourself. This command is important to understand because it defines a fundamental duty in worship.

First, recall that Jesus gave this second great commandment as an application and expression of the first, the commandment to worship God with all our heart, soul, mind, and strength, orienting every area of our lives around him. Jesus delivered these two commandments together because each is best understood in light of the other. Love, often understood as an emotion or confused with getting what we want from others, is a person. Jesus, God's Son and his perfect *image*, is love that we can see, hear, and have a relationship with. By following him, by worshipping him, we're schooled in what love really is. As the Bible teaches in 1 John 4:19, "We love because he first loved us." To say that our ability to love others is based on love for self is to neglect the truth that Jesus makes the second great command (love for others) dependent on the first (love for God).

In the command to "love your neighbor as yourself," what does "as yourself" mean? Why does Jesus not say, "Love one another as God loves you," as he does elsewhere? Just as with the first great commandment, Jesus again quotes from the Old Testament, this time from Leviticus. In Leviticus 19 loving your neighbor summarizes the preceding verses, which contain many commands that illustrate how we're to love one another in the details of life.

> Do not steal. Do not lie. Do not deceive one another.... Do not do anything that endangers your neighbor's life. I am the LORD.... Do not seek revenge or bear a grudge against one of your people, but *love your neighbor as yourself*. I am the LORD. (Leviticus 19:11, 16b, 18, italics mine)

In this context loving your neighbor as yourself means that you should give others the same kind of concern and care you would want them to give you. Jesus applies it this way in Matthew 7 (the Golden Rule): "So in everything, do to others what you would have them do to you, for this sums up the Law and the Prophets" (Matthew 7:12).

The Golden Rule probably sounds similar to things you heard from your parents or have said to your own children: "You don't want someone to take your things, so don't take her things. You don't like it when others lie to you, so don't lie to them."

But also, the phrase "as yourself" reminds us that because of sin we don't *want* to treat others the way we're treated. Deep down we don't want to be equal with others; we want to be superior to them. Sin entices us to exempt ourselves from the rules—to rationalize why we aren't bound by the same rules as everyone else. This is exactly what the Bible describes in James 2.

As discussed in an earlier chapter, our self-centeredness expresses itself in what we worship. Idolatry is a way of describing self-service in the language of worship. Through idolatry I elevate myself above all others, including God, and determine how others can best be employed to serve me and meet my felt needs.

In James 2:8, "as yourself" marks a boundary that you aren't to cross. You aren't to see yourself as better or more entitled than others; they're your equals, worthy of the same respect, honor, and care God demands that they extend to you. So, stated *negatively*, the second great commandment can be restated as, "Don't selfishly elevate yourselves above your neighbors." Or put even more simply, "Don't manipulate others."

Learning to Honor Your Spouse

If manipulation violates love, then honor fosters love. When you honor others you acknowledge their value and importance. Most often the Bible encourages giving more honor to others than we give ourselves. In his letter to the Philippian church Paul writes, "Do nothing out of selfish ambition or vain conceit, but in humility consider others better than yourselves" (Philippians 2:3). Paul understands this as a critical attitude of love because he sees it in Christ's attitude.

A few verses later he continues,

> Your attitude should be the same as that of Christ Jesus: Who, being in very nature God, did not consider equality with God something to be grasped, but made himself nothing, taking the very nature of a servant, being made in human likeness. (Philippians 2:5–7)

At first, this may sound like a sure path to being abused and taken advantage of. You may think, "If I let my husband know I consider him more important than me, I'd be waiting on him hand and foot." Remember, love doesn't mean being your spouse's yes-man but, rather, being determined to do what's best for him. As Jesus' own life illustrates, that doesn't always make others happy.

Attitudes of Honor and Manipulation

Honor Acknowledges That You Belong to God, not Me

Manipulation sees others as objects that exist to serve my own felt needs. Honor sees others as God's image bearers who exist for him.

God's image bearers belong first and foremost to God. Your identity as someone's spouse is secondary to your identity as a servant of God. In his letter to the churches in Rome, Paul addresses Christians that are disagreeing over an array of religious matters ranging from the kinds of food they should eat to what day of the week they should worship. What troubles Paul most is the attitude that these Christians have toward each other. He asks pointedly: "Who are you to judge someone else's servant?" (Romans 14:4a). In other words, "You act and speak as if this other person is your possession!"

Attitudes of Honor	Attitudes of Manipulation
You belong to God.	You exist to serve me.
You're made in God's image.	You're an object.
I give without expecting a return.	I give to get what I want from you.
I want you to be successful.	I need you to make me happy.
God is using you to make me like him.	You're the problem.
I'll love you, even if you don't respond with love.	I'll love you as long as it "works" (i.e. changes you).

To follow Christ is to accept him as your master. He's the owner and ruler of it all. Our acts of love are to be done because we worship him, not because other people own us, and we shouldn't demand the attention of others as if we own them. In marriage we have an obligation to fulfill our promises to love each other, but remembering each other's responsibility to love is very different from seeing the other person as someone (or some*thing*) who exists only for you.

Paul goes on to write,

> For this very reason, Christ died and returned to life so that he might be the Lord of both the dead and the living. You, then, why do you judge your brother? Or why do you look down on your brother? For we will all stand before God's judgment seat. (Romans 14:9–10)

Though in marriage we belong to each other in a very real sense, we don't belong to each other more than we belong to God. Your spouse has value and purpose far beyond his or her role as your spouse. We serve one another in marriage, but that service is only an extension or expression of service to God.

Remember, marriage was not created as a substitute or replacement for God. We *worship* God. We *love* our spouses. When we make our personal desires the measure of our spouses' worth, we're playing God. We want them to exist for us, to be devoted to us with their all, and we judge them if they fail to meet that standard.

> Your spouse has value and purpose far beyond his or her role as your spouse.

Manipulation Cries, "You're Mine, All Mine!"

Have you ever put your spouse on a pedestal, adored them, treated them like a prized possession, told them that you *need* them? There are people who wince to hear their spouse talk that way. Being needed in that way can be oppressive and suffocating because it's a sign of insecurity and neediness, not love. Being loved and being needed isn't the same thing. In the sense that we were made for relationship we need others, but that's very different from living out of a sense of desperation that communicates, "Without you I'm not going to make it."

Carl often told his wife how much he needed her. Whenever I heard him say this, I could see her fear. Why fear? Because whenever Carl felt lonely or insecure, he would look to his wife for affirmation and approval. If she didn't notice his bids for attention, he would often explode in anger and accuse her of not loving him. When Carl said, "I need you," it didn't mean, "I want what's best for you." It usually meant, "I feel like I have to have something from you to survive." When you need someone like a starving person needs a meal, you're putting him or her on the menu. No one wants to be eaten alive even if they're being told they're loved in the process. Anger comes when the person needing security and approval realizes that his spouse is unable to truly satisfy his hunger. Rather than recognizing that he's demanding the impossible, he punishes his wife for being unwilling or unable to meet his need.

Honor Considers How to Build You Up

Love isn't about getting your spouse to fill your sense of need. Jack Miller offers a great definition of what it means to serve one another in love: "Practically it means to labor to make others successful."[7] Love involves your effort to make your spouse successful. What does it mean to be successful?

Recall that being made in the image of God means you have a destiny. As we've learned, you were created to mature and grow to be more and more like God. Have you ever looked at your spouse and considered that he or she was made to be a picture of God here on earth? Sin has done a lot to make it difficult for us to see that image in each other at times. Understanding that it's your job to shine and polish that image is one way to think about what it means to love your spouse.[8] When you're in tune with the fact that you stand before an image bearer and child of the almighty God, it's hard to see that person as an object that exists for your purposes. C. S. Lewis explained the weightiness of this reality and the obligations it brings this way:

It is a serious thing to live in a society of possible gods and goddesses, to remember that the dullest and most uninteresting person you talk to may one day be a creature which, if you saw it now, you would be strongly tempted to worship, or else a horror and a corruption such as you now meet, if at all, only in a nightmare. All day long we are, in some degree, helping each other to one or the other of these destinations. It is in the light of these overwhelming possibilities, it is with the awe and the circumspection proper to them, that we should conduct all our dealings with one another, all friendships, all loves, all play, all politics. There are no ordinary people. You have never talked to a mere mortal.[9]

Manipulation Blames Your Spouse

Your desires are sure to conflict with your spouse's desires. What do you do when the inevitable conflict comes? One natural, sinful reaction is to view your spouse as a problem—as an obstacle to the things you want.

In the kitchen of the counseling center where I work there used to be an old soda machine. I don't know how old it was, but as I stood in the kitchen one afternoon sipping my afternoon soda I noticed how beat up the machine was. It had no casters and couldn't be moved around, and it was too heavy to carry or drop, so how did it get all of those dents and scrapes? I realized that most of those dents weren't accidental; they were the result of human hands and fists, maybe even mine. What do you do when you put your money into a vending machine and it doesn't give you what you've paid for? If you're like me, you give it a not-so-gentle swat hoping it will either digest your coins or free up whatever mechanism is keeping you from your soda. Within moments that machine can change from the beloved dispenser of a refreshing drink to a thief standing between me and what I crave. One minute it's the solution to my problems, the next minute the cause of them. One minute I love the machine, the next I hate it.

If you find yourself grumbling about your spouse, regarding him or her as an obstacle that stands between you and happiness, you're sliding into a mind-set of manipulation. You're focused on what you want and not seeing your spouse as a person.

Honor Learns from Others

When we're frustrated with our spouses, there's actually a very different way of thinking about them that can lead to real growth. If one of God's purposes in marriage is for us to love our spouses as his possession and build them up, it should dawn on us that he intends for them to have the same effect on us.

In other words, whereas manipulation means seeing your spouse as a tool in your hands, honoring your spouse means seeing him or her as a tool in God's hands. God is able to use our spouse's actions— noble or foolish—for his good purposes. One way to immediately begin to transform ordinary moments into extraordinary ones is to pause, no matter how annoyed you are, and ask, "What's God trying to teach *me*?"

> God is able to use our spouse's actions—noble or foolish—for his good purposes.

For example, when I was not able to reach Kim on the phone that frustrating Saturday, things would have been different if I had stepped back from my frustration and asked God to help me understand it and learn from it rather than immediately focusing on Kim as a threat to my plans. Even if Kim were actually wronging me, God could teach me something about my own heart and his love and care for me. The key is to pray for the humble attitude of someone who wants to learn and is even willing to ask for input.

Quite apart from how God can use our spouses' weaknesses and sins to teach us, we should be willing to learn from the positive ways that they're different from us. The Bible celebrates the ways that God has made us different from one another. It uses the image of the human body, describing its different parts and their functions (see Romans 12:1–8 and 1 Corinthians 12), to help us understand that our differences often complement one another and help us to move toward maturity as one. Living together as Christians we see that God has made and equipped us to do things differently from each other. Be willing to learn from them.

Manipulation Says That Won't Work

When we focus on changing our spous[e]
to learn from them, we often find ourselve[s]
action in terms of what works. Trying to fig[ure]
just another expression of the attitude of g[...]
our spouses the way God asks us to, there isn't always an immediate payoff. Love requires us to do difficult things, things that don't seem fair or may not even make much sense to us. Love requires us to define success in terms of God's agenda, not our own. What works from God's perspective is what causes us to grow.

Patterns of Manipulation

To admit that you can be manipulative is simply to say that you're a sinner. The question isn't whether you manipulate but how you manipulate. Taking the time to identify the typical ways that you manipulate your spouse can be a real advantage to growing in love. There are several typical patterns or styles of manipulation. As you read about them, consider which style you use. Each provides clues to heart issues or idols that drive you in your marriage.[10]

Moving toward Others

Sometimes acquiring the things you want or avoiding the things you fear means you need to get more out of the people in your life. Say, for example, you crave approval, affection, intimacy, belonging, or safety. Those are things you get from other people—and sometimes it takes other people to get what you crave, people that must be brought into your world. If acceptance is one of your chief desires, you may use any number of various strategies to attract others; you might hone a great sense of humor, be an extravagant gift giver, or be ready to help others out, for example. On the other hand, if you don't have much confidence in your ability to gain others' acceptance, you may employ more "negative" strategies like pouting, withdrawing,

ning clingy, or even taking more desperate measures like harm-
g yourself.

Moving Away from Others

Sometimes acquiring the things you want or avoiding the things
you fear requires *less* of the people in your life. Some people find that
peace, control, perfection, order, and safety are more easily secured by
having fewer people in their world or by exercising tight control over
those who are there. Some of the same "positive" strategies mentioned
above can also serve as a way of carefully controlling or limiting other
people's access to your world. For instance, a sharp wit can be an invitation to someone's company or a way to jab at those you want to keep
at a distance.

Moving Against Others

Sometimes acquiring the things you want or avoiding the things
you fear requires you to move *against* others. If you desire superiority, control, success, or power, you'll probably be moving against the
wishes of others in order to get them or to demonstrate that you have
them. Making sure that my plans succeed and yours fail can give me
a sense that my plans are better than yours and that I'm better than
you. When you fail I feel more successful, so I take steps to ensure that
you fail. Strategies for moving against others can be as elaborate as
dominating vacation plans or as small as nit-picking another person's
grammar.

You may have noticed that some desires and fears occur in more
than one pattern of manipulation (safety and control, for example). The
desires and fears are listed under their more typical pattern, but keep in
mind that, depending on how it's used, each pattern can serve any and
every desire or fear. The motives suggested above for each pattern provide a typical starting point for understanding what motivations might
lie beneath your relational patterns or those of your spouse.

The above patterns don't always suggest sinful manipulation. Love itself sometimes moves toward others, sometimes away from others, and sometimes against others. There's more to love than drawing near. Sometimes love requires moving away from one you love so as not to participate in evil. Or you may need to create distance in an abusive relationship. Love may even call you to move against someone you love—not to that person's detriment but in challenging sinful behavior or to protect others. In marriage, love will, at times, require you to say no or otherwise challenge your spouse just as God challenges us when we need it.

Start with an honest look at your own attitudes. Many couples stumble in their first attempts to change because they're expressing an attitude that undercuts every effort to love. When you look at your spouse, do you see someone who *should* be loved and given respect and honor as a person? Or do you see your spouse as an obstacle to the things that you desire or a shield that fails to protect you from the things you fear? Whose best interests most shape the way you think and feel about your spouse?

Think about It

- Recall an instance, apart from your marriage, when you were used by someone or treated like an object. How did it feel? Why?
- Think about your spouse's strengths and abilities as a person. How might you learn from them? How might God use them to help you grow? Think about some of the typical frustrations or ordinary moments of your marriage. How might God be asking you to learn and grow from those as well?
- What is your typical pattern of relating to people? Do you tend to move toward, away from, or against others? Do you respond differently in different relationships? Do you have a typical style in your marriage?

seven

Honesty Is Important

What You'll Learn in This Chapter:

- At the root of many communication problems is a lack of honesty.
- Because of sin and shame we often hide our thoughts and feelings from ourselves and our spouses. We hide from God, too, because deep down we know that sin has broken our relationship with him.
- Jesus makes it safe for us to face the things that we hide from ourselves, our spouses, and God. He came to touch and make clean the desires, fears, shame, and sin that we don't want to face or aren't even aware of.

Talking around the Problem

KEVIN AND BRENDA came to counseling because of a conflict they weren't solving on their own. Like many couples they had a sense that the way they were communicating was part of the problem.

"I think we need more than help sorting out a few problems; I think we need help communicating," Brenda explained. "Somehow we aren't hearing each other." Kevin nodded in agreement. Brenda continued, "It's frustrating because we've always been able to connect easily, but recently we don't seem to be connecting at all."

Kevin and Brenda had been going through financial difficulties for some time, and recently Brenda had been considering taking a part-time job. She was a registered nurse but had left nursing when they started a family. Now that the kids were all in school and money was tight she thought it might be a good time to return to it. Kevin was not convinced.

Within a few minutes I witnessed the communication problem Brenda had described. "Kevin, I don't understand what the big deal is. It will only be part time, and I promise I'll be home before the kids get out of school. I really think you'll hardly notice," Brenda urged.

"I don't think you're being realistic," Kevin replied. "You know how exhausting nursing can be. I don't see you doing nursing work without it having a negative impact on our home life."

Brenda rolled her eyes. "Kevin, what's the big deal! Having everything at home the way you like it isn't everything. Look, we need the money and I can earn it. Stop being such a baby about it!"

"Why are you determined to get out of the house!" Kevin snapped. "I swear, it's like you can't get away from us fast enough! And why the sudden obsession with money! Why can't we just leave things the way they are and ride out this financial rough patch?"

Within minutes both appeared sullen and defeated. Brenda's eyes were filling with tears, and Kevin had turned away from her and was staring at the far wall.

Brenda was right. There were real communication problems here. The rapidity with which their conversation escalated into a full-blown fight was a clue that they were trying to talk about something much deeper and closer to the heart than jobs and finances. What made Brenda think Kevin was acting like a baby? Why did Kevin think Brenda was trying to get away from him and the kids? These are clues to the deeper underlying issues that they weren't talking about openly and honestly. The inflammatory things that were being said were reactions to and an inability to deal with what *was not* being said.

> The kind of honesty that reflects God's love requires sharing the right information in the right way, a way that leads to oneness and growth.

Honesty and Oneness

As Kevin and Brenda's conversation illustrates, honesty isn't just communication free of lies. In one sense, we could say that Kevin and Brenda were being honest (way too honest) letting words and thoughts fly that had more to do with judging each other than with understanding each other. Honesty doesn't mean saying the first thing that pops into your head or just getting something off your chest. The kind of honesty that reflects God's love requires sharing the right information in the right way, a way that leads to oneness and growth.

In Ephesians 4:25 the apostle Paul puts it this way: "Therefore each of you must put off falsehood and speak truthfully to his neighbor, for we are all members of one body." In explaining the importance of honesty Paul uses the image of the body. Remember how Genesis 2 described the creation of marriage. Eve was created out of Adam's body. It was a picture of two persons being created out of one and the two being joined together as one: "For this reason a man will leave his father and mother and be united to his wife and they will become one flesh" (Genesis 2:24). The body is often used as a word-picture to describe intimate relationships, people joining together in a relationship of trust, the different parts working together for common goals and the common good.

The Bible also describes the church, God's community, as a body. The phrase "one flesh," used to describe marriage, is another way of saying the same thing. Although Paul is speaking to everyone in Jesus' church, his words can be applied directly to marriage; both are relationships of intimate connection.

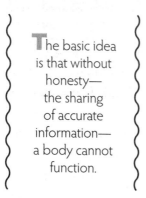

The basic idea is that without honesty— the sharing of accurate information— a body cannot function.

The basic idea is that without honesty— the sharing of accurate information—a body cannot function. My wife, Kim, is a physical therapist. When she first started practicing, she worked in a hospital with acute-care patients. Many of these patients had suffered strokes or head injuries. Frequently a stroke causes a breakdown in communication between the brain and part of the body. Kim came home with story after story of the hard work her patients had to do in order to function again, to reestablish communication so they could walk and talk. She told of patients who walked into doorjambs, banged their arms into tables, or simply stumbled and fell because they'd lost communication with part of their body. Sometimes patients complained that the limb felt like it belonged to someone else, someone working against them. The automatic coordination of our bodies is something that we all take for granted; when we lose it, it can be devastating.

Sometimes our marriages function, or stop functioning, as if we've suffered a stroke. We stop sharing important information with each other. We lose our ability to coordinate our lives and move forward. We no longer know what's going on with the other, and, therefore, every effort to move along the path of life together leads to a stumble, a fall, or a painful collision.

The Problem of Hiding

Paradise Lost, The Problem, Genesis 3

The Bible tells us that, in a sense, we've all suffered a spiritual stroke. Everyone lives with a communication breakdown that makes honesty difficult, sometimes impossible. This problem has been with us from the beginning.

The picture of relationship that the Bible gives in the beginning is one of amazing openness. Genesis 2 tells us that Adam and Eve "were both naked, and they felt no shame" (Genesis 2:25). Don't miss the significance of this statement. Nowhere else in the Bible do we find nakedness without shame. Adam and Eve's physical nakedness is a visible expression of the total openness they enjoyed with each other and with God. They lived with literally nothing to hide, inside or out.

Having never experienced life without sin, we can only imagine what it would be like to live in complete openness and safety, with no need to hide or cover up. You may have glimpsed this in your marriage or other intimate friendships, but no matter how much you love and trust your spouse or best friend there are things that you never want them to know about you. Maybe you said or did something terrible. Maybe lustful, dark, or angry thoughts are racing through your mind. Or, maybe other people have done awful things to you. There are things we don't like to face about ourselves, things we certainly don't want on view to others. Before the Fall, Adam and Eve, with nothing to hide or avoid, knew nothing of that feeling. Nakedness without shame is a picture of complete openness, honesty, and safety.

Things soon changed dramatically. Adam and Eve turned away from God and trusted in the lies of the Serpent. Notice that the first thing they did was to hide. Genesis tells us, "Then the eyes of both of them were opened, and they realized they were naked; so they sewed fig leaves together and made coverings for themselves" (Genesis 3:7).

Clearly, they were hiding from God who had warned them not to disobey him and eat from the forbidden tree, saying, "when you eat of it you will surely die" (Genesis 2:17b).

Adam and Eve were hiding from one another as well. Because of sin it was no longer safe to live openly before God or each other. Remember what sin and idolatry are really about: attempts to play God, to make everything and everyone serve you and your desires. To sin is to treat people as objects. It simply isn't safe to live openly before someone who's willing to reduce you to a *thing* that exists for his or her pleasure. You need protection from someone like that. Imagine what it must have been like for them to move, in the blink of an eye, from a state of complete openness and safety to one of shame and fear.

But what isn't obvious from Genesis 3 is the hiding that happened *inside* Adam and Eve. They didn't just conceal themselves from God and each other; they also hid from themselves. They began to cover up and deny what they knew about themselves. Genesis tells us, "The man and his wife heard the sound of the LORD God as he was walking in the garden in the cool of the day, and they hid from the LORD God among the trees of the garden" (Genesis 3:8). Did Adam and Eve really believe they could hide from God?

Adam and Eve may have been simply naive about God's absolute knowledge, but more likely, their actions illustrate how sin not only keeps us from knowing each other but from knowing ourselves. Adam and Eve couldn't bear to face a God who saw them and their naked guilt clearly. They didn't want to see the plain truth: they were wicked, sinful, without excuse, and living in plain view of a holy and angry God.

On a kinder note, who can blame them? Can any of us bear knowing how sinful we really are? Do you really want to see yourself clearly? Do you want to remember all of the shameful things you've thought and done over the last five years, five days, even five minutes? To know that *and* to know that God sees it as well is more than we can handle.

But as much as we might like to avoid it, this knowledge is inescapable. Because we're made in God's image we can't fully escape knowledge of ourselves, and of God's purity, holiness, and wrath. We were made to be like him and at the deepest level, at the level of your spiritual DNA, God is hard-wired into your system. When you look at yourself in the mirror you can't help but be reminded of who God is and what he is like. All of your thoughts, feelings, and observations are imprinted with reminders of God. They all, in some way, point to him.

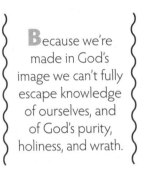
Because we're made in God's image we can't fully escape knowledge of ourselves, and of God's purity, holiness, and wrath.

Do you become angry when mistreated? So does God. Are you sad over loss and pain? So is God. Do you enjoy the good things of this world? God created them. Even in your sinfulness you bear the family resemblance. Because you're reminded of God when you reflect on yourself, you can't help but also feel shame over being sinful. To be a human and fallen image bearer is always to experience the simultaneous knowledge that you're both an image bearer of God and a sinful person. In each of us, two things that couldn't be more different are woven together.

Warp Core Breach!

When we were kids, my brother and I loved watching *Star Trek*, the original series, with Captain Kirk, Spock, Dr. McCoy, and the whole gang. One of the things I learned from *Star Trek* is that the worst thing that can happen on a starship is a "warp core breach." It seems that the *Enterprise* was propelled by bringing together matter and antimatter, two substances that are completely opposite from each other and that release an enormous amount of energy when they come into contact. Under the right circumstances, when carefully controlled, the matter/antimatter fusion propels the starship *Enterprise* through the galaxy at multiples of the speed of light. But we always knew we were in for a nail-biting episode when Mr. Scot, the chief engineer, radioed the bridge and warned Captain Kirk that a warp core breach was imminent. In other words, the matter and antimatter were about to lose containment, and the *Enterprise* would soon explode like a supernova. (Fortunately, that never actually happened.)

In a sense, we all live in regular danger of a spiritual warp core breach. The "matter" of being the image of God is always in danger of coming into conscious contact with the "antimatter" of our sinfulness, the fact that we'd rather be God than love God. On the one hand we're wired to know and love him, and on the other, our sinfulness compels us to rail against him and avoid him. Thus we live as divided people, always of two minds. Sometimes we genuinely desire to draw near to God, to embrace him, to love him, and to love others. In the very next moment we can feel the complete opposite impulse. Wild desires seize us, animosity and anger flare up, and we inwardly shake our fists at God and others.

The apostle Paul describes this internal warfare this way:

> For I have the desire to do what is good, but I cannot carry
> it out. For what I do is not the good I want to do; no, the evil
> I do not want to do—this I keep on doing. Now if I do what
> I do not want to do, it is no longer I who do it, but it is sin
> living in me that does it. (Romans 7:18b–20)

Have you ever felt that way? Have you felt the madness of having two minds, one that wants to do what's right and one that wants to do what's evil?

This is the dynamic that shows up when we try to communicate in marriage. On the one hand we want to be known and loved. On the other hand, we avoid knowing ourselves and, what's more, know that it isn't entirely safe to be known by another sinner. We don't know what should be said and what should be left unsaid. We tell selective truths, sometimes hiding from our spouses the most important things that are going on inside of us. What are we to do? Like victims of a stroke, we struggle to communicate with others; we struggle to communicate with ourselves, and at best we stumble through marriage without really connecting with our spouses.

God's Solution to Our Problem with Honesty

Covered by Christ

The tension of living as both a sinner and an image bearer of God can seem hopeless at times. But when Jesus came something happened that changed everything. In Jesus, the two things that must never touch—the matter and antimatter of holiness and sin—touched. *But there was no explosion.* We weren't destroyed. In a shocking turn of events, God's holiness swallowed up and destroyed sin, not us, so that we could live once more with him in peace and intimacy.

That warp core breach shocked and offended some. Jesus didn't just tolerate the sinners that thronged to him; he reached out and touched them. He visited tax collectors in their homes; invited prostitutes to follow him; touched and cured the lepers, the blind, and the lame, all of whom were considered unclean. A holy Jesus reached out and touched these broken and rebellious image bearers, not to punish but to rescue. Their unholiness didn't contaminate him; rather his holiness invaded their hearts and they were changed; they became clean. God solves the problem, not by destroying us, but by destroying our sin.

We no longer need to hide behind fig leaves. We no longer need to cover ourselves to avoid the truth that we live naked and defiled in the world of a holy God. In Jesus, God says, in effect, "I see you and I don't want you to be afraid. I'll make you new again. You no longer have to hide. I'll cover your sinfulness and shame with my Son's perfection. Step out and be seen."

Part of the challenge for us is that, although we're truly forgiven and accepted by God, we still experience the presence of sin in our hearts. We still experience the tension of our own sin and God's holiness. The battle rages on. That doesn't mean that we aren't accepted by Jesus. Being forgiven by God and becoming one of his children is an event. It happens the moment we admit our sinfulness, brokenness, and need and commit to depending on Jesus. But as we explored in an earlier chapter, being transformed into the perfect image of God, the image of Jesus, is a process that takes a lifetime. During that process we still experience the activity of sin in our hearts, but we now have the power of Jesus' own Spirit living in us to help in every moment of temptation and need. If you're one of God's children, sin is no longer at the center of your identity. You're fundamentally different. Love has replaced animosity for God at the core of your being. Gradually, over the rest of your life, you'll grow and mature as that love grows and the power of sin diminishes within you.

> True honesty, not just the basic skills of speaking and listening, requires faith: it's a matter of worship.

The love and forgiveness God gives you in Jesus mean that you can now live an open life before him. These gifts also mean you can live open lives before one another and your spouse. You can give your spouse the same wonderful gifts that God has given you. You can invite your spouse to live an open life before you, to be honest about his or her thoughts, the good and the bad. And your spouse can be sure that you won't turn away. This is the gift we all want—to be truly *known* and *loved*.

But knowing your spouse can be just as scary as knowing yourself. To invite your spouse to that kind of honesty requires as much faith on your part as it does for your spouse. If your spouse tells you what's really going on inside, what will you hear? True honesty, not just the basic skills of speaking and listening, requires faith: it's a matter of worship. Will you continue to trust in your efforts to hide from God and your spouse, or will you trust God to love and protect you as you face what you'll hear as you and your spouse practice true openness?

Learning *how* to be honest with your spouse still requires wisdom and care because as sinners you're quite capable of misusing each other's honesty. We will explore the hows of honesty in the next chapter.

The Truth about Kevin and Brenda

So how do Kevin and Brenda need to be honest with each other? First, there are truths they need to acknowledge to themselves before they can share them with each other—truths central to the way they understand themselves and what relationships are all about.

Kevin was raised in a family of four boys of which he was the youngest. It was a difficult childhood. His father's work required him to travel a lot, and he was an alcoholic. When he was home he kept to himself, slept a lot, and was often irritable and occasionally abusively angry with his wife and kids. Kevin's mother did the best she could to raise Kevin and his brothers on her own, but her stress and unhappiness were plain to her sons. The boys were often left to fend for themselves. Being the youngest, Kevin was often at the mercy of his older brothers who could at times be bullies. It's no surprise, then, that Kevin tends to avoid conflict and cherishes a home that's different from the one he knew as a boy. He craves relationships (and a marriage) that are soothing and comfortable. He gets irritated and anxious when problems with Brenda aren't resolved quickly. But he's not always aware of how and why these feelings are so powerful. The feelings themselves make him feel ashamed, and he's embarrassed when he knows he's overreacting.

Brenda was raised in a family with two younger brothers. A powerful shaping influence in her life was her mother's unexpected death when she was eleven. Her mother had been a warm nurturer, and Brenda assumed that role after her mother's death. Her father continued to work hard supporting the family, while Brenda stepped into many of her mother's roles, keeping house and supervising her brothers. She never complained and found satisfaction in doing things that were meaningful and that she was good at. Becoming a nurse seemed a natural fit to her after leaving home and graduating from college. Nursing, more than simply a job for her, is an expression of a deeply held sense of calling and importance. Caring for others feels central to her identity as a person. Now that her own kids need less of her attention at home, she's eager to expand her calling as a caregiver. But Brenda doesn't fully realize why nursing is so important to her, and part of her is afraid that she does, in fact, sound like a wife and mother just trying to get out of the house. She doesn't know how to face these conflicting feelings, and she certainly doesn't know how to discuss them with Kevin, especially when he seems to have already assumed the worst.

Kevin and Brenda need to realize that they aren't arguing just over the logistics of finances and jobs. They're each fighting for and defending deeply held desires, fears, and beliefs, some of which they've lived with for so long that they're hardly aware of them. Brenda had lived in her role as caregiver for so long and with such satisfaction that it hadn't occurred to her that it could be flawed or might need to be adjusted in any way. Kevin, on the other hand, battled real anxieties about conflict and feeling neglected. These feelings made him feel weak. To the extent that he was aware of them he chose not to think about them, and he certainly didn't want to share them with Brenda. But to live life as one body they must learn to face them and then share them.

The Pathway to Honesty

Look again at Ephesians 4:25: "Therefore each of you must put off falsehood and speak truthfully to his neighbor, for we are all members of one body." The first word, "therefore," indicates that everything that follows is based on what has just preceded. The "therefore" of verse 25 points us to the work of Jesus and the process of change that I've just explained. Honest communication is an important expression of how Jesus has freed us from hiding.

In Ephesians 4:17–24 Paul describes the process of maturing into the image of Christ as one of "putting on" and "putting off." We put off all of the sinful and useless ways of thinking and acting that have corrupted our lives before we knew Jesus, and we put on all of the new truths and ways of living that Jesus has taught us. It's an image of taking off one set of clothes, dirty smelly old clothes, and putting on new ones, clean white, fresh ones.

Paul's instruction to "put off falsehood and speak truthfully," isn't just helpful advice on communication but a product of being connected to Jesus. It's the fruit of growing and maturing in him. It isn't something that we do as a strategy to change our spouses; rather it's a change that results from being in relationship with Jesus. Rescued and redeemed by Christ, you no longer have to live a life of inward shame and fear. Remembering that God knows you and loves you and that you no longer have to hide who you are can be the difference between communication that's an expression of sincere love and communication that's manipulative and self-centered.

But honesty isn't just an expression of our personal growth in Christ. Our willingness to speak the truth has everything to do with the growth of other followers of Jesus. In the first half of Ephesians 4, Paul explains how Jesus has equipped us with everything we need to grow and mature in his love. In particular, Paul writes, "speaking the truth in love, we will in all things grow up into him who is the Head, that is, Christ" (Ephesians 4:15). In other words, our willingness to speak truth to one another is part of how we help others to grow in love and maturity in Jesus as well.

Think about It

- How would you rate your honesty with your spouse on a scale from one to ten, one being least honest and ten being most honest?
- How do your desires or fears—or idols—shape the way you talk with your spouse and others? How do you argue for them? How do you hide or disguise them?
- What things have you avoided seeing in yourself and sharing with your spouse that you can begin to share with Jesus?

eight
Being Honest about Yourself

What You'll Learn in This Chapter:

- Our attempts at communication often backfire because rather than revealing our own thoughts and feelings we tell our spouses what we believe is wrong with them.
- Emotions play an important role in honesty. When we're able to share our emotions with our spouses we're more effective at expressing sincere love.
- Anger and fear are emotions that require extra care. Both can tempt us to cover rather than reveal ourselves.
- Double binds, indirection, and misdirection are common but subtle forms of dishonesty that we need to be especially careful to avoid.

Reveal Yourself, Not Your Spouse

"KEVIN, WHAT'S THE big deal! Having everything at home just the way you like it isn't the most important thing. Look, we need the money and I can earn it. Stop being such a baby about it!"

"Why are you determined to get out of the house?" Kevin snapped. "I swear it's like you can't get away from us fast enough! And why the sudden obsession with money! Why can't we just leave things the way they are and ride out this financial rough patch?"

> The truth that your spouse desperately needs—and the truth that only you can give—is truth about yourself.

Kevin and Brenda's conversation derailed at the moment they became defensive and stopped listening to each other. In a sense, both were being honest: Brenda honestly believed Kevin was being childish and selfish, and Kevin honestly believed that Brenda didn't care about him and just wanted to get away. The aim of their honesty was to remain hidden while exposing the other. They delivered honest *accusations,* not honest *disclosures* about themselves.

This is perhaps the most common mistake couples make. Spouses describe each other's actions, thoughts, feelings, and motives while ignoring, even hiding, their own. They expose the other while concealing themselves. The truth that your spouse desperately needs—and the truth that only you can give—is truth about yourself.

Only you know what you're thinking and feeling, and only you can share that with your spouse. Instead of focusing on your spouse's thoughts, feelings, and motives, concentrate on your own. Simple phrases like "I think . . . ," "I feel . . . ," or "It seems to me . . ." can help you stay on track. Offer your observations not as indisputable facts but as what you think, feel, and observe. You might be surprised at the difference it makes in your communication.

Above all, when you speak, maintain an attitude of humility. Recognize that your understanding is always shaped and limited by your own perception. You never see everything; you only see what you see. You never hear everything; you only hear what you hear. Remember, too, that we live with desires and fears that shape what we hear. Worship shapes communication. The idols that you worship erect a filter that screens out information that doesn't match up with expectations. Idols also amplify other messages that you're sensitive to. Approach every topic with humility—a willingness to learn something new and correct faulty understandings. Communicate a humility that allows room for more information or a different perspective.

The Importance of Sharing Emotions

Emotions can get us into trouble. In the heat of the moment we've spoken rashly, vented anger, or caved in to fear. Emotions don't always help us obey God, and yet they're a part of who we are as God's image bearers. The Bible displays a full spectrum of emotions— e.g., joy, fear, grief, anger—and describes God as expressing these same emotions. Following Christ isn't a call to deny emotions and live life as a stoic. In fact, emotions are a critical ingredient in the meaningful expression of honesty.

In Romans 12:9 Paul writes, "Love must be sincere." The word *sincere* means "without hypocrisy." In other words, love must not be a put-on or a show; it must be genuine through and through. Paul goes on to describe genuine love: "Honor one another above yourselves," and "Bless those who persecute you; bless and do not curse"—give even when you do not get—(Romans 12:10, 14). Then he writes, "Rejoice with those who rejoice; mourn with those who mourn. Live in harmony with one another" (Romans 12:15–16a). Sincere love requires sharing in each other's emotions—the good and the bad, the joys and the sorrows. Love requires us to *feel*.

What is the connection between emotions and love? Jesus Christ is Love. The Bible describes Jesus as a man who expressed emotions. He shows anger as he challenges the cruelty of religious leaders and the pride of his own disciples (Mark 3:1–6; 8:31–33). He grieves over the death of a friend (John 11:34–36). Jesus "offered up prayers and petitions with loud cries and tears" (Hebrews 5:7), and he was "a man of sorrows, and familiar with suffering" (Isaiah 53:3). God wants us to know that Jesus cares for and understands us.

Jesus didn't just peek down from a cloud and say to us, "I know it's hard to live down there in a broken world with broken people"; he came and lived in our broken world vividly expressing his pain and sorrow. Jesus' emotional expressions, which convince us of his empathy and care, encourage us to trust and draw near. The Bible puts it this way:

> For we do not have a high priest who is unable to sympathize with our weaknesses, but we have one who has been tempted in every way, just as we are—yet was without sin. Let us then approach the throne of grace with confidence, so that we may receive mercy and find grace to help us in our time of need. (Hebrews 4:15–16)

For you husbands who have more trouble sharing your emotions than your wives: Imagine inviting a friend over to watch your favorite team compete in a playoff game. You invite him because you both root for the same team. He reads the sports page, knows the team roster, and even knows the team's history and statistics. It should be great fun watching the game with him. But to your dismay, during the game he's an expressionless zombie. When your team makes an incredible play you toss potato chips in the air and howl with joy; your friend simply crosses his legs. When there's an unfair call on the field you scream through the TV at the refs; your friend folds his arms and looks at his watch. When your team loses in the final seconds you're in agony; your friend comments impassively on the statistical significance of the loss, and how it will affect the careers of the coaches and team members.

Most sports fans would never watch another game with this person. Why? His impassivity communicates that he doesn't really care. Loving a team isn't about memorizing *facts* but about being in the game with the team and those who love it.

Now apply this to your marriage. Just saying "I love you" isn't enough. Do you rejoice when your spouse rejoices? Do you weep when she weeps? It isn't enough to know facts and stats; it's about being in the game together—caring about the struggles, victories, and defeats.

Emotions communicate the value you place on something the same way a price tag does.

Emotions are the currency of personal involvement. Emotions communicate the value you place on something the same way a price tag does. When you spend a lot of money on something it demonstrates how great a value it has to you. When you feel deeply about something it means that it has great value to you. Your emotions tell you—and, when you express them, they tell others—how important something is to you and how you value it. The stronger the emotion, the more important it is to you.

What do your emotions communicate to your spouse? As with the sports example, the absence of emotion doesn't communicate neutrality, logic, or intelligence; it communicates indifference. Indifference can be just as painful as rage, rejection, or betrayal. The bottom line is this: if you're unwilling to share in your spouse's emotions, your spouse isn't likely to feel loved.

But also understand that your unwillingness or inability to share your emotions makes it difficult for you to experience their sincere love for you as well. Again, your emotions communicate what's important to you; if you, therefore, haven't really shared with your spouse what's important to you, how can you believe that your spouse knows you? And if someone doesn't truly know you, how much does it mean when he or she says I love you. To claim to love someone you don't really know is to love only the image the person projects. If you've revealed nothing but a carefully constructed image of yourself, your spouse couldn't possibly love the real you. At some level you feel the pain and loneliness of that.

There's no one right way to experience and express emotions. Spouses with different backgrounds and personality traits will have different ways of expressing emotions. Instead of insisting that our spouses match our style or preferences, we should show love by letting them know how we're sharing in their experiences.

Emotions That Make Honesty Difficult

Anger and fear are two powerful emotions that can sometimes make honesty difficult. In different ways both emotions can reinforce our temptation to hide rather than reveal ourselves to our spouses.

Anger

Anger can be seductive. It has a powerful physical and psychological appeal. Psychologically, anger usually highlights the wrongs of others. It tells us that someone has treated us unfairly, injured us, or threatened something that's important to us. It's seductive because it reinforces our tendency to cover ourselves. As we saw with Kevin and Brenda, anger invites us to expose our spouses, blaming them for what's bothering us. It invites us to reveal their faults, their nakedness, all the while directing attention away from our own.

The psychological appeal is only reinforced by anger's powerful physical appeal. You *feel* anger in your body. Adrenaline flowing and blood pressure rising, you feel hot and invigorated. Anger infuses you with energy and prepares you for action, readying you to launch a counterattack. It's unsurprising that some people develop an addiction to their anger. The physiological rush combined with an innate desire to elevate self above others is a powerful one-two punch that can do serious harm to a marriage.

Anger, however, doesn't have to be the enemy of honesty. In fact, when we examine God's anger we find that it can be an emotion that generates constructive honesty that protects and restores relationships. It may seem odd that we can know God as both loving and angry, but it's God's love, in fact, that drives his anger. Human anger can be destructive and dangerous, but you may, on occasion, have seen it accomplish good. You may have seen a mother dash to pull her child out of harm's way and then angrily scold the little tot. Her anger is motivated by genuine concern for her child, anger that moves her immediately to instruct her child about the importance of being careful around traffic. Anger can be polluted by impure motives, but that doesn't negate the fact that there are good and constructive reasons for anger.

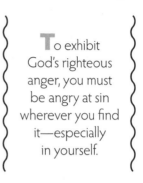

To exhibit God's righteous anger, you must be angry at sin wherever you find it—especially in yourself.

God's anger is motivated by his holiness, yes, but also by his love. His anger moves him to speak and act to rescue his children from danger and restore his relationship with them. In loving anger he speaks to the real problem, our sin, warning, pleading, and wooing us away from danger. He uses consequences to instruct us. Ultimately, he gave his only Son to right our wrongs and pay the penalty for our sins that we deserve. Christ's death on the cross is both an act of love and an act of anger. In his love, God attacks our true enemy, sin, pouring out his anger and judgment on it and creating a way for us to be restored to him.

Your anger can become more like God's as you worship him. You can use the energy of your anger to examine yourself, not just your spouse. To exhibit God's righteous anger, you must be angry at sin wherever you find it—especially in yourself. After you've identified your own sin, turned from it, and received God's forgiveness, then you can address your spouse's wrongs with humility and love. We will take a closer look at this in the chapter on conflict. For now, remember that the real problem isn't anger; the real problem is using anger to serve self instead of God and others.

Fear, Shame, and Hurt

Fear, unlike anger, has no psychological or physical appeal. Fear keeps me focused on what might happen next. Fear gets the adrenaline flowing and the blood pumping as well, but it doesn't feel like power. It gives you no sense of control; it makes you want to run and hide to cover up and protect yourself. In a sense, fear is an emotion of exposure to danger. Given that we all struggle with sinful hearts and actions, we can assume that honesty and fear will often accompany each other. We know that we need to be honest, but we're afraid.

> With the graciousness and love that God gives us, we can reveal ourselves to our spouses.

Our fear of honesty is legitimate. When we tell our spouses how they've hurt or offended us, or when we confess how we've hurt and offended them, we give them power to attack us where we're vulnerable. If I say to my wife, "I was really hurt when you said that I should lose some weight," I run the risk of hearing her say it again. If she *wants* to hurt me she can use that information as a weapon and call me "fatty" or make snide comments at the dinner table. Obviously, if my spouse has a track record of abusing my honesty then my fear tells me that I should be cautious about how I practice honesty with him or her. In such instances we must first talk about how previous honesty has been abused and how that's damaging to the marriage.

Often our fears predate our history with our spouses. We fear honesty because as Adam's descendants we're convinced, from birth, that if we're truly known we will be rejected and punished. That's when we need to hear the gospel—God has loved us by revealing himself as our gracious and loving Savior. With the graciousness and love that God gives us, we can reveal ourselves to our spouses and allow them to cover our nakedness with graciousness and love; we, in turn, cover their nakedness in the same way. That's how worshipping God moves us toward honesty.

Untangling Fear and Anger

Getting to the truth about yourself is often more complicated than admitting how you feel. Sometimes your experience with anger or fear (or some other emotion) leads you to confuse one with the other, or cling to one and deny the other.

For instance, some people choose to be angry rather than afraid. They prefer the proactive self-justification of anger, to the cringing weakness of fear. Consequently, they avoid fear (or other emotions that make them vulnerable), channeling it through anger. For example, instead of telling my wife that I am hurt because she told me to lose weight, I lash out at her. "I can't believe you just said that!" I say as I stomp out of the room and slam the door. Perhaps I bury the hurt further by launching a counterattack. "I need to lose weight? Maybe you should take a look in the mirror!" Not only do I avoid the pain of facing my hurt, but also I stroke my ego by labeling my wife a hypocrite.

Other people have had such negative experiences with anger that they can't acknowledge it in themselves let alone in others. They may have grown up in abusive homes where anger raged unchecked, and where its carnage made them want to distance themselves from it as much as possible. Then there are people who have never seen anger modeled at all. Perhaps they grew up in a home where peace and tranquility were the dominant values and anger had no role at all. Or perhaps they were severely punished or shunned for expressing anger. For these people anger is sometimes channeled into fear or sadness. With no way to express legitimate anger and address wrongs, they become anxious about their anger, either unable to identify it or fearful that they'll become the abusive angry people they've known.

Whatever the case, we ourselves may be our own biggest obstacle to honesty. Sometimes we believe we're being honest and open as we express our emotions, but the emotions themselves are a foil to avoid deeper issues. As we explore common forms of dishonesty, be alert to how your emotions may play a role.

Common Forms of Dishonesty

With the exception of outright lies, much of the dishonesty that cripples communication is subtle, of a kind that you might not even recognize as dishonesty. There are three forms of dishonesty that regularly short-circuit honest communication: double binds, indirection, and misdirection.

Double Binds

Our reluctance to be honest can put our spouses in a real bind. We conceal the truth by joining it to a contradictory message that makes it almost impossible for them to know how to respond. No matter which message they respond to, they lose—this is the "double bind."[11]

The double bind that we've all seen parodied on TV involves a wife modeling an outfit for her husband. She asks, "Do you think this new blouse makes me look fat?" Every bulge screams the answer at her from the mirror. Beads of cold sweat begin to form on her husband's brow. What is he to do? On the one hand, she seems to be asking for honest input. It *does* make her look fat. But experience has taught him that she doesn't respond well to that message no matter how carefully he phrases it. On the other hand, if he's dishonest and tells her she looks great, she'll probably accuse him of lying because from the way she's looking at herself in the mirror it's obvious that she sees the same bulges he does. The conflicting messages, "Be honest with me," and "Don't tell me I look fat" create a double bind that makes husbands cringe, or at least avoid the bedroom when their wives are getting dressed.

Husbands are equally capable of creating double binds. One that I've come to recognize in myself is pouting. Pouting is just what you think: a look of sadness or irritation accompanied by silence and withdrawal. It works this way: Kim does something that angers me or hurts my feelings. Rather than speak honestly about it, I begin to look sullen and withdraw. If she asks me what's wrong I say, "Nothing." But with my tone, facial expression, and body language, I answer, "Everything!" What is she to do? If she listens to my body language and challenges my words, then I become increasingly angry with her for doubting me. If she listens to my words and ignores my body language, the pouting intensifies and I smolder on the inside thinking, "See, she really doesn't care! If she did she'd be asking me what's wrong!" My dishonesty has put her in a no-win situation.

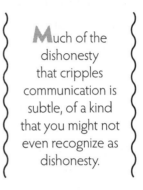

Much of the dishonesty that cripples communication is subtle, of a kind that you might not even recognize as dishonesty.

Watch for contradictions in your communication. Try to notice when your tone of voice, facial expression, or body language contradicts your words. Have you ever screamed, "I'm not angry!" while your face turns purple and veins stand out on your forehead? Have you ever said, "I'm sorry," with a tone of utter contempt and disgust that immediately destroys any conciliatory effect your words might have had? You're putting your spouse in a double bind. Double-bind messages conceal the truth and make difficult situations worse.

Indirection

Sometimes we try to soften the truth by communicating indirectly or dropping hints. We make comments that, if properly understood, might offend our spouse. So we hide the message in an offhand comment or behavior. It gives us wiggle room to deny that the offensive message was the one we intended.

For instance, a wife wishes that her husband were more helpful around the house but has found that asking for his help only irritates him. So she looks for opportunities to get the message across in other ways. She knows that he values their time together in the evenings, so she goes to bed an hour or two early for a few nights making sure to explain to him that she's just too tired from all of the housework to stay awake another minute. (Hint: If you'd just help me, I'd be more available to spend time with you.) How should the husband respond? Even if he takes the hint, it's hard for him to respond well. His wife isn't being honest and he feels manipulated. If he takes offense and angrily responds, "I know, you're trying to tell me I need to do more to help out around here," his wife can deny that she was trying to send a message at all and tell her husband he's too sensitive and overreacting.

Misdirection

Sometimes the truth is too hot to handle. We can't contain our anger and frustration over something, yet we're afraid to tackle the real issue. So rather than talk about the real problem, we manufacture another.

For instance, although sexual intimacy is often important to husbands, they're reluctant to talk about it with their wives. A husband may get upset if he feels there hasn't been frequent or regular sexual intimacy, or if he just feels his wife hasn't shown much interest. Yet discussing the issue openly and honestly with his wife seems too risky. As his frustration builds he finds it more and more difficult to conceal it, but he would rather talk about anything else than let his wife know that he misses her. Instead, he vents his frustration and anger on anything and everything that stands between him and his wife's affections. Everything is fair game, from children who need help with their homework to his wife's extended phone call with her mother.

"I don't understand why you have to hold our kids' hands the whole time they're doing their homework! They have to learn to do it on their own! You aren't going to go to college with them are you!"

"I'm tired of the phone constantly interrupting our evenings! We need uninterrupted family time. That's it! I'm drawing a line! No more phone calls after 7:00 p.m.!"

The real issue is never put on the table. Venting anger may bring some temporary relief for the husband, but his wife is certainly no closer to understanding what's really bothering him, and she's certainly not romantically inclined after being attacked for what normally goes unnoticed.

At the Root of It All

In all three forms of dishonesty, a message is camouflaged to protect the sender. The speaker tries to stay safely hidden, while coaxing or goading the spouse out into the open.

At their root, these strategies are about selfishness and self-protection—about getting the results we want without loving our spouses. In the act of dishonesty we're refusing to believe that we can really trust Jesus and come out of hiding. Instead, like Adam and Eve we allow hiding and shame to rule the day. We say we believe the truth of God's love and forgiveness in Christ, but the way we communicate says otherwise. We trust ourselves and try to manufacture safety at the expense of our spouses and our marriages.

Think about It

- How do you express your emotions? How hard is it for you to put them into words? Is your anger ever a covering for fear, shame, or hurt?
- Replay in your mind a recent disagreement with your spouse.

What percentage of your statements were disclosures about your own thoughts and feelings versus statements you made about your spouse's actions and motives?

- What strategies do you most often use to avoid being honest with your spouse? When have you used double binds, indirection, or misdirection to avoid honesty?

nine

Speaking the Truth to Your Spouse

What You'll Learn in This Chapter:

- Honest communication doesn't mean saying the first thing that comes to mind. The goal is always to speak the truth in love with the purpose of building up the other.
- Exaggerations, trait names, mind reading, and shaming are typical ways that couples distort the truth and communicate destructively.
- Honesty that builds relationship affirms God's love for our spouses, is based on a careful understanding of them, and is sensitive to the timing of our words.
- Sometimes a spouse's destructive behaviors and words make it unsafe to communicate honestly. In those situations share thoughts and feelings cautiously or even remain silent.

Pointless Truth

WHEN KIM MARRIED me she took on a burden she hadn't expected —in a sense, she became anonymous. Kim's maiden name is Leith, and when we married she took my last name and became Kim Smith—a name that isn't much more distinct than Jane Doe. We'd been married only a few months when during an eight-hour drive on vacation she shared with me that sometimes she wished she'd kept Leith as her last name. I was shocked. After all, I'd been a Smith all my life and was proud of my last name and my heritage. I didn't think of Smith as *common* but *popular*. And in addition to feeling offended, I couldn't help but wonder, were there other things she didn't like about being Mrs. Kim Smith? Was this just the tip of the iceberg?

For hours we jousted over the relative strengths of both family names, toyed with the notion of hyphenating them, and debated the reasons why the wife traditionally takes her husband's name. All the while our emotions and defensiveness escalated. With one hour to go, I said, "Look, it just hurts my feelings that you don't like my last name and I wish you'd just drop it!" To her credit, she's been Kim Smith ever since, without objection. We laugh about it now as one of our first memorable fights. Perhaps there was more to that spat than either of us remembers. But we remember that episode as an example of misguided honesty. Almost twenty years later I can completely sympathize with the loss of the distinguished name she's always known, but, at the time, telling me how boring mine was really served no good purpose. Sure, she was being honest, but it was not honesty that was very helpful.

Unwholesome Talk—Language That Tears Down

You may have suffered much more serious moments of honesty in your marriage. A wife tells her husband she wishes she'd married someone else. A husband tells his wife he dreams of being single again.

No matter how true those statements may be, saying them just because they're true is like throwing a lit match into a keg of gunpowder. Is this the kind of honesty that God is after—honesty that tears down a marriage like a demolition charge? Is honesty always the best policy?

Recall the apostle Paul's words in Ephesians 4:25: "Therefore each of you must put off falsehood and speak truthfully to his neighbor, for we are all members of one body." Remember, Paul's admonition to speak the truth is about God's desire for us to grow to be more like Christ.

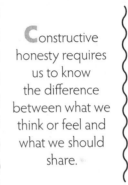

Constructive honesty requires us to know the difference between what we think or feel and what we should share.

God doesn't simply tell us to speak the truth but to speak the truth *in love* (Ephesians 4:15). As we've learned, the word *love* isn't defined by our personal preferences but by God and his purposes. The truth speaking that Paul describes is about sharing information in a way that moves you and your spouse along the path of maturity in Christ. Marriages need truth shaped and guided by love, not as a result of venting or clearing the air. In fact, the Bible calls it foolishness to speak whatever is on your mind without reflection, whether it's true or not. Proverbs 12:23 states, "A prudent man keeps his knowledge to himself, but the heart of fools blurts out folly." This proverb along with others (Proverbs 12:18; 17:27; 18:6–7) reinforces the wisdom that just because we think or feel something doesn't mean we should say it.

The wise person understands how powerful words can be and uses them carefully. Constructive honesty requires us to know the difference between what we think or feel and what we should share. Wisdom also means that we know our spouse well enough to decide what should be shared and how and when to share it.

Paul describes truth and love working together this way, "Do not let any unwholesome talk come out of your mouths, but only what is helpful for building others up according to their needs, that it may benefit those who listen" (Ephesians 4:29). Constructive honesty, or *wholesome* talk, is what's most beneficial in the moment, whether it be a kind word, encouragement, correction, warning, or even silence.

Just as there are forms of dishonesty that creep into our communication, there are also several forms of honest expression that are loaded with corrosive content.

Exaggerations—Only, Always, Never

Sometimes one spouse has something legitimate to share with the other but exaggerates it in a way that makes it almost impossible for the other spouse to receive it. For example, imagine you've just blown it and in a flash of anger you spoke harshly. After a few minutes you cool off and realize that you need to apologize. As you try to apologize your spouse says, "You know, it would help if you weren't so critical *all* the time! You *never* say anything nice to me!" How would you respond to that? You might think, *Am I critical "all of the time"? I "never" say anything encouraging? Okay, I blew it; and I've blown it before, but haven't I gotten it right at least once?* Your first inclination is probably to defend yourself by finding examples of times when you were, in fact, supportive and encouraging—which, of course, your spouse will immediately discount. Are you still ready to apologize?

Your spouse was right to let you know how hurtful your angry criticism can be, but the truth was distorted by offensive exaggerations that made it hard for you to hear what you needed to hear. Instead, you ended up on the defensive.

Notice how in the heat of the moment a few simple words exaggerate a truth and create a new offense. To say that someone *always* or *only* does the wrong thing, or *never* does the right thing, is an offensive exaggeration. Words like *always*, *never*, and *only* are absolutes that make the truth hard to take and create an offense rather than repair one.

Consider how different it would have been if your spouse had listened first or started by saying, "You know it really hurts me when you lose your temper like that. And sometimes I feel like you're disappointed with me more often than you're happy with me." It might have deepened your understanding of what happened, which would have deepened your apology rather than negating it.

Trait Names

"You're a liar!" "You're such a jerk!" "You're a monster!"

In the heat of battle, spouses say things that are especially destructive. They use trait names, taking the behavior that's angered or hurt them and using it to label the other. Instead of saying, "I feel like you weren't being honest with me," they say, "You're a liar." Instead of saying, "You really hurt me when you said . . . ," they say, "You're a jerk!" *Loser, liar,* and *jerk* are just a few that I often hear as a marriage counselor.

You know all too well that these words sting, but you may not understand why they're so damaging. Trait names and exaggerations work the same way and have a similar effect. (Trait names are a type of exaggeration.) Both, in effect, reduce a spouse's identity to his or her sinful behavior. Trait names and exaggeration communicate, "You're no more and no better than what you've just done." That's a powerful statement, and, if you let it sink in, overwhelming. When your identity, *who you are*, is under attack, it's very hard to respond in a positive way.

Mind Reading—Assuming the Worst

Stewart and Tammy had a real blowout this morning, yelling and screaming ugly things. Five minutes ago Stewart came through the door with a dozen roses, planted a passionate kiss on Tammy, and announced that he had arranged for a babysitter and that they were going out to a fantastic restaurant, Tammy's favorite.

Tammy angrily pushed Stewart away and proclaimed, "Don't think I don't know what you're up to! You want me to just forget everything that you said to me this morning, pretend that it didn't happen and then you're just going to sweep me off of my feet, buy me dinner, and even expect me to have sex with you tonight! Well, you can just forget it!" Tammy stormed off to their bedroom, slamming the door behind her. In effect, Tammy acted as if she'd read Stewart's mind, as if she not only knew what Stewart was doing but why he was doing it—and that it was awful.

> Marriage gives us an opportunity both to give and to receive the same kind of love that God gives us, a love that communicates that we can be known and loved.

Was Tammy right about Stewart? Who knows? Surprises and gift giving have become Stewart's regular response to fights. The gifts have the effect of burying the conflict rather than resolving it. But does that mean Stewart is being manipulative? Does that mean he's just after sex? Does that make him callous? Maybe, but it could also be that Stewart simply doesn't know any other way to recover. Maybe he doesn't know how to solve the problem and is afraid to engage in it again. The point is, we don't know; Tammy doesn't know; Stewart himself may not even know why he's doing what he's doing. One thing we do know is that now Stewart and Tammy are both angrier than ever, and they're no closer to solving their problems.

Sometimes mind reading is a strategy of self-protection. When you assume the worst, you believe you can defend yourself from unpleasant surprises or being wounded in the same way you've been wounded in the past. But whatever benefit you believe you get from mind reading is far outweighed by the damage done to your marriage.

For one thing, mind reading tends to extinguish whatever good was motivating your spouse. When you read your spouse's mind, you punish him or her for even attempting the good. Of course, everyone can be manipulative, but God can work in everyone. If God is at work, Stewart could be reaching out to repair the damage he's caused. First steps are always awkward and often ineffective, but that's why they're called first steps.

Second, mind reading destroys the heart of communication, the need to share information. If you already know what I'm thinking and why I'm doing what I'm doing, why should I bother to explain it to you? And if the result of all my efforts so far is that you believe the worst about me, why would I hazard offering more information? Anything I say will only go to prove the conclusion you've already reached, the worst possible conclusion.

If you're afraid of being taken in, then just say it. If Tammy had thought more carefully before she spoke, she could have said, "I want to believe you're trying to do something nice, but I'm afraid of being hurt again. I don't want to sweep what happened under the rug." Or, "I very much want to enjoy your company at dinner tonight, but I'm not ready to stop talking about our problem, and I'm not ready to be intimate with you tonight. Can we go to dinner as a way of calling a truce so we can figure out a better way to talk about things?"

Shaming

At one point during a counseling session with a desperate couple, the wife was so angry, distraught, and desperate for me to side with her against her husband that she blurted out, "You don't understand how sick he is! Did I tell you what he did once in college!"

Her husband jerked his head around and stared wide eyed at her. Before she could continue, I held up my hands and said, "Stop! Don't say another word!" I couldn't have been more emphatic or determined to stop her if she'd pulled the pin on a hand grenade and threatened to throw it at him. To this day I don't know what she was going to say, but I do know that if she'd said it, marriage counseling, and possibly the marriage itself, would be over. Her husband would have been humiliated, and likely enraged, by whatever she was going to share.

One of the biggest challenges to honesty is shame, our sense that there are things about us that make us unacceptable and unlovable, things that we feel we must hide. Marriage gives us an opportunity both to give and to receive the same kind of love that God gives us, a love that communicates that we can be known and loved. It's especially egregious, then, when in a moment of anger a spouse takes something you've shared in a moment of intimacy and safety and uses it as a weapon against you. When you shame your spouse in this way, you're not only humiliating your spouse and breaking trust; you're actively attacking the work of the gospel in his or her life. Where God says, "You're forgiven," you're saying, "You will always be guilty." Where the gospel says, "You're now clean," you say, "You're still filthy." When you shame your spouse, you're not offending only your spouse but God himself.

Spiritual Roots

These categories of destructive speech express a disconnect from God's love. Exaggerations, trait names, mind reading, and shaming our spouses all reflect our beliefs, however momentary, that we must defend ourselves by attacking the other. They reflect a fearful mind-set that doesn't find safety or protection in God's love—a mind-set that cannot believe that love is more powerful than evil. They also represent a fist in God's face—insistence on doing it our way rather than trusting him.

In those moments we aren't thinking of ourselves the way Paul describes us in Ephesians 4. We aren't thinking of ourselves as children of God, members of one body, who are to put off the old, ignorant ways of doing things and put on the new ways of doing things as we become more and more like Jesus. Instead, we speak as if we were still cowering in the trees with Adam and Eve, having to go it alone, expecting the worst from God and our spouses. Furthermore, to speak that way is to deny that God is at work in our spouses. "You're just fooling yourself," that language says. "You're as lost as you ever were."

All of these destructive ways of speaking share the goal of trying to change our spouses by telling them how hopelessly rotten they are. We aren't just telling them that they are people with problems, children of God who need to grow, but that they *are* the sinful things that they do, that they are sinners without hope. And by the way, it never works. Rarely, if ever, do people genuinely change because they're told that they're so rotten that even God can't change them! In fact, if they really believed the exaggerations, trait names, mind reading, and shaming, it wouldn't make sense to expect them to change. If I *am* a liar, a liar at the core of my being, then of course I'll always lie. I don't have the ability to be anything else. If I *am* a jerk, I'll always behave like a jerk.

What is the alternative?

Wholesome Speech

Wholesome Speech Affirms Identity

Having three children, I've spent more time watching Disney movies than I care to admit, but one movie has stuck with me over the years—*The Lion King*. You may remember the story line: The hero of the story is a young lion cub named Simba, the son of the king, Mufasa, and heir to the throne. But Simba's evil uncle Scar murders Mufasa and convinces Simba that it's his fault. Out of guilt and shame Simba runs away, and Scar assumes the throne. Simba grows to adulthood in the jungle with two newfound friends (a warthog and a meerkat) who teach him their philosophy of life, *hakuna matata*, which means, "no worries." Simba tries to forget about the past and live a life of ease in the jungle with his friends.

Meanwhile Scar plunders Simba's homeland and decimates the pride. One evening the spirit of Mufasa appears to Simba in a vision. His words and their impact are striking:

Mufasa begins, "Simba, you've forgotten me."

"No. How could I?" Simba replies.

"You've forgotten who you are, so you've forgotten me. Look inside yourself, Simba. You're more than what you've become. Remember who you are. You're my son, and the one true king. Remember who you are."

Taking the message to heart, Simba hurries home to overthrow his wicked uncle. Shame and fear have evaporated. How did his father, with just a few words, completely turn Simba around and give him the courage to do battle? He reminded him of his *true* identity. He reminded him that it didn't make sense for him to hide in the jungle. For Simba, *hakuna matata* was a denial of who he really was and what he was meant to be.

How do you think Simba would have responded if Mufasa had said, "I can't believe how you've squandered your life. I can't even believe you're my son. You're such a disappointment. I can't even look at you. In fact, don't even think of yourself as my son anymore. I don't recognize you!" My guess is that Simba would have slunk back into the jungle trying harder than ever to forget.

Inviting others to change by reminding them of their true identity is God's trademark. If we expand our study of Ephesians beyond chapter 4, we see that the entire letter is organized around the principle of asking people to become who they really are. The letter starts,

> Praise be to the God and Father of our Lord Jesus Christ,
> who has blessed us in the heavenly realms with every
> spiritual blessing in Christ. For he chose us in him before the
> creation of the world to be holy and blameless in his sight.
> In love, he predestined us to be adopted as his sons through
> Jesus Christ, in accordance with his pleasure and will—to the
> praise of his glorious grace, which he has freely given us in
> the One he loves. (Ephesians 1:3–6)

Paul reminds us that from the beginning of time God had a plan for us, a plan to love us, to make us his children, and to make us like Jesus. And he reminds us that this plan is all about God's grace. The plan is based not on our goodness or ability but on God's love given to us through Jesus' heroic rescue. Paul develops these ideas throughout the first three chapters. By chapter 4, it's crystal clear that we're loved and have God's full support and approval. God asks us to grow, not as a condition of his love but as the result of his love.

Follow Paul's example when you ask your spouse to look at a problem. Even a few well-chosen words can provide a compass heading and reorient a couple in danger of losing their way. Consider how different difficult conversations would be if they were punctuated with statements like these:

> From the beginning of time God had a plan for us, a plan to love us, to make us his children, and to make us like Jesus.

- *"I know God wants better for us. Let's take some time to cool off and pray."* Bring God into the discussion, not to seem spiritually superior but to remember that he's as real a part of your marriage and your problems as anyone.
- *"We aren't just husband and wife but brother and sister in Jesus. Let's listen to each other and help each other grow."* I recently met with a couple struggling in their marriage, and the wife shared that one of the things that's helped her the most is remembering that her husband isn't just her husband but a child of God and her brother.
- *"One of the things I've always loved about you is your _____.* [Fill in the blank with whatever fits your spouse and the situation.] *We don't have to hide from this problem."* How can you draw on the strengths that each of you brought to the marriage? How can you remind each other of what they are and activate them? This is a way of remembering and recognizing that God has given us gifts to strengthen and bless each other.

Wholesome Words Are Based on Understanding

"He who answers before listening—that is his folly and his shame" (Proverbs 18:13). For our words to be wholesome, they must be based on an accurate understanding of the other person.

Sometimes our marriages suffer a communication breakdown because we don't understand what's going on with our spouse. Armed with faulty assumptions, we speak in a way that totally misses the point. The framework of Ephesians 4, that we're all members of one body, provides a bedrock of understanding for every Christian marriage.

Every husband and wife faces the same *basic* temptations. We're all depicted by Paul as those who are putting off the old manner of life, which included living in unbelief enslaved by the lusts and fears of the heart. Your spouse's inner world is similar to yours; you both experience shame, desires, lusts, and fears. You share the same spiritual heritage, a sinful nature inherited from Adam and Eve. You both need to know that you are known and loved by Jesus. These bedrock truths form the basis of understanding every person on this planet.

Being Incarnational: Visiting Your Spouse's World

History, experience, and personal makeup are all factors that make your spouse different from you. You both experience shame, but your spouse doesn't experience or deal with it exactly the way you do. The particular desires they serve and the ways they serve them aren't the same as yours. When you know a person in the details of his life, you know how to build him up; you know what he needs in the moment. To know someone that well requires a visit to his world.

God didn't love us from a distance; in Jesus, he visited our world, experienced what we experience, and faced what we face—God's love is incarnational. Because God has visited our world and shown us he understands, we trust him. Likewise, we need to visit our spouses' worlds, understanding and communicating that we truly understand each other. Here are some ways to be incarnational:

- *Let your spouse know that you want to understand.* Ask honest questions—questions you want answered. Don't bait your spouse. Don't act like a lawyer hoping to trap your spouse with his or her words. If you're going to act like a lawyer, you can expect your spouse to take the fifth! Be willing to hear something new and learn from it.

- *Verify your understanding.* Don't assume that you understand; to be sure, ask. Put what you hear into your own words and see if your spouse agrees with you. Repeat this process until your spouse knows that you understand. There's no point moving on to the next idea or responding to what you heard if your spouse doesn't believe you understand what's been said.

- *Emotionally respond to what you hear.* Your spouse needs to know that you're affected by what he or she has shared. That doesn't mean generating phony emotions; just be honest about what you feel. If you feel uncertain about what you've heard, then share that. If you need more time to process it, share that. But your spouse needs to know that you care about what's important to him or her.

Timing

One of the results of knowing and understanding your spouse is developing a sense of timing. Not only about word choice, speaking the truth in love includes knowing when to speak. "A man finds joy in giving an apt reply—and how good is a timely word!" (Proverbs 15:23). Saying the right thing at the right time brings joy to you both.

Husbands, there's a time to give your wife advice and a time to listen. Early in our marriage Kim would come home from work and tell me about a problem she had with a coworker, a friend, or a patient. I'd immediately troubleshoot her problem, analyzing, offering explanations, and suggesting different courses of action. Over and over again Kim explained that when she came home upset, she needed me to be a listener, not a fixer. Eventually I realized that there are times when she's not ready for advice.

Don't take that anecdote as a lesson about the differences between men and women. Your wife or husband may be completely different. Some people look for solutions first and feel the weight of the problem later. The point is, take the time to find out the kind of truth your spouse needs *when* he or she needs it. When do they need encouragement? When do they need advice? When do they need time to think things through on their own before talking about it? If you aren't certain, ask!

A Time to Be Silent

Some of you are reading this and thinking, "It doesn't matter what I say or how I say it, my spouse isn't going to listen or care. I'd only be asking for trouble."

That could well be. What's been written so far applies to two spouses who want things to be better and need help knowing how. But there are marriages that don't fit that description. For some, marriage isn't a journey with a friend and lover, but a life with their enemy, with someone who gives no thought to harming them.

There are times when a relationship is so destructive that even careful, well-intentioned honesty is dangerous. In Matthew 7 Jesus warns us not to be hypocrites when we criticize others, exhorting us to get the "plank" out of our own eye before getting the "speck" out of theirs (Matthew 7:3–5). But in the next verse he adds, "Do not give dogs what is sacred; do not throw your pearls to pigs. If you do, they may trample them under their feet, and then turn and tear you to pieces" (Matthew 7:6).

Baring your heart, sharing concern, offering help—all the ways you'd naturally want to speak to your spouse—are, in effect, pearls, the sacred discharge of your marital vows. If your spouse, however, acts like your enemy, speak only with special care. Your well-intentioned words may become an excuse for more nasty words or even physical abuse.

Proverbs 9:7–8 puts it this way: "Whoever corrects a mocker invites insult; whoever rebukes a wicked man incurs abuse. Do not rebuke a mocker or he will hate you; rebuke a wise man and he will love you." If your spouse is unwilling to examine himself or herself honestly, ridicules attempts at honest conversation, or resorts to verbal or physical abuse when you try to communicate, repeated attempts at honesty are unwise. You're in a marriage that requires delicacy and wisdom. Don't try to navigate alone the dangerous waters of this marriage. Seek counsel from trusted pastors, friends, and counselors. To live with a fool, a mocker, or a wicked person is dangerous. Seek counsel from others, be frugal with your words, and if in doubt about what to say, be silent.

Think about It

- Think of a time when you spoke in haste and hurt your spouse. What did you say that was hurtful? Did you exaggerate, use trait names, mind read, or shame him or her? What did your words, tone, or actions communicate to your spouse?
- Think of specific ways that you can affirm God's love for your spouse. Where do you see God's goodness reflected in his or her character? How is your spouse growing as a child of God? How can you communicate this to your spouse?
- How does your spouse typically feel misunderstood by you? If you don't know, then ask. Remember that understanding doesn't mean that you necessarily agree with him or her.

ten

God Is Up
to Good in Conflict

What You'll Learn in This Chapter:

- The Bible tells us that conflict doesn't have to be destructive. In fact, God promises to use conflict to expose and eradicate sin and help us to grow in love.
- To solve conflict biblically, before looking critically at your spouse, examine yourself. Conflict is aggravated by blame shifting, defensiveness, and pointing out our spouse's faults when we haven't dealt with our own.
- Conflicts are often battles for things that we want. Examining your heart and thinking carefully about what you really want is an important step in solving conflicts biblically.

Dangers of Conflict

MOMENTS OF MARITAL conflict can be some of the most discouraging and destructive moments of all. The Bible describes the danger this way: "Starting a quarrel is like breaching a dam; so drop the matter before a dispute breaks out" (Proverbs 17:14). A hairline crack appears in a dam and a drop of water slowly forms. As the crack widens imperceptibly, the drop becomes a trickle. Moments later the trickle becomes a jet of water firing through an ever-widening hole. Soon the entire dam gives way, water and rubble exploding downstream and destroying everything in its path.

Does it feel like your marriage is built at the base of a cracked dam? The message is clear: given how devastating conflict can be, sometimes avoiding it is best. Wisdom advises us to consider the destructive potential of conflict before engaging in it.

Peace is one of God's inherent qualities. The prophet Isaiah gives the coming Messiah, Jesus, the title "Prince of Peace" (Isaiah 9:6). Peace is a fruit that God's Spirit produces in us (Galatians 5:23). The Bible urges Christians to live at peace with others. "Make every effort to live in peace with all men" (Hebrews 12:14a).

If peace is a hallmark of the Christian who's following Jesus, then conflict can be doubly discouraging for Christians. Not only do we live in the marital wreckage it creates, but we feel like spiritual failures as well. Conflict can leave us feeling that we haven't only failed as husbands and wives but as Christians.

God's Good Purposes for Conflict

The Bible also teaches that conflict is a sign that God is at work. It isn't inherently wrong, a sign of failure, or evidence that God has somehow abandoned you or your marriage. In fact, God uses conflict to accomplish good in the lives of his people by destroying sin and establishing the very peace he desires.

Surprising Words from the Prince of Peace

Listen to the way Jesus describes his mission:

> I have come to bring fire on the earth, and how I wish it were already kindled! But I have a baptism to undergo, and how distressed I am until it is completed! *Do you think I came to bring peace on the earth? No, I tell you, but division.* From now on there will be five in one family divided against each other, three against two and two against three. They will be divided, father against son and son against father, mother against daughter and daughter against mother, mother-in-law against daughter-in-law and daughter-in-law against mother-in-law. (Luke 12:49–53, italics mine)

How can this be the mission of the Prince of Peace? He came to bring division? Even division within the family! Do I really want *this* Jesus involved in my marriage? How do we make sense of Jesus' words in light of everything else the Bible says about conflict and peace?

Conflict, a Blessing Wrapped in a Curse

As we've already learned from the first chapters of Genesis, when sin entered the picture marriage became a badly distorted version of what God had intended. God created unity, but sin brought division. God created safety, but sin brought danger. And God created peace, but sin brought conflict. The first couple's rebellion brought division and danger, and it brought conflict as well. By disobeying God, in effect trying to overthrow him, Adam and Eve fired the first shot of a battle, a conflict, between God and sinful humanity that's still going on. They unwittingly also created marital strife the first moment they realized that they needed to protect themselves from each other. Remember, they not only covered and hid themselves from God but from each other. They were not only exposed and vulnerable to God's wrath but also to each other's sinfulness. Where sin exists people will battle; there will be conflict with God *and* each other.

God confronts Adam and Eve and doesn't destroy them. There are, however, painful consequences. In Genesis 3:14–19 God pronounces a series of curses in response to their rebellion, but even the punishments are laced with God's goodness, love, and promises of redemption—promises not only to restore what was broken but to make things better than ever.

> Conflict, far from being a sign of moral or marital failure, is God's chosen means of rescuing his people and destroying sin.

God pronounces a curse on the Serpent in Genesis 3:15: "I will put enmity between you and the woman, and between your offspring and hers; he will crush your head, and you will strike his heel." The conflict that Adam and Eve started will continue, accompanied by enmity, strife, crushing, and striking. But the curse of conflict is also laced with blessings and hope.

First of all, notice that the curse of conflict is pronounced upon Satan, not Adam and Eve. Satan may have started the fight, but God is going to finish it. The conflict that Satan provoked has become a curse that will ultimately destroy him, not us. Our mortal enemy—the one who created the temptations that ensnared Adam and Eve and challenge us today—is going to be destroyed. The author of the discouragement, suffering, even misery that we experience in marriage will be destroyed: temptation, itself, will be destroyed. This battle will be decisive; Satan's head will be crushed, sin will be destroyed, and Paradise will be restored.

This conflict is going to be an epic battle that spans years and generations; it's a battle between offspring, Satan's and Eve's. Not only did God spare Adam and Eve; he also made a way for us, their offspring, to be a part of the solution.

Although Satan desires to use conflict for his purposes, God has overruled his plans and claimed conflict for himself. God has taken the conflict that Satan started and turned it against him. Notice that God "places enmity" between Satan and Eve's offspring. We struggle against sin, hating it in ourselves. If God hadn't placed enmity between the seed of the Serpent and the seed of the woman, we would be given over to our sinfulness, willing slaves to Satan's evil purposes. But God blesses us by giving to us and preserving in us a hatred for what is evil. God gives us new hearts when we put our trust in Jesus, but we still must battle the sin nature that remains. The fact that there's a battle at all is a result of God's grace and part of his plan to eradicate the enemy.

We can all agree with the Bible that conflict is painful, sometimes destructive, and not to be entered into carelessly. Conflict, far from being a sign of moral or marital failure, is God's chosen means of rescuing his people and destroying sin. *Don't lose sight of this fact: God will rescue us, and marriage, through* conflict.

Jesus, the Promised Offspring

In the Old Testament, many people battle against Satan (Abraham, Moses, and David to name a few), but they're only forerunners of the great Deliverer, Jesus. In Luke 12, when Jesus says that he has come to "bring division," he is identifying himself as *the* offspring promised in Genesis 3:15. In Christ, the great conflict that started in the beginning reaches a climax. He crushes the Serpent's head, even as he is wounded—"struck in the heel"—on the cross. Jesus is wounded on the cross for our sins, but it's Satan who receives the fatal blow. By forgiving our sins and giving us new hearts, Jesus makes it possible for us to join God's family and grow and mature to be like him.

Although we still must battle sin that lingers in our hearts, we no longer have to be mastered by it. In Jesus the tide of the battle took a decisive turn. Despite appearances, Jesus' power is increasing and Satan's is decreasing. As God's children through Jesus, we have the freedom to say no to sin and yes to God. That's where the battle continues for us. Jesus landed the fatal blow, but we have to join the battle to see it fulfilled in our lives and our marriages.

In Luke 12 Jesus is letting us know that we will continue to have a role in this conflict, a conflict that sends shock waves through families. In the early years of the church, Jews who followed Jesus often faced punishment and persecution; they were disowned by their families, thrown out of the synagogues, and even imprisoned or put to death (Acts 8:1–3; 9:1, 13, 21). Jesus wants his people to know that following him means walking a hard road. The cost can be high; you might even lose your family. The two lines of offspring, God's and Satan's, might be mixed and do battle within one household.

Being rejected by family because of Jesus isn't just a relic of church history. Some of you may have experienced rejection by your family because of your relationship with Jesus. Some of you may be experiencing it at present with an unbelieving spouse.

If you and your spouse are both Christians, what does this have to do with your marriage? Consider the broader principle behind Jesus' words. His presence doesn't always result in peace and tranquility in the home—and Jesus doesn't apologize for that! Jesus is willing, even expects his rule to be established through conflict, including conflict in intimate relationships. Even if husband and wife are both offspring of Jesus' line, the sin that remains in their lives will surface in marriage. It needs to be addressed, even if it means engaging in the messy business of conflict. Jesus is willing for conflict to exist in your marriage.

Everyday Battles

Paul closes his letter to the Ephesians with the image of the Christian as a warrior. He writes,

> Finally, be strong in the Lord and in his mighty power.
> Put on the full armor of God so that you can take your stand
> against the devil's schemes. For our struggle is not against
> flesh and blood, but against the rulers, against the authorities,
> against the powers of this dark world and against the spiritual
> forces of evil in the heavenly realms. (Ephesians 6:10–12)

If you didn't know it was a passage from the Bible you might well think it was an excerpt from *The Lord of the Rings!* Do you, in any way, see yourself engaged in a battle of such cosmic importance? The Bible does because the battle against the devil's dark power doesn't just happen in heroic moments as we typically think of them. The battle against darkness doesn't just happen as Christians are imprisoned for their beliefs or demons are cast out of the possessed. As Jesus teaches in Luke 12, it happens in the relationships of everyday life. For all its language of battles and armor, Ephesians 6 comes right after Paul's boots-on-the-ground advice about the everyday life relationships in Ephesians 4 and 5.

> It's in the context of everyday life and relationships that the Christian must be fully armored, prepared, and ready.

As he finishes directing husbands and wives to live together in love and respect (Ephesians 5:22–33), as he directs children to obey their parents and parents to raise their children wisely (Ephesians 6:1–5), and as he instructs even slaves and masters to treat one another as followers of Christ (Ephesians 6:5–9), Paul urges us to put on the armor of God. It's in the context of everyday life and relationships that the Christian must be fully armored, prepared, and ready. Where are you most tempted to be selfish? Callous? Impatient? Home is usually one of the places we let our guard down, where we're most likely to be ourselves around people we no longer feel the need to impress—the people who are stuck with us anyway! At home we find the people we depend on most to meet our expectations and to serve the desires of our hearts. So home is where the enemy finds ample opportunity to strike, attacking when we don't see life through a spiritual lens but through our own sense of entitlement.

We follow Christ into battle. Our ultimate enemy is Satan and the sin of our own heart, and our weapons are the weapons of faith. Paul continues in chapter 6,

Stand firm then, with the belt of truth buckled around your waist, with the breastplate of righteousness in place, and with your feet fitted with the readiness that comes from the gospel of peace. In addition to all this, take up the shield of faith, with which you can extinguish all the flaming arrows of the evil one. Take the helmet of salvation and the sword of the Spirit, which is the word of God. (Ephesians 6:14–17)

Doing battle may involve conflict with our spouses, but we have to learn that they aren't enemies. Also, we must learn to fight with the weapons of faith and love that God supplies.

The Battle Starts with Yourself

In conflict how do you attack the problem and not your spouse? The book of James provides a surprising answer, "What causes fights and quarrels among you? Don't they come from your desires that battle within you?" (James 4:1)

I seldom meet with a married person who isn't convinced that his or her spouse is the source of the problems in the marriage. The fact that we're told to begin by examining ourselves is revolutionary—and contrary to our nature. An effect of the Fall is our tendency to blame shift and look for the cause of our problems outside ourselves. A basic tenet of the Bible, however, is that once you know yourself as a broken image bearer, a worshipper gone wrong, a rebel against God, you must look for the source of your problems by examining yourself first.

Beneath the battles that we have with our spouses are the battles that our own desires fight within us. We've already learned how our hearts can manufacture idols out of our harbor of desires and fears. Cravings for approval, control, or comfort and safety are natural desires that, because of sin, can become obstacles to love. Before we explore how these desires show up in our conflicts, let's look at another natural desire, our desire to defend ourselves.

Defensiveness

"An offended brother is more unyielding than a fortified city, and disputes are like the barred gates of a citadel" (Proverbs 18:19). This is a fitting image because, on occasion, arguing with my wife has felt like I was banging my head against a wall. She refused to see things from my point of view. Not surprisingly, my wife has had the exact same experience with me!

In ordinary moments of conflict we've all tried to break through walls and squeeze through barred gates. At the same time we've built our own walls, locked our own gates. Attempts at getting to the real issues and resolving conflict seem doomed from the start when hearts are hidden within fortresses of defensiveness.

The disputes themselves aren't difficult; the difficulty lies with the "offended brother." Conflicts become unconquerable strongholds when one spouse takes offense at the words or actions of the other. Of course, most conflicts start because someone is offended, but the proverb is pointing out the simple relationship between walls and offenses: The greater or more numerous the offenses, the higher the walls that protect the other's heart. If we want conflict to serve God's good purposes we need to do our utmost to minimize defensiveness.

Hypocrisy, the Most Common Offense

The most common way we offend each other is with hypocrisy. Jesus explains the relationship between hypocrisy and defensiveness this way:

> Do not judge, or you too will be judged. For in the same way you judge others, you will be judged, and with the measure you use, it will be measured to you. Why do you look at the speck of sawdust in your brother's eye and pay no attention to the plank in your own eye? How can you say to your brother, 'Let me take the speck out of your eye,' when

all the time there is a plank in your own eye? You hypocrite, first take the plank out of your own eye, and then you will see clearly to remove the speck from your brother's eye. (Matthew 7:1–5)

Everyone seems to know at least one verse from the Bible: "Do not judge, or you too will be judged." This verse is usually employed to thwart criticism of behavior. But, in context, this verse means the complete opposite. It instructs how to gain another person's ear when he or she needs to hear criticism—how to avoid hypocrisy, the offense that so often is the cornerstone of defensiveness.

Let the image speak. Your spouse complains that you're blind to things because there's a speck in your eye. They say this as a plank sticking out of their own eye almost takes your head off and knocks the lamp off of the bedside table. If you weren't so offended by their hypocrisy it would be laughable. Have you ever told your spouse, in a sinful way, that he or she was sinning against you? Have you ever used a murderous tone to tell your spouse that he or she hurt you? Have you ever rejected your spouse for rejecting you? Yelled at your spouse for yelling at you?

Jesus' point isn't that you've no right to address your spouse's sin if you've ever sinned. His point is that you need to deal with your own sin first. You must "remove the plank out of your own eye, and then you will see clearly to remove the speck from your brother's eye." Start with defensiveness itself. If you've responded poorly to your spouse's attempt to get you to look at yourself, or if you approached your spouse full of pride and intent on blame shifting, then you need to admit your fault and ask for forgiveness.

Defensiveness and hypocrisy are fueled by a host of subversive desires, such as the desire to be right; the desire to avoid anxiety, shame, or guilt; the desire to feel justified; or the desire to feel superior. When you find yourself quarreling with your husband or wife, and aren't sure what desires are "battling within you," begin with the desires that fuel defensiveness and hypocrisy. Clearing the decks in this way will set the stage for productive problem solving.

What Do You Really Want?

According to James, in tackling conflict start with self-examination. He follows up with a simple observation: "You want something but do not get it. You kill and covet, but you cannot have what you want. You quarrel and fight" (James 4:2). Frustrated or blocked desires battle within you. When I'm fighting with my wife, usually I want something that I'm not getting. I want her to say yes to my desire for time with her, but she chooses to spend time with a friend instead. I want her to say yes to my desire to watch a ball game on TV, but she wants me to mow the lawn as promised. When she says no to my desires, I often, without thinking, engage in battle to get what I want.

As you try to figure out how you're contributing to the quarrel, the Bible suggests that you ask yourself a question: "What do I want?"

Often, combative spouses draw a complete blank when asked, specifically, what they want. Bear in mind, the question "What do you want?" is a different (though related) question from "What are you fighting *about?*" What you're fighting about is an *event*, a set of circumstances that are the occasion for the conflict. What you want is the question of what you're fighting for—the desires that are the real *issues* driving the conflict. The Bible challenges us to dig beneath event details to uncover deeper heart issues.

Let's say, for instance, you're the wife and you're angry because your husband didn't help you put the kids to bed. You could describe what you want by saying, "I *want* my husband to help me with the kids." True enough. But is there a deeper want that you haven't put on the table for discussion? Describe your wants in relational terms: How would you like your husband to think about and treat you differently? Maybe beneath the bedtime event is a sense that your husband doesn't value time with the kids. You want your husband to place a higher value on his relationship with the children. Or maybe you feel your husband doesn't value or respect your role as a parent. You want him to express appreciation and respect for what you do, even if he doesn't view those duties as being part of his role. Or perhaps, at root, you simply don't feel like your husband values you as a wife. It feels as if he just considers you domestic help—a nanny, cook, and maid. It isn't

> **R**emember, love is about seeking what is best for the other, not about getting what you want.

so much that you want him to help you put the kids to bed; you want your husband to treat you like you're more than hired help. You want him to want you for you. These are issues that, if they truly reflect the concerns of your heart, likely touch on many areas of the marriage and drive many conflicts.

When we accurately identify the wants or issues that drive a conflict, we often find that those same issues are driving other conflicts. The same issues create different conflict events. So not only does your sense that your husband regards you as hired help more than as a wife show up in conflicts over putting the kids to bed; it also shows up in conflicts over laundry, mealtime cleanup, and other household tasks. Additionally, it shows up in areas you might not suspect, like the bedroom. Your sense that you're simply "used" as a household servant contributes to the feeling of being used sexually. Rather than feeling like intimacy, sex feels like one more chore performed for your employer.

If you're unaware of the underlying issue then you might have two different conflicts that are about the same thing. Sometimes, after hearing a laundry list of conflict events, I'll tell a couple that they have a "conflict with a thousand faces." A thousand different conflicts might express only one basic underlying issue that the couple is either unaware of or that they have no idea how to tackle.

At what point does identifying the "want issues" become an exercise in removing the plank from your own eye? To the extent that your desire has driven your words and actions more than love for God or your spouse, you've sinned against them both. Remember, love is about seeking what's best for the other, not about getting what you want. Even if in the conflict, your spouse has done wrong—been harsh and defensive—you need to admit that you've been so driven by what you want that you were willing to be unkind and sin against God to get it. You might say, "I just realized that when I was angry at you for not helping me put the kids to bed, it was really about something else we need to talk about. But first I want to tell you I'm sorry I snapped at you in my anger. It was wrong, and I ask you to forgive me."

We will explore more carefully what it means to confess sin and ask for forgiveness in the next chapter, but first heed one last warning about how deceitful desires can ruin our attempts to be humble. When you're removing a plank from your eye, don't confess something just to make yourself look good or throw your spouse off balance, or so that you can take a shortcut to pointing out their faults. If you do, you'll simply be replacing one plank with another. Take time to honestly reflect on what's going on in your own heart. Think, pray, journal. Remember, one of the foundational truths we've emphasized is that to sin against your neighbor, your spouse, means you've violated worship and sinned against God in the same moment. Before trying to repair your relationship with your spouse, repair your relationship with God. Experiencing his mercy, love, and forgiveness will give you the support you need to be Christlike with your spouse.

Think about It

- What is your attitude toward conflict? How might your attitude change if you understand conflict as something that God uses to help you?
- How are you guilty of the very things that you typically point out to your spouse?
- Think about the recent conflicts you've had with your spouse. What did you really want? What desires do you typically bring to relationships? How do your desires fuel conflict?

eleven

Moving Forward in Conflict

What You'll Learn in This Chapter:

- There are several common strategies that we use in conflict. Some of us try to *appease*, some try to *ignore*, and some try to *win*. The strategies that we prefer are sometimes a clue as to the motives that may complicate our conflicts.
- Similar to those identified above, there are three biblical approaches to conflict: to yield, to wait, and to confront. These strategies are expressions of love.
- Decide which approach to use in conflict by discerning which one will best serve the needs of your spouse.

Common Strategies for Handling Conflict

IF YOU'RE HAVING trouble understanding how your wants and desires contribute to conflict, don't worry. Sometimes the desires that are fueling our quarrels can be difficult to spot. But even our typical strategy or style of handling conflicts can provide clues to what those desires may be. Here are three general ways to respond to conflict:[12]

- *Appease: Find a way to appease or satisfy others so that there's no reason for conflict.* Spouses who appease often say things that they don't really mean and agree to do things they don't really want to do. On the one hand, there seem to be many perks to appeasement. You appear very laid back and easy to get along with. Your spouse and others seem to think well of you and enjoy your company. On the other hand, relationships are hard when you always have to hide what you think and feel to avoid the possibility of offending others. When you misrepresent your thoughts and feelings you don't feel known, understood, or loved. When you do things you don't really want to do you feel frustrated and unhappy. When you say yes to every request you become burdened and overwhelmed. When you get angry you don't have the freedom to talk directly to the person you're angry with, so you stew silently or perhaps talk to someone else about it. When appeasing fails and conflicts with a particular person are frequent or intense, appeasers usually find a way to cut off the relationship.
- *Ignore: Pretend the problem doesn't exist.* These people avoid the conversation entirely. They may avoid sharing their opinion, or they may share it and then shut down any attempts to dialogue about it. Rather than saying yes to requests, they delay decisions, try to avoid being pinned down, or, when pressed, tend to say no. Conflict is still a possibility, but only if it's unavoidable. This strategy seems to have the advantage of

avoiding all of the frustrations of being overcommitted, but it doesn't make problems go away. In other words, though you choose not to acknowledge them, there are still problems and conflicts in your marriage and relationships that will only get worse over time if they aren't directly addressed.

- *Win: Settle problems by prevailing.* Spouses who seek to win work hard to make sure their interests prevail in conflict. They don't seem intimidated or reluctant to engage in conflict; in fact, some seem to enjoy it at times. Winners tend to be skilled in communicating, persuading, and even intimidating. Their emotions (anger, fear, frustration) are an active part of the argument. You not only hear their words but experience pressure to agree based on how emotional they are. While this strategy escapes most of the pitfalls of avoiding and appeasing, it can fail in that it simply drives problems underground. Others may not be genuinely convinced or persuaded by the winner but simply cave into the emotional pressure, realizing that they aren't going to be heard.

Can you see yourself in any of these descriptions? One may describe you perfectly. You may see yourself in some combination of all three. To the extent that you tend toward one strategy or the other, ask yourself, why? Perhaps you saw conflict modeled that way during your childhood. Maybe it's the style you've found most effective in relating to your spouse. In any case, examine yourself to see if there are deeper reasons.

Does your preferred strategy play to the desires and fears that show up in other areas of your marriage? These three approaches roughly correspond to the three patterns of manipulation that we explored in chapter 6 (see the table "Strategies for Handling Conflict" on the next page). Does your preferred strategy for conflict reflect a pattern of interaction that's rooted in the ruling desires and fears of your heart?

- Is your tendency to appease others part of a larger pattern of movement *toward* others? Does it reflect cravings for acceptance and peace or fears of rejection?
- Is your tendency to ignore part of a larger pattern of movement *away* from others? Does it reflect desires for peace, comfort, and control or a distaste for messiness or other fear?
- Is your strategy of winning part of a larger pattern of movement *against* others? Does it reflect cravings for success, a desire to be superior to others, or a fear of failure, or being dominated or controlled by others?

Strategies for Handling Conflict

Strategies	Appease (Move Toward)	Ignore (Move Away)	Win (Move Against)
Desires	Acceptance, intimacy, belonging	Comfort, security, perfection, order, control	Success, power, control, admiration
Fears	Rejection, isolation, shame	Hassles, chaos, punishment, being controlled	Failure, humiliation, being dominated, weakness

When the plank in your eye keeps you from seeing the truth about yourself, the way you handle conflict can help you to see yourself more clearly.

Biblical Strategies for Handling Conflict

So which is the correct strategy for handling conflict—appeasing, ignoring, or winning at all costs? All three have downsides and are easily corrupted by the deceitful desires and fears of our heart. What does love look like in conflict? Let's look at some passages from the Bible that can help us to construct a godly strategy governed by love.

Yield

We've already explored how defensiveness can be an obstacle to resolving conflict. Jesus exhorts us to defuse defensiveness by examining ourselves first. "You hypocrite, first take the plank out of your own eye, and then you will see clearly to remove the speck from your brother's eye" (Matthew 7:5).

Sometimes you engage in conflict with your spouse and realize you're in the wrong—you've misunderstood or misinterpreted your spouse. You may even see your own sinfulness at work. At that point you need to yield and admit your mistake or confess your sin.

> Sometimes, even when you're right, yield to the desires or preferences of the other because to do otherwise might cause harm.

Sometimes, even when you're right, yield to the desires or preferences of the other because to do otherwise might cause harm. For example, when Kim and I first married I enjoyed a good horror movie every once in a while. I enjoyed an occasional scare. The scare didn't last long, and it didn't bother my conscience. Kim has never enjoyed horror movies; in fact, she despises them. So what should we do if I want to see a horror movie on a Friday night but she doesn't? Are horror movies taboo simply because Kim doesn't like them? She should tolerate movies she doesn't like for my sake every once in a while, right? In fact, we don't watch horror movies together. I yielded to her on this over the years because I understand that her dislike of horror movies is more than simply a matter of taste. Kim has seen enough horror movies to know that they leave troubling images in her mind. I love her and don't want her to have to suffer that way just so I can indulge my preference. Out of love for her, I sacrifice whatever right I may have to watch horror movies, with or without her.

In these instances, we follow the path of love that Christ has laid out for us. Would God not have been within his rights to look on our sinfulness and reject or even destroy us? God, however, sacrificed both his rights and his Son's life to restore relationship with us. Sometimes loving our spouse means surrendering, for their benefit, what we may be entitled to.

Wait

"It is to a man's honor to avoid strife, but every fool is quick to quarrel" (Proverbs 20:3). As we saw in Proverbs 17:14, starting a quarrel is like breaching a dam. When possible, avoid arguments.

But the Bible's advice to avoid or postpone conflict is based on other important truths. For one, it reflects the way God loves us. No matter how aware you are of your sins, you can assume that you're guilty of countless others that you aren't aware of. God's holiness exceeds anything we can imagine, and as sinners who live in a sinful world we've been desensitized to most of our sins. If God were to confront us every moment we sinned, it would be unbearable. In this sense, God postpones challenging us until we're ready for it; until his loving challenge will lead to our growth and change. As you try to love your spouse as God loves you, it may mean postponing a conflict when your spouse isn't in the right frame of mind to hear what you have to say. It may mean overlooking a minor offense altogether because it's out of character for your spouse, and you can sympathize with the circumstances or pressures that tripped him or her up. Or it may mean taking a longer view and understanding that some of your spouse's weaknesses and sins are part of a long-term battle. Rather than addressing every instance of failing, we need to be patient with our spouses as God is with us.

Confront

"Do not hate your brother in your heart. Rebuke your neighbor frankly so you will not share in his guilt. Do not seek revenge or bear a grudge against one of your people, but love your neighbor as yourself. I am the LORD" (Leviticus 19:17–18).

Once you realize that sin, not your spouse, is your real enemy, then you can begin to understand that sin can't be ignored. This passage highlights some of the temptations we face in handling conflict. Both payback and turning a blind eye are off the table. We aren't to react angrily, pursuing revenge by giving our spouse a dose of their own medicine. But we must also resist the temptation to think we've overlooked an offense when we've really tucked it away and allowed it to become a silent grudge. The Bible teaches that there are times to speak directly and honestly about a problem. Notice how God jolts us out of the ways we mishandle conflict: if our spouse is entangled in sin and we fail to act in love, it's considered hatred. The Bible teaches us to love one another as God has loved us. Through the Bible, God speaks to those who have wronged and betrayed him. Rather than ignoring the problem and walking away or destroying us in anger, God speaks to us openly about both our sin and his desire to restore the relationship.

Love Is More Than Right and Wrong

Biblical strategies are strikingly similar to the strategies we examined at the beginning of this chapter. Yielding looks a lot like appeasing; waiting, like ignoring; and confronting, like winning.

The Bible gives us more than one strategy because different people and situations require different approaches. How do you know which one to use? Since our foundation is God's love, ask yourself which approach would most benefit the other. Answering that question requires more than a technical understanding of one approach or another; it requires you to know yourself and your spouse.

Knowledge Puffs Up, Love Builds Up

The Corinthian church was beset with a multitude of problems disrupting the community. There were disputes over which leaders they should follow (1 Corinthians 1:10–17), sexual immorality (1 Corinthians 5:1), divorce (1 Corinthians 7), even how to maintain order during worship services (1 Corinthians 11:20–22; 14:39–40). The letter is full of practical advice; Paul wisely, however, does more than just give instructions on what to do. He gives a principle to guide them in solving any problem.

The principle captured in the phrase, "knowledge puffs up, but love builds up" (1 Corinthians 8:1b) tells us that in a conflict, being right and doing right aren't always the same thing. In other words, we can be right in principle, but so wrong in the way that we act on that principle that we're harming others; we're not acting in love. Paul contrasts two images here, the image of those puffed up in pride, because they're right, and those who in humility work to build up others, helping them to grow through love.

> We can be right in principle, but so wrong in the way that we act on that principle that we're harming others; we're not acting in love.

Paul applies this principle to a problem of the early church: there was debate as to whether it was acceptable for Christians to eat foods that had been sacrificed to idols. In the ancient world, followers of pagan religions would sometimes sell meat that had been used in ritual sacrifice. Some Christians had no qualms eating such meat. Others felt that this was wrong, that the meat had been defiled because it had been used in pagan sacrifice. Who was right? How should this conflict be resolved? The issue of ritually sacrificed meat may seem strange and irrelevant, but Paul's strategies for handling the conflict are helpful for dealing with conflict in your marriage.

Paul reminds the Corinthians that since idols aren't true gods the meat sacrificed to them is acceptable to eat (see 1 Corinthians 8:4). Later he writes,

> Eat anything sold in the meat market without raising
> questions of conscience, for, "The earth is the Lord's, and
> everything in it." If some unbeliever invites you to a meal
> and you want to go, eat whatever is put before you without
> raising questions of conscience. (1 Corinthians 10:25–27)

In other words, God created the meat, and it belongs to him as the only true God. Christians are free to eat meat that's been sacrificed to idols.

But Paul qualifies this truth with an important principle of love: *How are others affected by this?* How are others affected when someone sees a Christian eating meat that's been sacrificed to an idol? Paul writes, "But not everyone knows this. Some people are still so accustomed to idols that when they eat such food they think of it as having been sacrificed to an idol, and since their conscience is weak, it is defiled" (1 Corinthians 8:7). Paul recognizes that some Christians in Corinth come from pagan backgrounds and have strong and shameful associations with these sacrifices, or some simply don't think clearly about the issue. For those who can't eat the meat without feeling disloyal to God, eating it would indeed be wrong.

Christians who understand that the meat isn't defiled must not eat it in a way that tempts others to eat it and feel guilty. Paul puts it this way:

> Be careful, however, that the exercise of your freedom does not become a stumbling block to the weak. For if anyone with a weak conscience sees you who have this knowledge eating in an idol's temple, won't he be emboldened to eat what has been sacrificed to idols? So this weak brother, for whom Christ died, is destroyed by your knowledge. When you sin against your brothers in this way and wound their weak conscience, you sin against Christ. Therefore, if what I eat causes my brother to fall into sin, I will never eat meat again, so that I will not cause him to fall. (1 Corinthians 8:9–13)

Notice the question shift from "Who is right?" to "How do I love my neighbor?" It isn't enough for those eating the sacrificed meat to be right and expect the rest simply to deal with it. That isn't love. Love means caring about how your actions affect others.

A couple, counselees, was having difficulty in their sex life. In general, the husband was much more adventurous in the bedroom than his wife and this was causing tension between them. The wife was especially troubled by the way her husband would ask her to role-play with him, urging her to assume an imaginary identity complete with costume and props during lovemaking. The wife was uncomfortable with this, while the husband seemed perplexed and irritated by her reluctance. They wanted to know who was right?

> You might think of it this way: we're tempted to think of peace as the absence of conflict, but real peace is established by destroying sin.

I asked the wife to share with her husband how she felt about the role-playing. She said, "I guess what really bothers me is that I feel like you'd rather be making love to someone else. Why can't you just be excited to be with me? Why do I have to pretend to be someone else? I married you because I want to be with you, not another man. It really hurts me to think that we have to pretend to be other people for lovemaking to be exciting."

At that point, right and wrong became perfectly clear. You don't need a Bible verse that specifically allows or prohibits role-play during sex to know that the role-playing was wounding the wife and damaging the relationship. Even if you were to argue that the Bible grants husbands and wives the freedom to engage in role-play, the Bible would argue that you must not use your freedom in a way that harms others. To do so is to sin against Christ. Paul also summarizes it this way, "'Everything is permissible'—but not everything is beneficial. 'Everything is permissible'—but not everything is constructive. Nobody should seek his own good, but the good of others" (1 Corinthians 10:23–24).

Conflict resolution is about more than figuring out who's right and who's wrong. It requires us to know more than the facts of the issue at hand. We also have to know enough about each other and love itself to plot a course that leads to growth. As Paul walks the Corinthians through this issue, we learn that working through conflict successfully, in a godly way, is about love, not about marshalling enough facts to claim victory.

Putting It All Together

Jesus, the Prince of Peace, is our only hope of ever living in peace. But Jesus doesn't establish peace by ignoring sin; he establishes peace by defeating sin. You might think of it this way: we're tempted to think of peace as the absence of conflict, but real peace is established by destroying sin. And, often, the only way to locate and defeat sin is through conflict.

Conflict can be painful, dangerous, and destructive, and we should heed the Bible's cautions. But we must take equally seriously the Bible's call to do battle against sin where we find it—in our hearts and in our relationships. When spouses learn the difference between attacking each other and attacking sin, conflict takes on a whole new meaning.

Learning to work through conflict in a godly, constructive way will always be more than following a three, five, or ten-step process. It requires that you grow in wisdom and act in love. Let's quickly review the themes presented in chapters 10 and 11:

- Remember the big picture of conflict and don't give in to discouragement.
- Be alert to the dangers of defensiveness.
- Deal with your own sin first.
- Adopt the biblical approach that fits your knowledge of yourself, your spouse, and the need of the moment.
- Don't get stuck on who's right and who's wrong; always act to build up the other in love.

Think about It

- What strategy do you use most in conflict: appeasing, ignoring, or winning? Why? Are there particular desires or fears that shape your approach?
- Which biblical approach is most difficult for you: yielding, waiting, or confronting? Why?
- Can you think of a way that you may need to yield to the needs of your spouse out of love?

twelve

Foundations
of Forgiveness

What You'll Learn in This Chapter:

- Forgiveness is supernatural and rooted in God's forgiveness of us through Christ. There are many biblical images and stories of forgiveness that can help us understand how God asks us to forgive each other as he has forgiven us.
- God's forgiveness reflects several decisions that we need to make to forgive our spouses: decisions to let go, to sacrifice, to trust, and to grow.
- Learning how to take responsibility for our sins against our spouse and confess them is important too. In confession, there are several important elements to include and several pitfalls to avoid.

What It Means to Forgive

FORGIVENESS IS INCREDIBLY powerful. If it could be bottled, a daily dose would probably save a lot of marriages. But what, exactly, does it mean to forgive? What are the "active ingredients"? How do we learn to forgive?

Recently, I looked at a book on the topic of forgiveness, and within the first few pages read this admission: "Clearly, scientific research on forgiveness is on the rise. However, at the time of this writing, individual researchers' conceptualizations of forgiveness are quite diverse. In particular, no consensual definition of forgiveness exists."[13] In other words, more and more psychologists are studying forgiveness, but they all have different ideas about what it is. Nonetheless, this tentative definition was offered a few pages later: "We propose to define forgiveness as *intraindividual, prosocial change toward a perceived transgressor that is situated within a specific context.*"[14] My best shot at a translation: forgiveness is something that happens inside of you that makes things better with the person you're angry with. I already knew that much.

To be fair, no one sentence can adequately define forgiveness, especially without understanding what the Bible has to say about it. In a sense, psychologists have an impossible task. While forgiveness is something that people do and can be observed, it's ultimately a supernatural act. God invented forgiveness, and his love is its foundation. Rather than starting with a definition, it might be easier, then, to let the Bible paint a picture of it.

A Curtain Is Torn and the Dead Are Raised

The Bible's most powerful and dramatic picture of God's forgiveness and love is Jesus' death on the cross. In agony physically and spiritually as God places the penalty for our sin on him, Jesus willingly suffers for us to set us free. Jesus' death is accompanied by some dramatic events:

And when Jesus had cried out again in a loud voice, he
gave up his spirit. At that moment the curtain of the temple
was torn in two from top to bottom. The earth shook and
the rocks split. The tombs broke open and the bodies of
many holy people who had died were raised to life. (Matthew
27:50–52)

A curtain is torn in the temple, the earth shakes tombs open,
and the dead are raised. Those, too, are powerful images of God's
forgiveness.

To understand the significance of the torn temple curtain, remember that sin creates separation at every level of relationship. It separates parent from child, church member from church member, friend from friend, and husband from wife. Sin even divides our own hearts. But nowhere is this separation starker than between God and his people. Apart from Jesus, it's inconceivable that a sinner would approach God without being destroyed.

In the law, God encoded and symbolized both this separation and his determination to rescue us. His law contains numerous commands explaining what behaviors made people unclean—unacceptable to God—along with the rituals, washings, and sacrifices required to cleanse. In many instances cleansing requires an animal sacrifice; the shedding of its blood, signifying the seriousness of sin and reminding us that the appropriate punishment for sin is death.

Once a year, the high priest would make atonement for all of Israel. After careful cleansing, attired in special garments, the high priest entered the Most Holy Place, the inner room, which housed the ark of the Testimony, God's earthly throne (see Exodus 25:10–22). This inner room was separated from the rest of the temple by a heavy curtain. In this room the high priest sprinkled the blood of sacrificed animals on the atonement cover of the ark (Leviticus 16:1–19). This annual atonement was done according to God's specific detailed instructions; to do it carelessly would result in immediate death (Leviticus 16:2).

Imagine living under this system of ritual cleansing and sacrifice. There are daily reminders that your sinfulness requires bloodshed, and that an impenetrable curtain stands between you and God because of your sin. Not a moment passes without an acute awareness that seeing God face to face would kill you. On the one hand, there's hope because God provides cleansing so that he can live among his people. On the other hand, however, the unending bloodshed and that curtain, are constant reminders of a debt that's never repaid. How the people long for the day when sins are forgiven once and for all.

> When Jesus was crucified and the temple curtain was torn in two, God's message was unmistakable: his people had been forgiven once and for all.

When Jesus was crucified and the temple curtain was torn in two, God's message was unmistakable: his people had been forgiven once and for all. The obstacle of sin was removed. There was no longer a need for separation between God and his people. Likewise, death, the ultimate form of separation and punishment, is no longer our final destiny. Along with Jesus himself, the dead came out of their graves with new life. And now nothing separates God from his people. We can approach him without fear.

> Therefore, brothers, since we have confidence to enter the Most Holy Place by the blood of Jesus, by a new and living way opened for us through the curtain, that is, his body, and since we have a great priest over the house of God, let us draw near to God with a sincere heart in full assurance of faith, having our hearts sprinkled to cleanse us from a guilty conscience and having our bodies washed with pure water. (Hebrews 10:19–22)

Jesus has become a perfect sacrifice that removes our sins from us once and for all so that there's no need for a curtain of separation and death. We can now draw near to God in an intimate way, without fear of rejection or judgment.

Learning to Forgive as God Does

Embracing what Jesus has done for us and extending that in thought, word, and deed to others is the essence of forgiveness. In forgiving one another, we draw on the forgiveness that Jesus has given us by making a decision to release another from the penalty of sin. Rather than drawing a curtain and pushing each other away, we push sin and judgment away and draw near to each other. Put as simply as possible, forgiveness is releasing the other from the penalty of sin so the relationship can be restored.

Think about forgiveness in terms of four basic *decisions* that reflect the way God forgives us:

- *God decided to release us from the penalty of our sin.* God's forgiveness isn't a decision he waffles on. He doesn't dwell on our sin or bring it to mind. In the same way our forgiveness must be a decision to let go of how our spouse has wronged us. Sticking to that decision requires us to refuse to dwell on how we have been wronged.
- *God decided to sacrifice in order to forgive.* God decided to absorb the cost of our sin. Repairing the relationship means accepting the wound and choosing to draw near to the one who has sought to harm him. He doesn't seek revenge or look for opportunities to pay us back for our sin. Likewise, we choose to draw near to our spouse without the lingering threat of payback.
- *God decided to accomplish good even through our sinfulness.* God doesn't just forgive our sins, he promises to use even our worst failures to do good in our lives and in our relationship with him. When we forgive our spouses we trust that God will work for our good and the good of our marriage.

167

- *God decided to allow us to grow.* God didn't simply forgive us once and place us on eternal probation: "Okay, one more sin and you're finished!" He knows we will continue to battle with sin even as he helps us to grow. Likewise, we forgive our spouses, but we don't expect perfection and we allow them to grow. Our ability to forgive also grows.

Don't think of these as sequential steps but as different aspects of forgiveness. In forgiving there will be times when you'll need to focus on one aspect more than others, and it's likely that you'll have to revisit each aspect numerous times.

A Decision to Release

Forgiveness means letting go of your right to punish another and choosing through the power of God's love to hold onto the other person rather than his or her offense.

In the process of forgiving, the first barrier you have to remove is within yourself. You have to decide to let go of the offense along with your desire to punish the offender. You have to decide to see your spouse instead of the offense. Often the decision to let go has to be renewed daily, hourly, or even more often. The bigger the offense, the more challenging it can be to let go; but the less you ruminate on the offense and feed your anger, the easier it becomes.

Understanding forgiveness as a decision to let go is important because we often confuse forgiveness with our emotions. When this happens forgiveness ebbs and flows as our emotions ebb and flow. When we don't feel angry, we think we've forgiven, but when anger resurfaces it seems we're back to square one. Just when we think an issue has been laid to rest for good, it pops up again. While forgiveness affects and can bring relief to our emotions, it's much more than an emotion. It's a decision we make based on our worship of God to forgive as he forgives. God's forgiveness isn't a declaration of emotion but a declaration that his people are forgiven and pardoned from their sins just as a judge would dismiss a case from a courtroom. In that sense, forgiveness is a decision, a declaration, a once-for-all-time pronouncement.

But what if you can't stop thinking about it? When you dwell on an incident, it may mean there are lingering questions or anxiety about what's happened. Look for unresolved issues or unanswered questions. Are there hurts that you never revealed? Is there something missing or wrong in the way your spouse is dealing with their sin?

Also explore the possibility that there's a hidden benefit to dwelling on the incident. Sometimes feeling angry is preferable to feeling anxious or helpless. Sometimes we prefer to live in a self-protective cocoon of anger rather than risk the trust required to forgive. Holding onto an offense may afford

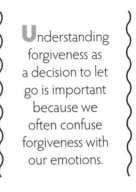

Understanding forgiveness as a decision to let go is important because we often confuse forgiveness with our emotions.

a sense of moral superiority over our spouses and distract us from having to look at our own hearts. If this is the case, focus on God's love and mercy and ask him to help you forgive. You may also want to enlist the encouragement and prayers of wise friends or a counselor.

Forgiving isn't the same as forgetting. It isn't a divine form of amnesia. God doesn't ask us to live as people without a history or pretend that sins never happened. In fact, being able to recall how God has delivered us through marital storms, empowering us to confess, forgive, and overcome, can give us hope and an anchor in future storms. Stories of forgiveness and reconciliation can also become part of the way you seek to strengthen and encourage others in their marriages. Remember that it's one thing to dwell on an incident with thankfulness for how God has worked in your marriage but quite another to dwell on it and find your anger and hurt reawakened.

A Decision to Sacrifice

God's forgiveness required the sacrifice of his Son to pay the penalty for sin. Our forgiveness requires sacrifices, too, though of a different sort. Your suffering doesn't atone for your spouse's sin, but you'll have to sacrifice in several ways:

- You'll have to accept the wound that you've received from your spouse. Forgiveness doesn't mean pretending it didn't happen or running from it. Face the pain of the offense and the discomfort of talking about it, so your spouse can know how you've been hurt and have an opportunity to turn from sin and receive mercy and forgiveness. Forgiveness is a sacrifice in the sense that you're choosing the more difficult path. You're sacrificing the temporary comfort of ignoring the problem or the temporary pleasure of erecting a wall of bitterness and instead doing the hard and sometimes painful work of moving toward the one who has wounded you.
- It also means that you're letting go of any future payback. You're sacrificing all of the moments that you'll want to remind them of how they've wronged you, wanting to cause them the same kind of pain they've caused you, taking comfort in the power of making them earn back your love and affection.

An important way that you sacrifice your claim to justice is by refusing to bring up the matter in a harmful way. That means, for example, no subtle digs and not using it as a trump card in the next argument. This is an extension of your decision to release your spouse from penalty. If you're successfully putting off negative musings then you're much less likely to use the incident against your spouse in the future. If you repeatedly bring up the matter for the purpose of hurting your spouse, reaffirm your decision to release them from penalty. Reflect to see if you're regularly reviewing the hurt in your mind and why.

The key phrase in this commitment is "in a harmful way." Even in the context of a conflict, it may be helpful to understand how a current problem is related to a past problem. Being able to identify a pattern of problems in marriage can lead to a deeper understanding of what's going on beneath the surface. So, for example, a wife who has recently sinned by losing her temper over several different incidents may need to be encouraged to notice the rising tide in her anger. A loving husband would naturally want to help her think through and understand what's driving the recent spike in anger, to get beneath events to underlying issues. That doesn't demonstrate a lack of forgiveness but wisdom and love.

Don't gossip about the issue. Talking to others about the incident probably means that you're nursing your memory of the offense. Notice how often you're thinking about this incident, what your attitudes are about it, and why.

A desire to talk to others may also be a sign that you need to talk more to your spouse about the incident but can't. If you're afraid that raising the issue again will hurt your spouse or if he or she has asked you not to bring it up again, remind yourself and your spouse that forgiveness is a process, that you're committed to forgiving, but that you need help thinking and talking it through if your forgiveness is going to grow.

A Decision to Trust That God Is Up to Good

As Jesus sacrificed he had to entrust himself to God. He had to trust that God would really deal with the sin that he, Jesus, was paying for. He trusted that forgiveness would make a difference and that his sacrifice was not in vain. He trusted that God would protect him, even raise him from the dead. He trusted that God would renew and restore his people.

You, too, have to trust God when you choose to forgive. You have to trust that God will both heal your hurts and use your sacrifice to restore your relationship. When you forgive you have to trust that you aren't being a fool, but that God will work through your forgiveness. Your forgiveness doesn't guarantee a change in your spouse, but it does guarantee that you'll grow and that you'll be protected from bitterness. Trust that forgiveness is the path that God provides to draw back the curtains that separate you and your spouse. Trust that forgiveness will renew your marriage.

Your decision to forgive is a decision to do everything you can to keep this incident from standing between you and your spouse.

This decision is a culmination of the others. If you refrain from dwelling on the incident, and choose not to use it destructively against your spouse or talk about it with others, you're already doing a lot to remove obstacles in your marriage. But sometimes we allow the offense to come between us in more subtle ways. For instance, you and your husband successfully worked through the issue of his working late without calling home to let you know what's happening.

> The forgiveness that God gives us based on Jesus' one-time death on the cross is bestowed on us day by day for the rest of our lives.

He apologized, acknowledging that it was thoughtless and selfish not to think of its effect on you, and committed to do better. Now, two weeks later he calls home as promised to explain that he has to work late and that your dinner date will have to be pushed back an hour. You find yourself fuming again. He's made good on his commitment, and yet your emotions are roiling and you just want to withdraw and tell him to forget going out that night. What is happening?

It's possible that the emotions you experienced several weeks back are resurfacing because this situation is similar to what happened before. He's working late and that affects your plans. But the situation is also wonderfully different. Remind yourself of your decision to forgive, and thank God that he helped you both to work it through. Be thankful that your husband is keeping his word, and focus on enjoying time together when he gets home.

It may also be the case that there's some unfinished business you need to consider. You dealt with the incident of his not calling when he has to work late, but the issue goes deeper for you. He didn't call when he was working late, but more than that, he was working so much in general, and you feel that you aren't the priority to him that you should be. That's good to recognize, but it needs to be dealt with as a separate issue from tonight's dinner plans. Enjoy your date tonight, but think and pray about how and when to discuss the issue of his work demands.

A Decision to Grow

No matter how sincere the confession and commitment to change, your spouse may again sin against you. Remember that change is a process. The forgiveness that God gives us based on Jesus' one-time death on the cross is bestowed on us day by day for the rest of our lives. A purpose of that forgiveness, restoring us to his perfect image, is a process that takes a lifetime.

As God perfects his image in you, forgiveness is something that you'll become better at. On some days, forgiveness will seem natural and easy. On other days you'll feel ready to overturn the decision you made the day before. Jesus has begun a wonderful work in you but you aren't fully mature. Growing in forgiveness will require you to stay focused on Jesus, interacting with him and learning from him just as you must do in every other area of life.

Confessing Sin and Asking for Forgiveness

"I know I need to learn to forgive, but shouldn't I expect to hear an apology from my spouse?"

For complete restoration, forgiveness must be offered in a context of confession. (We will deal with forgiving the unrepentant in chap. 13.) Forgiveness in marriage should involve both parties: one or both acknowledging and confessing sin, and one or both forgiving.

What to Keep in Mind When Confessing Sin

Sin is such a treacherous enemy that it even finds its way into our confessions and can actually aggravate the wounds we hope to heal.

There are a few simple principles that can help you avoid the most common mistakes and pitfalls of confessions gone awry.

Confession is about being restored to God, not just saying you're sorry

For many of us, confession means saying, "I'm sorry." Important though it is, expressing sorrow is only part of confessing sin. The foundation for confession is acknowledging your rebellion against God. Only after seeking God's forgiveness can confession to your spouse be effective. King David writes,

> For I know my transgressions, and my sin is always before
> me. Against you, you only, have I sinned and done what
> is evil in your sight, so that you are proved right when you
> speak and justified when you judge. (Psalm 51:3–4)

David has a clear view of his sin and knows it's evil committed against God himself. Notice the phrase, "against you, you only, have I sinned." This is a remarkable statement in view of the sin that occasioned this repentance—David's adultery with Bathsheba and subsequent murder of her husband Uriah (see 2 Samuel 11).

David doesn't discount the human victims of his crimes, but he knows that at its core, his sin is an expression of hatred toward God—an effort to dethrone God. David admits that his sins against Uriah and Bathsheba were ultimately actions rooted in his perverse desire to be his own god. Addressing the root of his sin, David asks God for complete and thorough cleansing. Cleansing and restoration with God will empower David to take every possible step to right the wrongs he's committed, continue as king, and face the inevitable consequences.

Lasting reconciliation in marriage must be rooted in repentance that gets to the real problem. Remember, relationship problems are worship problems, and the only way to correct worship problems is to be restored to God. When reconciliation with your spouse is built on a foundation of confession and repentance before God, its depth and authenticity make forgiveness more natural and easy for the other. At the same time, real repentance empowers the confessor to live with the real-life messiness that characterizes the process of forgiveness and restoration.

Confession isn't about getting something off your chest

Confession can make us uncomfortable, but it's often a relief. Have you ever had a guilty conscience that just gnawed at you day after day? A guilty conscience is a good thing when it helps us to see our sins and take action to set matters straight. But sometimes, we ease the burden of our conscience by telling our spouse something that will do more harm than good.

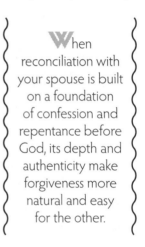

When reconciliation with your spouse is built on a foundation of confession and repentance before God, its depth and authenticity make forgiveness more natural and easy for the other.

Consider, for example, lustful thoughts. It's sinful to fantasize and entertain adulterous thoughts, but it would be hurtful to mention it to your spouse *every* time such a thought crossed your mind. Your daily confessions would, in effect, create an injury that might cause your spouse to live in anxiety and concern over something that, if it's a significant struggle, would best be handled by talking to a trusted friend. The point of confession isn't to soothe your conscience but to deal with sin. Don't launch into confession without considering how it will affect your spouse. Before you confess sin determine whether or not he or she has been or will be affected by your actions.

Even when we're confessing something that we ought, we can be in such a hurry to relieve our conscience that we rush through our confession, demand immediate sympathy or understanding, and give no thought to how our confession is impacting our spouse. Remember, confession isn't a strategy to ease your conscience but an act of love that should benefit your marriage.

Don't blame shift

Quick to blame shift, we even build it into our confessions of sin by using the words *if, but,* and *maybe.* Introduced into a confession these words have a sneaky way of turning a confession into an accusation or at least an invitation to share blame. For example,

When you say . . .	You mean . . .
"*If* I hurt your feelings I'm sorry."	You aren't sure you hurt your spouse's feelings? Maybe it's all in your spouse's head.
"I know I lied to you, *but* I wouldn't have to if you didn't react so negatively."	You mean your spouse is responsible for your lie. Are you confessing your sin or your spouse's sin?
"*Maybe* I shouldn't have spent that money without talking to you first."	If you aren't sure, then your confession is premature. If you're sure, don't use the word *maybe.*

If you aren't really taking responsibility for what you did, then you aren't confessing sin; you're simply explaining how somebody else is responsible for what you've done. Sometimes we essentially offer and retract our confessions in the same breath.

Get specific

When you confess sin, describe what you did, why you did it, and even ways that you're aware this is a spiritual battle. Confessing the specifics of what you've done demonstrates that you've taken a close look at yourself and your situation.

For example, if you lost your temper with your spouse, don't stop at, "I'm sorry that I lost my temper with you." Dig deeper.

Exactly how did you lose your temper? "I raised my voice with you and slammed a door. I know that's very scary."

What was going on in your heart? "I was feeling sorry for myself and wanted you to feel sorry for me too. I didn't get what I wanted so I punished you with my anger. That was selfish and wrong."

What was the spiritual battle? "I know God wants me to learn to love you more, and slow down and think about what I'm doing. He's showing me how sinful it is to focus on myself and forget that I love you. He's showing me, too, that I need to love him more."

When you're able to describe yourself that accurately then you're going to be more successful at changing and your spouse is going to find it easier to forgive you.

Express genuine sorrow

Granted, saying you're sorry doesn't constitute full confession; it is, however, critically important. Your spouse needs to know that you're pained by the hurt you've caused him or her. Remember, a basic element of love is an ability and willingness to visit the world of the other. Sincere love calls us to "rejoice with those who rejoice; mourn with those who mourn" (Romans 12:15). As part of your confession, take the time to ask about and listen to how your sin affected your spouse. To hear how you've hurt your spouse is a painful but important expression of love that may deepen your understanding of your sin, your repentance before God, and your appreciation for Jesus' forgiveness.

Plan to be different

If you're truly sorry for what you've done, then you'll want things to be different in the future. As you describe your sin and your desire to be different, be ready to discuss ideas that will make that more likely: be willing to accept consequences for your sin.

"Consequences? I thought forgiveness was about releasing the other from punishment?" Yes, in forgiveness we do release the other from the penalty of sin, but sometimes wisdom and love require that consequences follow.

For example, if you've spent money secretly knowing that you should have discussed it with your spouse first, you might say, "I know that I've broken your trust, and I'm willing for you to hold the checkbook for a while." If you've been having trouble with online pornography or gambling, accept the need for an accountability partner, Internet filter, or other limitations on your computer use.

> When your confession is explicit: your spouse knows how to respond and you avoid making false assumptions.

Accepting consequences like these shows humble recognition that you need fences to prevent further injury to you, your spouse, and your marriage. A willingness to accept consequences is evidence of a truly repentant heart.

Turning away from sin is a process. To repent is to acknowledge that what you did was wrong, so obviously you don't want to do it again. Without promising that you won't ever sin in the same way again, you can demonstrate genuine repentance by talking about how you plan to do things differently. It could be as simple as saying, "The next time I'm tempted to lash out I'm going to step out of the room and cool off," or as intentional as, "I'm going to ask Kevin to pray with me about this and hold me accountable." Let your spouse know that you don't just *want* things to be different, but that you're taking steps that will lead to growth.

Ask for forgiveness

Whether the confession is long or short, one essential element must be a clear request for forgiveness. When you explicitly ask for forgiveness, two important things happen.

First, your spouse knows how to respond. Your spouse may be as inexperienced at forgiving as you are at confessing. If so, explicitly asking for forgiveness gives them tracks to run on.

Second, you avoid making false assumptions. You don't want to walk away from this issue thinking it's resolved if it really isn't. If your confession is misunderstood or fails to take into account things that are important to your spouse, you need to know that. You don't want the issue to be dropped prematurely, only to come up later after bitterness or other complications have made things worse.

Allow your spouse time to absorb what you've confessed. Remember that forgiveness is a process and he or she may not yet be ready or able to extend it.

Conflict Is Ordinary, Forgiveness Is Extraordinary

In forgiveness we practice and extend to others what God has done for us. Just as God has dealt with sin so that it no longer obstructs our relationship with him, we must learn to forgive each other to resolve the sins and damage done in our marriages. God is the author of forgiveness, and we must learn it from him. Remember, the key to lasting change in marriage is learning to see the ordinary moments of life as extraordinary opportunities to embody the love of God. In moments of conflict God brings opportunities to make his love visible in powerful and amazing ways. A willingness to admit and forgive sin is nothing less than the good news of God's forgiveness of sin being proclaimed through your marriage.

Think about It

- Recall a time when someone sincerely forgave you. What did he or she say or do? How did it impact you and the relationship? Recall a time when someone refused to forgive you. How did it impact you and the relationship?
- Which aspects of forgiveness are easier or harder for you than others? Explain the differences.
- How do your confessions typically get off track? Why?

thirteen

Forgiveness in Marriage

What You'll Learn in This Chapter:

- Forgiveness can be a challenge in any relationship, but it can be especially difficult in marriage. The intimacy of marriage makes us more vulnerable to the sins and weaknesses of the other.
- There are common obstacles to forgiveness in marriage: using forgiveness to take the issue off of the table (i.e., rushing the process); fearing that it will just happen again; and failing to recognize the differences between forgiving and enabling, consequences and payback.
- Forgiveness can be facilitated by focusing on how your spouse has blessed you, how much you've been forgiven, and how you're subject to similar temptations and weaknesses.
- If your spouse doesn't accept responsibility for how he or she has harmed you, though you can't offer forgiveness in its fullness, you can still commit to avoiding bitterness and staying open to your spouse.

Obstacles to Forgiveness in Marriage

NO MATTER HOW practiced you are in forgiveness or how success-fully you've navigated the stormy waters of every other relationship, you'll likely find practicing forgiveness in marriage difficult. This is because the more intimate you are with someone, the more power he or she has to wound you deeply. As wonderful as your spouse may be, you're still intimate with a fallen image bearer, a sinner. When the per-son you trust most sins against you, the wound is deeper than in less intimate relationships. God's love, however, is deeper, and the forgive-ness he gives us in Jesus and teaches us to give to others is powerful.

Using Forgiveness to Take the Issue Off the Table

Knowing that forgiveness means that the incident should become part of the past, spouses sometimes rush through the process to get it over with. After all, even when you know that God accomplishes good things through reconciliation, that doesn't mean it's fun or pleasant.

The offended spouse may rush to grant forgiveness, short-circuit-ing the offending spouse's need to confess fully. Sometimes he or she feels pushed to forgive prematurely, in effect closing up a wound that's still filled with debris.

If your spouse is pushing you to forgive, while you feel important aspects of the incident haven't been discussed, explain that you fully intend to forgive, but that you want your forgiveness to have its full effect. Humbly and gently try to explain what's missing from your spouse's confession. Or if you simply need more time to reflect and process the confession and the events leading up to it, assure your spouse that you aren't rejecting the confession but rather taking it seri-ously and trying to respond thoughtfully to it.

A critical key to helping your spouse forgive is taking the time to put into words how your sin has affected your spouse, and then gen-uinely expressing heartfelt sorrow for it. Before you try to put your spouse's hurt in your own words, make sure you've taken adequate time to let your spouse verbalize their own the hurt. Expressing hurt isn't easy, and it can take time.

Writing out your confession can help you connect more deeply with your sin and its effects as well as help your spouse absorb your words. It demonstrates that you're thinking deeply about your sin, and it gives your spouse something in hand that can remind them of that when they may doubt it. If your spouse has been deeply wounded by your sin, don't rush this part of the process. If you do, it will only appear that you're minimizing your sin.

> The more complete the confession, the easier it is to have faith that, even if it happens again, God will continue to effect change and growth.

Believing That Your Spouse Will Just Do It Again

Another prominent obstacle to forgiveness is the belief that the offending spouse will inevitably commit the same sin again. If forgiveness means being a doormat for a spouse who doesn't care how his or her actions affect you, forgiveness seems futile and humiliating. On the other hand, we all know that turning from sin, even sin that we hate and repent of, is a process. We often repeat offenses even when we're trying to grow.

Several things can help when this concern becomes an obstacle to forgiveness. First, the more complete the confession, the easier it is to have faith that, even if it happens again, God will continue to effect change and growth. For example, most spouses understand that someone who's battling an addiction will have lapses even as he or she breaks free from the addiction. As long as the offender is genuine in his or her repentance and committed to staying on the path of growth, offended spouses are able to forgive and recover.

Second, when forgiveness is blocked by the fear of a repeat offense, it can be especially important to talk in detail about steps to take to prevent it from happening next time. No plan is foolproof, and we don't want to have more faith in our own plans than in God's work; still whenever possible, it's wise to erect barriers to sin and map out a path forward. Make sure a spouse with this fear has a voice in the plan; and make sure his or her concerns are taken seriously.

Forgiving, Enabling, and Setting Consequences: Knowing the Difference

We've learned that there are typical strategies that we use in handling conflict: appeasing, ignoring, and winning. We also learned that these strategies may resemble actions love requires (yielding, waiting, and confronting), but they are, at root, as different as night and day. The strategies that we arrive at on our own are often shaped by our desires and fears rather than love. In the same way there are elements to forgiveness that may seem to be elements of biblical love but are really veiled ways of serving ourselves.

For instance, we know that forgiveness means releasing our spouse from the debt of their sin. We shouldn't ask our spouse to suffer to satisfy our desire for payback. Love does, however, sometimes require consequences to protect both spouses from especially damaging sins, e.g., abusive behavior and various addictions.

If temptations to sin aren't taken seriously and consequences not put into place, a sincere desire to forgive can lapse into a form of enabling that will endanger our spouse and our marriage. A spouse addicted to pornography, for example, needs forgiveness, not unrestricted access to the family computer. Consequences, however, can easily become a cover for payback. Restricted use of the family computer is a reasonable and loving consequence for viewing pornography, but locking them out of the bedroom for six months is more likely an expression of revenge.

To escape the pitfalls of enabling and revenge, examine your heart to determine why you're either removing or asking for consequences. Our motives will always be a mixed bag, but the more prominent motive ought to be love, not fear, anger, or resentment. Can you honestly say that what you're doing is best for your spouse and your marriage? Also consider your goal in adding or removing consequences. Is it likely to encourage your spouse to change? Is it likely to provide some form of protection so the relationship can heal?

Helps in Forgiveness

Fear, anger, bitterness, hopelessness, and even numbness can impede forgiveness. Emotions that keep us tied to past wounds, they rob forgiveness of its life-giving power. In addition to staying committed to the decisions of forgiveness, we can focus on other things that add leverage to those decisions and weaken the grip of painful emotions.

I Like This Person

In anger and hurt we can sometimes demonize our spouses, only seeing them through the tunnel vision of how they've hurt us. But however difficult your spouse may be, there are probably some good reasons you married him or her, things that you liked or admired that made you want to make that person a permanent part of your life. So there are good reasons to work to remove what's separating you. Take time to meditate and appreciate the things that you like about your spouse—things you may have lost sight of in the midst of your hurt and anger. Paul spoke to this when he wrote,

> Finally, brothers, whatever is true, whatever is noble, whatever is right, whatever is pure, whatever is lovely, whatever is admirable—if anything is excellent or praiseworthy—think about such things. (Philippians 4:8)

This Person Has Been a Blessing to Me

To build on the ways that you like and appreciate your spouse, consider how they've blessed you. This is broader than just recalling what you like about them. Being blessed by your spouse includes how

God has used him or her to help you grow; this includes the irritating things. Consider how God uses his or her shortcomings and sinfulness to increase your patience, mercy, and forgiveness. How are you a better person because your spouse is in your life? How has God used him or her to make you more like him? How, then, can you give thanks for your spouse?

> When we remember how we complement each other, we find it much easier to forgive the sin that's sometimes involved.

At times, Kim's extroversion and my introversion collide. When this happens, it's an irritation; but when we remember how we complement each other, we find it much easier to forgive the sin that's sometimes involved. I'm a better person because I've been sharpened by Kim's extroversion. I've learned how to be more social and fun loving and, as a result, more loving to others because I've been schooled by her extroversion.

I've Been Forgiven Much

In the darkest moments of hurt, you may look inside of yourself to find some help in forgiving and feel that you're hunting for water at the bottom of a dry well. When you're consumed by your own hurt, where does forgiveness come from?

In Matthew 18, Jesus' disciples have been learning about the demands of forgiveness and find the idea as daunting as we do. Peter asks Jesus exactly how many times we're to forgive someone; maybe seven times, he ventures, trying to be generous. Jesus' answer: seventy-seven times (Matthew 18:22 [some translations say "seventy times seven"]). This doesn't mean you're supposed to keep a careful record of every forgiveness and walk away when the counter hits seventy-seven. It's Jesus' way of saying, "As many times as it takes."

Lest anybody doubt his intent, Jesus then tells the parable of a servant who owed a king a tremendous debt—ten thousand talents, the equivalent of millions of dollars. Amazingly, graciously, the king forgives the debt after the servant begs for mercy. But this same servant then goes to a fellow servant and demands repayment of a debt of one hundred denarii (about four months pay). When the king hears of this he is livid.

> "You wicked servant," he said, "I cancelled all that debt of yours because you begged me to. Shouldn't you have had mercy on your fellow servant just as I had on you?" In anger his master turned him over to the jailers to be tortured, until he should pay back all he owed. (Matthew 18:32–34)

Our ability to forgive comes from appreciating and living out of God's forgiveness. If you don't yet understand how much you've been forgiven, just remember that your forgiveness required the death of God's own perfect son. When you appreciate and live out of the joy and gratitude of God's forgiveness, it becomes easier to forgive others.

Notice that the parable recognizes how grievously we may have been sinned against as well. Jesus isn't minimizing the suffering you've experienced. One hundred denarii is a significant amount of money—one-third of an annual salary. Nonetheless, when placed on the scales, no amount of debt can compare with what you've been forgiven of. Bestowing forgiveness isn't about looking inside yourself to find an appropriate emotional response; it's about focusing on God's love and grace and asking for the ability to pass it on to your spouse.

Though it won't compare to the amount that God has forgiven you, stop to think, too, about sins of yours that your spouse has chosen to forgive or overlook. Forgiveness is easier when you remember how you yourself have been forgiven.

My Spouse and I Are More Alike Than Different

Sin encourages us to elevate ourselves above our spouses. In general, we evaluate others by determining if and how they can serve our ends, but sometimes we find comfort in how we're better than they are. "Sure, my spouse hurt me," you think, "but at least I have the comfort of knowing I'm the better person. After all, I could never do to her what she did to me." Thinking this way can be a tempting trap when you've been wounded; comforting for a season, this mind-set poisons every attempt to forgive.

In his Sermon on the Mount (Matthew 5–7), Jesus teaches his disciples and the gathering crowds that life in his kingdom requires a deep understanding of the law—an understanding that penetrates our judging hearts. As he teaches about various commandments—the prohibitions against murder, adultery, lying—he drives home one point again and again: under the law we're all sinners; therefore, we never have the right to elevate ourselves above others and judge them.

If we feel superior to the murderer we're reminded that we murder in our hearts when we harbor anger:

> You have heard that it was said to the people long ago, "Do not murder, and anyone who murders will be subject to judgment." But I tell you that anyone who is angry with his brother will be subject to judgment. (Matthew 5:21–22)

If we feel superior to the adulterer we're reminded that lust makes us adulterers at heart:

> You have heard that it was said, "Do not commit adultery." But I tell you that anyone who looks at a woman lustfully has already committed adultery with her in his heart. (Matthew 5:27–28)

In our hearts, we're all more alike than different. Instead of giving us grounds to feel superior to others, the law shows that we're all in equal need of God's forgiveness. Actions matter, of course, but we've little to brag about when we compare our hearts to those who have wounded us.

Has your spouse deceived you? Think of the ways you've kept yourself hidden. Has your spouse spoken harshly? Think about the harsh things you've said or thought about saying. Is your spouse an addict? Think about the things that you crave, can't live without, or turn to when you're suffering. Whether or not you've actually done

> Confessing sin is a proclamation of the gospel: a proclamation that there's a way back from failure, that there's rescue and healing from brokenness.

what your spouse has done, you can be certain that in your heart you've craved and served similar things.

God Will Use This

"He who heeds discipline shows the way to life, but whoever ignores correction leads others astray" (Proverbs 10:17). This proverb means that if I receive God's correction, own up to my sin, and ask for forgiveness, I benefit myself along with whoever is watching. God can use anything—even my failures—to accomplish good things.

Confessing sin is a proclamation of the gospel: a proclamation that there's a way back from failure, that there's rescue and healing from brokenness. We don't have to hide our sin from each other.

The reverse is also true. Refusal to confess and forgive is a proclamation of hopelessness and despair. It proclaims that the only hope of overcoming sin is covering it in the same pointless way that Adam and Eve tried. It proclaims that sins may be forgotten if enough time goes by and you work really hard to make the other person feel good about you again, but that sins are never really forgiven.

Sin and failure will accompany you throughout your marriage— throughout your life. Take courage, however, because your confession and forgiveness proclaim God's love and give life to your spouse and others.

What If Your Spouse Isn't Sorry?

When your spouse isn't ready to admit they've wronged you, making some of the commitments that forgiveness requires isn't appropriate.

For instance, you can't commit to not bringing up the matter to them again; in fact, you probably need to bring it up again carefully and humbly so that the issue can be resolved.

You may have to talk about it with others in seeking help for the sake of your marriage.

Still, commit to speaking about it prayerfully and constructively whether with your spouse or a counselor or friend.

To avoid bitterness, refrain from dwelling on it. Don't allow hurt feelings to erect a wall between you and your spouse. You'll be in a much better position to accept a request for forgiveness when it comes, plus your ability to remain open may soften your spouse's heart.

Repeated hurts make it difficult to remain loving and positive toward your spouse. In addition to steering clear of bitterness, consider introducing consequences to keep the offense from being repeated.

Offering encouragement for this situation, Jesus says,

> If [your brother] sins against you seven times in a day, and seven times comes back to you and says, "I repent," forgive him. The apostles said to the Lord, "Increase our faith!" He replied, "If you have faith as small as a mustard seed, you can say to this mulberry tree, 'Be uprooted and planted in the sea,' and it will obey you." (Luke 17:4–6)

The pain of being sinned against, especially when augmented by a spouse who refuses to repent, can feel as stubborn as the roots of a tree. Jesus' encouragement is that even tiny faith is more powerful than the most entrenched bitterness. You don't have to be tormented by bitterness. By faith it can be cast into the sea.

There's no hidden formula here, just a reminder to keep your eyes fixed on Jesus. He's your guide and helper as you battle the temptation of bitterness. To unrepentant people he continually extends his love and an invitation to repent.

Perhaps here, more than in any other chapter, we need to be mindful of worship. If you aren't focusing on God as your Savior, the source of all forgiveness, your efforts at forgiving will always fall short. The Bible teaches us how to forgive, but its foundations are found in God himself and the power of the gospel. As you move forward, keep your concrete expressions of forgiveness rooted in the wonder and joy of knowing God's forgiveness of you.

Think about It

- In what ways do you find forgiveness hard in marriage? How do you make forgiveness difficult for your spouse?
- Take a few minutes to write down at least five things that you especially appreciate and like about your spouse. Keep the list handy and read it regularly. The next time you feel you've been wronged by your spouse, review the list and thank God for your spouse before and after you talk to them about the offense.
- List some ways that God has helped you grow since marrying the person you did. Review both lists regularly.

fourteen
Understanding Your Role

What You'll Learn in This Chapter:

- Conflicts about marital roles often reflect more than a misunderstanding of what the Bible teaches about them. They also reflect assumptions about the differences between men and women and about the unexamined heart issues that shape our understanding of them.
- Confusion over headship and submission is often the result of a distorted understanding of authority. Jesus taught that authority is to be exercised sacrificially for the benefit of others, not for personal satisfaction and glory.
- Marital roles are all only different expressions of love and must serve the purposes of love. Recognizing how typical patterns of manipulation creep into the way we exercise our roles in marriage is important.
- Loving your spouse in his or her role includes knowing your spouse, not just his or her gender, and valuing his or her individual gifts and abilities.

Do I Need to Read This?

EVEN IF MARITAL roles aren't a battleground in your marriage—or are little more than an occasional annoyance—they're worth thinking through and discussing. In this ever-changing world you may encounter unexpected hurdles that require thinking more deeply about why you do things the way you do them. God brings us these challenges to the ordinary as a way of keeping us rooted in his extraordinary love.

"Mr. Mom"

I'll never forget the first year of my son Gresham's life. Who can forget those first experiences of parenthood? Holding your child for the first time. Letting your tiny baby sleep on your chest. Seeing that first smile.

But, despite the joys, Gresham's first year was a real battle for me as I played the role of "Mr. Mom." In school it was not uncommon for one spouse to work, while the other finished school, but now that I'd graduated I was eager to take my place as the family breadwinner and have Kim at home as much as possible. I'd just graduated from seminary and was counseling only a few hours a week. A full-time counseling position hadn't materialized, and having a new home and our first child made role adjustments tricky. So for the time being, I was the designated feeder, wiper, burper, nap-giver, and all around caretaker.

At first I relished my new role. After all, how many dads have the privilege of uniquely shaping the first year of their son's life! But after a few months, with no job prospects on the horizon, I began to feel down. The praise I'd received for being so flexible and secure faded, and I found myself struggling at many different levels. The biggest struggle was that I didn't feel like I was doing what husbands and fathers are *supposed* to be doing, earning a paycheck. Sure, staying at home with Gresham was fine for a month or two, but there was no end in sight, and as I watched TV, while feeding Gresham applesauce and pureed peas, the culture only reinforced my sentiments. Watching *Hawaii Five-O* reruns during lunch I noticed that there were three kinds of commercials during the day: Commercials for trade schools (trucking, heating and cooling repair, etc.), injury lawyers, and feminine hygiene products. The message was clear. If you're watching TV right now you're either unemployed, wrongfully injured, or a woman. What had felt like a novel opportunity for a few months began to feel like exile from the world of responsible husbands.

> God brings us these challenges to the ordinary as a way of keeping us rooted in his extraordinary love.

I began to wonder if I was really suited to care for Gresham. Sure, I could manage the logistics. I figured out how to feed, clothe, bathe, and get him down for naps, but I simply didn't relish it like I thought I should. So much of the time it seemed mechanical and forced. I wondered if Kim would be having an entirely different experience simply because she's a woman, and I wondered if maybe Gresham was missing out on something as a result. I wondered if women are somehow innately more nurturing than men, and men somehow more goal-oriented, designed, in effect, to be out of the home tackling a different set of challenges. Maybe my masculine wiring made it impossible for me to be an effective stay-at-home parent.

At the deepest level, I was struggling with issues that were bigger than being a husband, father, or even a man. I was battling a fear of failure and doubt before God. I wrestled with God. I wondered if I'd gotten it all wrong. What if I weren't really cut out to be a counselor? What if I couldn't support my family with the education I'd just spent so much time and money on? What if, now almost thirty years old, I was on the wrong career path? I was anxious and full of doubt. At its root, I doubted God and was overwhelmed with my own inadequacies. Much more than anything I saw on TV, it was that battle that was shaping the way I thought about my role as my son's primary caregiver.

Fortunately, Kim was supportive and encouraging throughout my entire tour of duty as "Mr. Mom." But imagining a wife who'd be as agitated by an unexpected change in marital roles as I was is easy. What if Kim had come home every day frustrated, even embittered, because she was not able to stay at home with Gresham? What if, on top of my own guilt and fear, Kim, speaking out of personal frustration, had accused me of lacking drive and grilled me daily about my job search? It isn't hard to imagine the ugly fights that might have erupted, making a bad situation worse.

Sorting Out Issues

As we explored the issue of conflict, we learned the importance of dealing with underlying issues rather than arguing about the obvious circumstances and events. This is especially important in working through conflicts about marital roles. There are several related but distinct issues to keep in mind as you examine your role in marriage:

- *General confusion over the differences between the roles of husband and wife.* Kim and I had to decide whether it was wise or even okay for husbands to be primary caregivers and wives, primary breadwinners. Some people say it's neither wise nor okay. Others will be offended that I even raised the issue because they don't believe such distinctions exist. What does the Bible say about this issue?
- *Confusion about the differences between men and women and how this shapes the way we think about marital roles.* Are there certain roles that husband and wife have by virtue of their gender? For instance, was I ill suited to care for my son because I'm a man? How much of our understanding is shaped by our culture and personal experience? Does how I think about men and women keep me from seeing myself, my wife, and our roles accurately? Does it keep me from loving wisely?

196

- *How my personal struggles play out in the way I define marital roles.* My angst over staying at home with Gresham was as much about my fears and doubts as anything else. If I hadn't been aware of how my own spiritual battles were influencing my thinking, I could have been driven by doubt and fear to make selfish and unwise decisions or even ended up in despair.

Recognizing that each issue is separate and yet influences and informs the others is important. For example, if a husband were to say, "My father never tolerated criticism from my mother, and I won't tolerate a critical word from my wife!" He might need to reflect more deeply and realize that his father didn't tolerate criticism from anyone else either. Maybe his approach to being a husband had more to do with his personal insecurity than a general truth about husbands and wives or men and women. We need to be careful not to read the challenges of our own hearts, our personal assumptions, and our cultural assumptions about gender into the Bible, creating roles that don't reflect the wisdom and love of Christ.

As you read this chapter keep in mind the purpose of this book: to help you take the ordinary frustrations of marriage and use them as opportunities for something extraordinary to happen. This chapter will focus on how the roles God has given are expressions of love, and how as husbands and wives we share in the calling to love each other as Christ loves us. We will take a look at how the desires, fears, sins, and idols of our hearts show up to frustrate those goals and how worship keeps us on track.

Headship and Submission

When you read New Testament passages on marriage (Ephesians 5:22–33; Colossians 3:18–19; and 1 Peter 3:1–7), you can't miss the prominence of the ideas of headship and submission. Each passage teaches wives to *submit* to their husbands and husbands to exercise *headship* over their wives. Exactly what these terms mean is a subject of debate, but there's no denying that the reason they're debated is because they've historically been interpreted to mean that within marriage, husbands are given a role of authority over their wives.

Talk about marital roles, especially the question of authority, can seem out of place in our culture, a culture that's suspicious of authority in every sphere. But if we're going to have a biblical view of marriage we've to take this question seriously because the Bible clearly does.

If it makes you bristle even to consider that there's a place for authority within marriage, consider how thinking through this issue may affect your life in general. Authority is a feature of most relationships and institutions. Authority touches us as fathers and mothers, employers and employees, as those who govern and are governed. Given its prevalence, it benefits us all to understand that God expects authority to be exercised as an expression of love, no matter the relational context. Though you may not reflect on it often, in almost every area of life, regardless of your gender, you either exercise authority over others or live under the authority of another.

You Don't Know What You're Asking

As it is today, the purpose and place of authority was a touchy subject in Jesus' day. The following passage illustrates how Jesus' followers must be willing to have their most basic assumptions about authority challenged:

> Then James and John, the sons of Zebedee, came to [Jesus]. "Teacher," they said, "we want you to do for us whatever we ask." "What do you want me to do for you?" he asked. They replied, "Let one of us sit at your right and the other at your left in your glory." "You don't know what you are asking," Jesus said. "Can you drink the cup I drink or be baptized with the baptism I am baptized with?" (Mark 10:35–38)

The disciples, like almost everybody else in their cultural milieu, expected that the Messiah would come, establish his kingdom, and overthrow their Roman oppressors. They expected a Messiah who operated the way kings and leaders ordinarily do but with the extra firepower of God himself. James and John wanted to be Jesus' top two deputies in his new kingdom. They wanted the glory and power of being his right- and left-hand men. Before we wag our fingers at James and John, we need to acknowledge honestly how much we're like them. We all bring baggage to the issue of authority. We've been the victims of those who abuse authority, and we are, at heart, like those who have abused authority. The disciples had been victims of Roman authority and of wealthy oppressors and had joined Jesus in ministering to the poor and downtrodden. But notice that didn't make them essentially different from those they despised. They wanted to slake their own thirst for power and advantage.

Jesus' response is stunning. He doesn't deny his role, authority, or power but rather points them to the radically different way he understands those terms. First, he reminds them that his role is to die a sacrificial death for his people, not to be pampered and waited on. The images of baptism and drinking from a cup are Old Testament symbols of God's purification and God's wrath, respectively. Jesus was reminding them of what he had already told them several times: he would die for their sins, suffering the punishment they deserve so that they could be forgiven and be resurrected from the dead (see Mark 10:31–32). Jesus added,

> You know that those who are regarded as rulers of the Gentiles lord it over them, and their high officials exercise authority over them. Not so with you. Instead, whoever wants to become great among you must be your servant, and whoever wants to be first must be slave of all. For even the Son of Man did not come to be served, but to serve, and to give his life as a ransom for many. (Mark 10:42–45)

Jesus' authority is so unlike what most of us have experienced we hardly recognize it as authority at all. We think of the person in authority as the person with all of the perks: the big office, the designated parking space, the season tickets, and all of the say so. When Jesus exercises his authority he assumes the position of a servant, meeting his people at their level, assuming their station in life, doing without for their benefit, making all of his decisions for their welfare. If authority is going to serve God's purpose in our relationships, then we must anchor all of our understanding in the foundation that Jesus has laid: Authority exists for the benefit of those who live under it. Authority must be an expression of love. As Jesus' followers our understanding and expression of authority should be as radical, surprising, and utterly concerned with others as Jesus' was.

Love Is the Foundation of Every Role

Jesus clearly teaches that authority must always be exercised in love. But the way we exercise authority and define our marital roles often doesn't seem informed by a biblical understanding of love at all. Some of the most basic elements of love drop out of the picture once we start talking about marital roles.

Sometimes I find it helpful, when counseling couples, to ask them to think of love as a large circle of responsibilities that we all share as followers of Christ. We brainstorm together, filling in that large circle. At the end, the circle is usually filled with words such as *kindness, patience, forgiveness, encouragement, honesty, openness, challenge,* and *correction.* These are the responsibilities we have in any loving relationship.

Within the large circle of love are two smaller circles, one for the husband's role and one for the wife's role. We brainstorm to fill them in. What often happens is the husband's circle will contain things like making decisions, handling finances, disciplining the kids (often elements related to power and control), and the wife's circle will contain things like housekeeping, preparing meals, helping kids with homework (elements related to caretaking and upkeep). It seems as if when thinking specifically about marital roles we effectively step out of the broader circle of love and focus on concrete, distinct, and isolated circles that emphasize cultural notions of authority. It's as if we believe the general duties of love are fundamentally different from our specific duties as husbands and wives.

The Bible is clear on this point: the roles of husbands and wives don't fall *outside* of our responsibilities to love. Rather, they're more particularized forms of love, and our understanding of headship and submission must operate *within* our greater responsibility to love.

We should expect husbands and wives to have more shared duties in love than distinctions. When you vow to love your spouse, you aren't promising to withhold correction; you aren't promising to withhold input or wisdom; you aren't promising to withhold encouragement or gentleness. You're actually promising to exercise love in a more dedicated form—to make your spouse your highest priority in love. You're promising to be focused in your love, consistent, and persistent—to keep at it as long as you both live. So, for instance, husbands, your responsibility to be gentle or to be an encourager didn't go away when you decided to marry your wife. It became particular and intensified. Wives, your duty to warn, admonish, and be honest didn't disappear on the day you promised to love this man as your husband. On the contrary, when you married your husband, you took up that duty in a particular way.

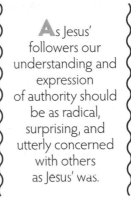

As Jesus' followers our understanding and expression of authority should be as radical, surprising, and utterly concerned with others as Jesus' was.

Why So Much Focus on Authority?

Because New Testament marriage passages are organized around the principle of headship and submission, getting the impression that authority is the centerpiece of marriage is easy. But though the

New Testament authors did highlight the significance of authority in marriage and other everyday life relationships, they weren't arguing that this was at the heart of these relationships. The emphasis on authority is actually needed to highlight the fundamental equality that all of God's children enjoy, while recognizing that the appropriate use of authority is an important aspect of love.

In the world of the early church, roles were rigidly defined and signified a person's status and worth. Much like today, having authority meant having more of everything—more perks, more opportunities, and more value. Being subordinate meant having less, or none, of those things. Like today, the exercise of authority had as much to do with maximizing and preserving privilege as anything else.

Jesus both taught and modeled that all of God's children have equal status and worth. As Paul explained in his letter to the Galatians,

> You are *all* sons of God through faith in Christ Jesus . . . .
> There is neither Jew nor Greek, slave nor free, male nor
> female, for you are all one in Christ Jesus. (Galatians 3:26–28,
> italics mine)

As children of God, all Christians have the same spiritual status. This essential equality is to be recognized in every cultural custom and institution. Christians are no longer to view each other through the worldly lens of status and power.

Husbands and wives are to view each other with this new understanding as well. Peter instructs husbands to understand their wives as "heirs with you of the gracious gift of life" (1 Peter 3:7). Peter warns husbands not to view their wives as objects that exist for their own personal happiness but as children of God who belong to God and share in all of the benefits of being united with Jesus. And, as we've seen, Paul expects husbands to view their wives as members of Christ whom they're to nurture as they mature in Christ (Ephesians 5:25–27).

Authority is a natural aspect of love. Christ's coming doesn't eliminate authority but redeems it. We understand its value in most other arenas of human relationship, and given the nature of our fallen world and the dangers within relationship itself, it seems as necessary as ever. The Bible acknowledges that authority can be abused, but God exercises his own authority to work in and through what's broken.

The Gift of Authority

God gives authority to some to ensure that in every arena of relationship someone is responsible for the care of others. Certain duties that need special attention or ability (income versus childcare, etc.) may be delegated, but the one in authority has the added responsibility of assuring that needs in *every* area are being met. Even if everyone else is dropping the ball, the one with authority is required to notice and take action.

"Should husbands and fathers just order their wives and children around all day?" you may ask. "In the happy marriages I've seen I see no signs of authority."

Think of your role as parents for a moment. When your children are toddlers, you exercise authority constantly. They're incapable of making decisions and directing themselves without risking catastrophe. Your day is filled with, "Don't touch that!" and "Daddy, said no!" and "I know you don't want a nap but you need one." We're comfortable exercising that authority because we know it's necessary for our children's welfare. But as they get older we let them make more and more of their own decisions, so that they'll become wiser and learn to depend on Christ and not us.

In marriage, we should expect authority to be almost seamless between mature Christians. Introducing the issue of authority in relationships, Paul writes,

Be filled with the Spirit. Speak to one another with psalms, hymns and spiritual songs. Sing and make music in your

heart to the Lord, always giving thanks to God the Father for
everything, in the name of our Lord Jesus Christ. Submit to
one another out of reverence for Christ. (Ephesians 5:18b–21)

As we live in relationship with each other, guided by the Spirit of
Jesus, we should live "musical" lives with each other. Our words and
actions should be hymns of praise to God and encouragement to each
other. Part of that music is a willingness to submit to one another in
relationships structured by authority. It should look and sound much
more like a dance than a forced march. In a march, one person sets the
tempo with the baton and everyone falls into lockstep. In the marital
dance, however, the husband leads as he listens to the music of Christ.
Because the wife hears the same music, they're able to keep time in
their own minds and move as one. In a clumsy moment toes may be
stepped on; on occasion, dance moves may have to be reviewed and
maybe an instructor consulted.

The Husband's Role

Husbands, love your wives, just as Christ loved the church
and gave himself up for her to make her holy, cleansing her by
the washing with water through the word, and to present her to
himself as a radiant church, without stain or wrinkle or any other
blemish, but holy and blameless. In this same way, husbands
ought to love their wives as their own bodies. He who loves his
wife loves himself. After all, no one ever hated his own body, but
he feeds and cares for it, just as Christ does the church—for we
are members of his body. . . . Each one of you also must love his
wife as he loves himself. (Ephesians 5:25–29, 33)

In this passage the word *love* is used seven times. Husbands have
one overarching duty: to love. All Christians have a duty to love, but in
the marriage relationship the husband has a unique responsibility and

faces a unique temptation as well. His unique responsibility isn't only to look to his own duty to love but to make sure everyone in the family is growing in meeting their duty to love. Where love is lacking, the husband must move to meet that need, especially for his wife. Likewise, he faces a unique temptation. He may sinfully choose to use his authority to serve himself instead of his wife and family.

Build Up Your Wife and Help Her to Grow as a Christian

As a husband, your love for your wife has a specific goal: her holiness. That means helping your wife to grow in reflecting the image of Christ—helping her to grow in holiness, love, and wisdom. As long as your goal is love, God gives you the freedom to work out the details of your life with your spouse in many different ways. Whatever issue is at hand, a husband's behavior should be guided by the question, "What do I need to do right now to love my wife in a Christlike way so that she becomes more like him?"

Serve Your Wife through Sacrificial Love

The goal of holiness carries a high price. Jesus' love for us was costly and painful, ultimately requiring him to lay down his life for us. Husbands are called upon to love in a similar way, to know and imitate Jesus' example of loving the church. Your love is to be sacrificial, placing the needs of your wife above your own. Husbands, in what ways will helping your wife grow require you to suffer loss? How will you have to say no to yourselves so you can say yes to love?

Sometimes when we think of loving sacrificially we envision martyrs being burned at the stake. A few husbands might have the opportunity to protect their wives from a bullet or shove them out of the way of a speeding car, but if you're observant you'll notice that your day is filled with ways to sacrificially love your wife. Maybe it's as simple as loading the dishwasher, tucking the kids into bed, throwing a load of laundry into the dryer, or as simple as taking a few minutes to pray with her over something she's anxious about.

Shortly after Gresham was born, John Bettler stopped me in the hallway at the counseling center to ask me how things were going at home. Specifically, he asked me how we were sleeping. I glibly replied, "I'm sleeping just fine, but I think Kim is tired from having to breast-feed Gresham in the middle of the night. I can do a lot of things to help her, but breast feeding isn't one of them." With a touch of humor John offered some gentle correction, "Then why don't you get up with her and just keep her company?" I hadn't thought of that one. Love doesn't settle for the easy answers but searches out the need of the moment (even if it means losing a little sleep!).

> **P**art of nurturing others is letting them exercise their own faith by making choices, sometimes even bad ones.

Don't Use Your Authority to Hinder Your Wife's Growth

Some husbands are tempted to use their authority in a controlling way and insist on making all the decisions in their marriage. But doing this won't allow your wife to grow in wisdom (nor will it allow you to benefit from her wisdom). This also keeps your wife from developing her own relationship with Christ. Part of nurturing others is letting them exercise their own faith by making choices, sometimes even bad ones. God has called you to protect your wife, but don't use that as an excuse for trying to control everything she does. Your wife needs to face situations that require her to trust God, grow in wisdom, and learn responsibility. Sometimes our desire to control others reveals our own lack of trust in God rather than another's "rebellious attitude."

If your wife complains that you're controlling, seize the opportunity to examine yourself. Controlling others can sometimes be a symptom of idolatrous desires and fears. For example, is your desire for control really a way of combating fear? Do you fear that your wife will reject, or even leave you, if you don't monitor her every move? Do you micromanage out of a sense of insecurity? Do you fear that if you don't hold everything together it will all fall apart? Or is control more about feeding appetites for power or simply having things done for your own convenience? To the extent that you use authority to manage your own fears and feed your own desires, you're subverting Jesus' authority and enthroning yourself.

Know Your Wife

You can't make wise decisions about how to love your wife if you don't know what life is like for her. You must know her hopes, dreams, fears, desires, strengths, and weaknesses—as much as you can know about her. If you haven't listened thoughtfully and worked to understand your wife's concerns, then you can't be confident you know what's best for her. And she won't be confident that your advice is useful. Patient, careful communication allows a couple to build unity in marriage and makes unilateral decision making unnecessary.

Once Kim came home from work so angry that she exclaimed, "If you'll call work and quit for me I'll do anything for you for the rest of your life!" As someone who enjoys pleasing others, this presented an easy way to be a hero to my wife. This was my chance to make one phone call and be the white knight rescuing my damsel from the evils of the working world. But would quitting her job be the best thing for *her*? Knowing Kim as someone who loves comfort and hates conflict, I suspected that fleeing from her problem was not what the Lord had in mind. Over the next several days we discussed our temptations, prayed, and asked for the Lord's wisdom. We decided that, for the time being, there were ways to work through her frustrations and represent Christ well at work. We often reflect back on that with gratitude as we recognize how her job has become an ideal place for her to exercise her gifts and display the love of Christ, as well as providing financial resources for our family with a flexible schedule that allows her to be home with the kids.

The Wife's Role

Wives, submit to your husbands as to the Lord. For the husband is the head of the wife as Christ is the head of the church, his body, of which he is the Savior. Now as the church submits to Christ, so also wives should submit to their husbands in everything. (Ephesians 5:22–24)

An understanding of biblical authority leads to an understanding of what submission looks like in a marriage. Like husbands, wives have a unique responsibility and face a unique temptation. They share the common duty to love, and, in addition, wives are responsible to love their husbands by accepting his authority and respecting his role as husband. There are many temptations in submission, but the most common is to reject or undermine authority. Paul urges wives to accept and respect their husband's authority as a way of entrusting themselves to Christ's care and submitting to Christ's authority, just as the entire church must do. God asks wives to allow their husbands to love and care for them, and to trust that God will care for them even when their husbands fail.

This will look different in each marriage, but the bedrock principle will be the same: love. When you're struggling in your relationship with your husband, return to that principle. Ask yourself, in the context of the role God has given you in your marriage, "How am I expressing love to my husband?" Remember, the duties of love that apply to your husband also apply to you. You share in the calling to "love your neighbor" just as your husband does. You're called to love your husband and encourage him to mature into the image of Christ. Love must be honest, gentle, patient, and self-controlled. Love always encourages, and sometimes even corrects. This means that the foundations of your roles are identical.

Exercise Your Full Responsibilities in Love

Be careful that your understanding of submission isn't missing important elements of love. For example, some couples feel that for a wife to correct her husband is improper. They consider correction to be a sign of disrespect and a lack of submission. But, as we've seen, the Bible considers correction a basic responsibility of love. Your obligation to love your husband is certainly not less than your obligation to a "neighbor." So respectfully correcting your husband is part of loving him.

Communication, too, can suffer because of faulty notions of submission. For some, submission means silence or noncommunication. Wives keep questions, concerns, or negative emotions to themselves. But this doesn't square with how the Bible describes communication in intimate relationships. The psalmist David writes,

> How long, O LORD? Will you forget me forever? How long
> will you hide your face from me? How long must I wrestle
> with my thoughts and every day have sorrow in my heart?
> How long will my enemy triumph over me? Look on me and
> answer, O LORD, my God. Give light to my eyes, or I will
> sleep in death. (Psalm 13:1–3)

To think that David can be that honest with God without being disrespectful is startling, but David's submissiveness is godly. He's being honest in a way that honors who God really is. David is saying, in effect, "God, I know that you're truly good and I'm having trouble understanding why you aren't doing things differently. Help!"

Healthy marriages that reflect God's love and relationship with his people require honest, godly communication.

Understand Respect as a Form of Love

In relationships where one member has authority, respect is an important element of loving the one in authority. In addition to urging wives to submit to their husbands, Paul reminds them to show respect.

In summary he writes, "However, each one of you also must love his wife as he loves himself, and the wife must respect her husband" (Ephesians 5:33).

Even in moments of disappointment, decide to respond in love. Remember, love speaks, exhorts, corrects, and says no to evil; the Bible doesn't advocate a life of mousy silence. *If you or your children are being verbally, physically, or sexually abused, love your husband by saying no to his sin.* You need help to do this. Please turn to a trusted family member, friend, or pastor to get the support that you need.

Act in Love Even When You're Disappointed

When you're disappointed, instead of turning away from your husband, turn toward him with encouragement, a kind word, even your prayers. His shortcomings can tempt you to grumble or to stroke your own pride or sense of spiritual superiority. More than a lack of respect for your husband, these responses reveal a lack of respect for God. Remember, you have a Savior who trusted God, and who can help you trust him too.

Typical Ways to Fail

In relationships we're always moving in one of three directions: toward others, away from others, or against others. Love can move us in any direction, but when we move exclusively in one direction it can be a signal that we aren't following love but desires and fears that may have become idols.

Idols can shape the way we live out our roles. When our hearts are ruled by desires or fears that move us toward others, we can become husbands who cave in to every whim or desire of our wives, all the while thinking we're serving as Christ does. Wives, likewise, can serve their husbands' every desire, while really serving their own desire for acceptance or living in fear of their husband's wrath, all the while calling it submission.

Idols also can drive us away from others. A husband can be under-involved in his marriage, only showing up to say no to things that inconvenience or trouble him. A wife can, likewise, use her husband's authority to fight her battles and shelter her from life by avoiding the difficult conversations, conflicts, and decision making that following Christ requires.

Idols can move us against one another. Husbands can be cruel tyrants, demanding and controlling the details of home life out of their own lust for power and control or out of their fear of rejection and failure. Out of their own distrust or craving for control, wives can be critical, picking apart their husbands' authority by second-guessing his every move.

> Remember, you have a Savior who trusted God, and who can help you trust him too.

Remember, every area of marriage is an expression of worship, either reflecting your love for God or your love for something else. Often a battle over marital roles or gender isn't about either of those but about deep heart issues.

Who Does What?

There's no simple, one-size-fits-all to-do list for husbands and wives. Husbands aren't commanded to take out the trash. Wives aren't commanded to change the baby. Instead of giving you set duties, God, in the Bible, does something much better. He gives a few basic principles to help you and your spouse define your roles in a godly way no matter what your life looks like.

Don't Recreate Your Parent's Marriage

God expects you to recognize and respect the gifts and abilities he's given to you and your spouse. It's common for couples to create their marriages in the image of their parents' marriages. If your father always managed the money, you may think this is a task that belongs to husbands. If your mother always ironed the clothes, you may feel that all wives should do the same. But the Bible tells us that God has given his people a variety of gifts—sometimes in ways that surprise us.

Consider How God Has Uniquely Gifted Each of You

Don't read the traditions of your families or culture into Scripture and make them mandates for your life together. If you're having difficulty sorting out your marital roles, ask a simple question: How has God gifted me? How has he gifted my spouse? If you're terrible with numbers and can't balance the checkbook, while your wife can do all of that in her sleep, then let her manage the funds. If your husband has a particular knack for helping the kids see their faults and pointing them to God for help, then let him use that gift in shepherding your children.

Don't Consider Any Gift Either Inferior or Superior

When the Corinthian church had difficulty in understanding how to exercise their abilities in various roles, Paul gave them some important advice. First, accept God's decisions about who has what ability (1 Corinthians 12:4–11). Second, be aware of the dangers of fear and pride (1 Corinthians 12:14–31). You shouldn't consider your gifts or roles to be inferior to or less important than others, nor should you consider them superior or more important than others. "All these are the work of one and the same Spirit, and he gives them to each one, just as he determines" (1 Corinthians 12:11).

Be Flexible

During World War II as thousands of American men took up arms and went overseas to fight, thousands of women donned work clothes, picked up tools, and reported to factories to produce weapons and machinery to equip their husbands and sons for war. Husbands and wives found themselves thrust into roles that neither had asked for, and yet the necessity of the moment required it. Sometimes life doesn't yield to our plans for our marriages. Like me, you may find yourself having to redraw the lines on a large scale to make your life work. Almost certainly, the unpredictability of day-to-day life will require it on a smaller scale. Don't become so wed to the details of your roles that you're unwilling to step into the world of your spouse to do what's necessary.

Know Your Spouse, Not Just His or Her Gender

It's silly to pretend that we don't have opinions about gender. Women talk more than men. Women are more emotional than men. Men are more logical than women. Those are some of the typical stereotypes that our culture shares. I'm not qualified to say how true they are and, if so, how much is the product of cultural influence and how much is a product of biology. But there seems to be more and more willingness to acknowledge that gender does influence behavior and that some of it has a physiological component.

Whether those are scientifically established facts, the result of your own observations, or simply the shared conclusions of our culture, the critical question for us is how they inform the way you love, or fail to love, your spouse.

I've already shared the dilemma I faced as Mr. Mom. There actually is research that suggests that women are biologically more inclined to be nurturing than men.[15] If true, how should we apply that information to marriage? Here are a couple of things to keep in mind:

- What is generally true of a people group may not be true of an individual within that group. In other words, to say that women are more inclined to be nurturing doesn't necessarily tell you anything about your wife anymore than saying that men tend to be taller than women tells you that every husband is taller than every wife. Some men are more talkative, affectionate, and emotional than their wives. Saying that women tend to be more nurturing doesn't tell me anything about what kind of job I'll do at home with my son.

- Facts are easily misinterpreted and misapplied depending on a person's perspective. A man could cite those studies to argue that, not only should he be the breadwinner, but that he shouldn't be asked to change a diaper, make a peanut butter sandwich, or hug his children. But the same man would wince to think a feminist divorce attorney could cite the same research and argue in divorce proceedings that men should have restricted custody and visitation rights.

- The Bible often shakes up the way we get comfortable with gender traits. For instance, in many places the Bible urges Christians to be gentle, as Paul does in Philippians 4:5: "Let your gentleness be evident to all." In our culture, many would classify gentleness as a feminine trait, and yet the Bible wants all Christians, male and female, to grow in gentleness. Likewise, women as well as men are exhorted to "be strong." As we've already seen, Paul encourages us all to "be strong in the Lord" putting on "the full armor of God." Again, many would classify strength as a masculine trait and wouldn't conceive of Christian women as warriors of any stripe.

To sum up, a general knowledge about gender only provides a vague clue to understanding your strengths and those of your spouse. It's folly to read them onto your spouse, especially without recognizing how your own heart issues could be coming into play. And besides, it doesn't negate both the demands and the power of the gospel to transform us. The Bible already has given us the most penetrating understanding possible in telling us that we're image bearers, worshippers, and sinners whose deepest need is relationship with Christ.

Your marriage is about loving your spouse, not your spouse's gender. Don't confuse what your parents said and what our culture says with what the Bible says and miss the most obvious truth of all: we were all created to grow into the image of Christ.

Remember Your Common Calling

Finally, understand that your marital roles, however you define them, must reflect the character of Christ. As you work to nail down the details of your roles, losing sight of the big picture is easy. The apostle Peter asks us to recognize differences in our roles, but interestingly, he begins his instruction to husbands and wives using same phrase: "Wives, *in the same way* be submissive to your husbands . . . . Husbands, *in the same way* be considerate as you live with your wives" (1 Peter 3:1, 7, italics mine).

The phrase "in the same way" refers to Christ's service that Peter described in detail in 1 Peter 2. He describes Jesus as the head of his people and as one who submits to authority.

As Jesus led and submitted he endured great hardship, but he trusted God to work through even the most difficult moments. Rather than lashing out at the sins of others, Jesus powerfully displayed love, mercy, and patience. Whatever your role, whether it's leading, following, or both, you're called to look to Jesus as your example and as the only one who can empower you to fulfill your ultimate calling to live in love and grace.

To people who were squabbling about their roles in the church, Paul wrote,

> If I speak in the tongues of men and of angels, but have not love, I am only a resounding gong or a clanging cymbal. . . .
> And if I have a faith that can move mountains, but have not love, I am nothing. (1 Corinthians 13:1–2)

No matter what your role is, no matter how important you think your job is, no matter how good you are at it, if you aren't acting in love, then what you do has no value. *No matter how marital roles are defined, they are only different expressions of love.* When discussing marital roles don't neglect the most important questions: Am I loving my spouse through this role? Am I carrying out my role in a way that benefits my spouse? God calls husbands and wives to act in love for the benefit of the other.

Think about It

- Do you believe the Bible teaches that husbands should be the head within marriage? Do you and your spouse have the same view?
- Make a list of the different responsibilities and roles that you and your spouse have. Describe how each of them is an expression of God's love for each other and/or the family.
- What desires and fears tend to trip you up in communication or conflict resolution? How might those same heart issues distort the way you think about marital roles?
- Make a list of your and your spouse's gifts and abilities. How are these gifts being used to the benefit of your marriage? Are there gifts that are being underutilized because they don't fit your view of what men and women should do?

fifteen

Intimacy and Sex

What You'll Learn in This Chapter:

- Problems of intimacy and sex are sometimes difficult to address because both can seem mysterious and unpredictable.
- Just as Christ is central to our understanding of marriage, he is central to our understanding of intimacy and sex. The understanding and safety he offers give us direction in creating intimacy in marriage.
- Sex is a specific form of intimacy that should grow out of the same foundational elements of intimacy that God offers us.
- God shows us how to entrust our hearts to and accept one another in building the kind of intimacy with our spouses that we have with him.

A Frustrating Mystery

Reid and Christy

Reid and Christy came to counseling distraught. They'd been married for ten months and had only been sexually intimate a handful of times. For the most part Reid was unable to perform, and when he did it seemed forced and mechanical.

Christy's eyes filled with tears as she spoke, "I just don't understand! It was so hard for us to keep our hands to ourselves while we were dating, and then we got married and there was just nothing! It doesn't make sense!" Christy's attitude varied from day to day, sometimes from minute to minute. Sometimes she was able to be warm and supportive; other times she was angry and demanding, and increasingly she was depressed and hopeless.

Reid had no answers. He claimed that he was very attracted to Christy and swore that he had no interest in anyone else. He had been to several doctors, been poked, probed, and questioned, but they found nothing out of the ordinary.

They'd even considered separating for a season just to escape the pain and embarrassment and gain some perspective.

What is the solution to such a mystery?

What We Don't Understand, and Don't Want to Talk About

Working through problems of sex and intimacy can be difficult for many reasons. For one thing, intimacy often seems to be more of an experience than a choice or behavior. Intimacy is hard to *do*: it just happens or not. How do you control or change something as unpredictable as intimacy? Intimacy often comes as a surprise. One evening, completely unplanned, you end up sitting on the floor with your spouse looking at old photos, reminiscing, and falling in love all over again. On another evening you hire a babysitter, go out to your favorite restaurant, and sit in awkward silence with no idea what to say.

Sex is especially mysterious. One spouse wants to have sex more often than the other. One spouse is more adventurous than the other. One spouse enjoys prolonged foreplay and the other doesn't. No one *asks* for these preferences. Are preferences problems to be solved? Who's to say one spouse's preferences are right and the other's are wrong? Or when the problem is more serious, like Reid and Christy's, what can be done when one spouse's interest in sex disappears altogether?

Making matters worse, we aren't accustomed to talking about sex—at least without either smirks and giggles or embarrassment and shame. Sex leaves us laughing or crying but not talking.

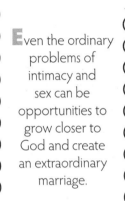

Even the ordinary problems of intimacy and sex can be opportunities to grow closer to God and create an extraordinary marriage.

There's much that's mysterious and wonderful about intimacy and sex, just as there is about marriage itself. The purpose of this chapter isn't to remove the mystery or "magic" from intimacy but to shed light on what we need to know to give us direction and hope as we deal with problems of intimacy. Even the ordinary problems of intimacy and sex can be opportunities to grow closer to God and create an extraordinary marriage.

Intimacy is made up of at least two critical ingredients: being known and being safe. We experience intimacy when we feel known and understood as well as safe, accepted, or cared for by our spouse. A breakdown of intimacy, therefore, usually means that one or both of us doesn't feel understood or safe. It makes sense, then, that an evening of looking at old photos can stir up both your shared experiences and the sense of safety that comes with years of marriage. On the other hand, there are no special date night or dinner plans that can overcome the barriers to intimacy created when we haven't shared enough of our lives recently to feel known and cared for or there are reasons to believe that if we do we won't be accepted.

Sex Is about Intimacy

Sex is a subset of intimacy, a particular form of intimacy reserved by God for the most intimate of all human relationships, marriage. Just as Christ is central to our understanding of marriage, so he is central to our understanding of sex.

Chapter 5 explored how marriage was created as part of God's plan for us to bear his image. God is relationship, three persons who are one, and he is the essence and definition of love. You may also remember that in Ephesians 5, Jesus' relationship with the church is given as our model for understanding marriage. That same model provides a powerful way to understand what sex is really all about.

- *Sex is a unique expression of marriage.* Biblically, God intended sex between his image bearers to take place within marriage. The "one-flesh" relationship of marriage described in Genesis 2 is both a picture of an inner connection—a spiritual and psychological intimacy—and a physical connection. Adam and Eve were created to become one at every level. Marriage and sex were designed to go together.
- *Marriage is a unique expression of Christ and the church.* Marriage was created so we could fully image God in the world. To be accurate image bearers, we need to exist in relationships of commitment and love. Jesus is *the* image of God, and his relationship with us, his church, is a model we're to follow. Marriage, in particular, mirrors Jesus' relationship with us in unique ways. It's a lifelong relationship based on a promise of love and grace that creates oneness.
- *Sex is a unique expression of Christ and the church.* If marriage is a unique expression of Christ's love for the church and sex is a unique expression of marital love, then the only logical conclusion is that marital sex is an image of Christ's love for the church.

As radical as this idea may seem, the Bible often describes God's relationship with his people using the language and imagery of marital intimacy. (See, for example, Jeremiah 2:1–2; Ezekiel 16:8–14; Revelation 19:7–9.)

One of the first things that this understanding confirms is that sex is about intimacy. Sex is an outward, physical, connection that should express and reinforce an inner connection. In other words, there are particular qualities of relationship, qualities that make up Jesus' relationship with us, that unite our hearts with his. While we aren't physically or sexually united with him, this sort of intimacy is the foundation of sexual union that we share in marriage. Essentially, the joy of being one at heart, "on the inside," leads to a joyful physical union, being one in body. Understanding that God intends sex to be an expression of intimacy has several important implications.

God is relationship, three persons who are one, and he is the essence and definition of love.

We can't simply think of sex as a function of biology. We don't have sex simply because we're animals, driven by biological urges that we can't understand. Sex is both a physical experience and an expression of our hearts. In other words, the mysteries of sex are more mysteries of our hearts than mysteries of our bodies.

The quality of our relational intimacy will shape our sexual intimacy. When we don't connect well "on the inside," we aren't likely to connect well "on the outside." A lack of intimacy in other areas of marriage will often result in problems of sexual intimacy. As many wives have tried to instruct their husbands, "Sex begins in the kitchen." In other words, good sex doesn't just happen in the bedroom; the foundation for good sex is built with loving, caring interactions in every other room of the house. An impatient, angry husband in the family room will often be an impatient, angry lover. A wife who has trouble expressing her wants and desires in the den will often have trouble expressing wants or desires in the bedroom.

Understanding how to improve intimacy in the bedroom means learning intimacy from Christ. The way Christ builds trust and intimacy with us teaches us how to build trust and intimacy with our spouses. As always, this involves more than simply imitating Jesus. It means worshipping him.

Learning Intimacy from Christ

What words come to mind when you start thinking about Jesus' relationship with us? When I ask couples that question I regularly hear words like: *faithfulness, safety, sacrifice, acceptance, unity, honor, service,* and *honesty.*

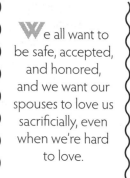

We all want to be safe, accepted, and honored, and we want our spouses to love us sacrificially, even when we're hard to love.

Most would agree that these qualities make for a great marriage. We all want to be safe, accepted, and honored, and we want our spouses to love us sacrificially, even when we're hard to love. But can you see how these same qualities are as important for sexual intimacy as they are for intimacy in general?

Think about the basic mechanics of sex. Husband and wife disrobe, allowing another to see them as few, if any, have ever seen them in their adult lives. There is, literally, nowhere to hide, no way to defend yourself from a critical eye or a violent hand. It would be devastating to be laughed at or criticized. You want to be physically valued, accepted, and embraced. What follows is mutual contact. You touch and allow yourself to be touched on the most sensitive parts of your body. The husband enters his wife, literally touching her on the inside. You give the other the power to bless you with pleasure and warmth—or to harm you in a terrible way. Can you see how safety and acceptance are important?

How about service or sacrifice? Men and women respond to sexual stimulation at different rates; men typically climax more quickly than women. If a man wants to be selfish, he can do so easily, leaving his wife unsatisfied, frustrated, and feeling used. To serve and bless his wife a husband needs to exercise self-control.

How about honesty and communication? Husbands and wives have their own preferences, wanting to be touched in some ways and not others. Without good communication, both verbal and nonverbal, how do you know if you're giving your spouse pleasure? How does your spouse know how to love you if you don't communicate it?

Almost every characteristic of heart-level intimacy has a critical counterpart in the area of physical intimacy. The outer is always a fruit of the inner.

Back to Reid and Christy

As I got to know Reid and Christy better it became clear that there were problems in other areas of their marriage that were damaging their intimacy. Soon after they married, Reid started a new job often working twelve-hour days six and even seven days a week. There was little time for connection of any kind, much less the time it takes to really share at heart level.

Both brought relational struggles into their marriage that weren't being addressed. Reid hated conflict and avoided it at all costs. This was complicated by an idolatrous drive for success. In their marriage, Reid would often avoid conflict with Christy by throwing himself into his work even more, which of course, only deepened Christy's sense of hurt and rejection.

Christy had been through many disappointing relationships with men in her life from family, to friends, to love interests. Reid's avoidance and workaholism only aggravated Christy's temptation to succumb to a disappointment and bitterness that had been building her whole life.

Fortunately, Reid and Christy had the faith to uncover and explore these dynamics together, seeking the Lord's healing from past hurts and learning new patterns of loving communication and conflict resolution. With guidance, they began a new journey of growing sexual intimacy.

Building Safety and Understanding

Safety and understanding are critical ingredients of intimacy, but creating both takes effort. Thinking carefully about how God offers both as he relates to us can help us take specific steps toward offering them to one another in marriage.

Entrusting

In chapter 7 we saw that the Bible tells us to be honest with each other because we're members of one body. As we learned how communication creates oneness, we were already learning about intimacy. Intimacy requires knowing each other well, so if you're applying the principles of communication covered in chapter 7, you're already doing a lot to improve intimacy in your marriage. Intimacy is about sharing things your spouse may not know and, also, about sharing things that you both already know.

Our relationship with God provides a good example of how entrusting another with what he or she already knows is an important part of intimacy. As God becomes intimate with us, he reveals himself to us and, in turn, asks us to reveal ourselves to him. Obviously, God needs to reveal himself to us, otherwise it would be impossible to know him. But it seems odd that God asks us to reveal ourselves to him. After all, he knows absolutely everything about us—more than we know about ourselves! In Psalm 139 David wonders at God's knowledge of him,

> O LORD, you have searched me and you know me. You know when I sit and when I rise; you perceive my thoughts from afar. You discern my going out and my lying down; you are familiar with all my ways. Before a word is on my tongue you know it completely, O LORD. (vv. 1–4)

Why talk to God when he knows what you're going to say before you say it? God asks us to pray, and not just laundry list of wants and needs, to actively share our deepest thoughts and concerns with him. The Bible puts it this way: "Trust in him at all times, O people; *pour out* your hearts to him, for God is our refuge" (Psalm 62:8, italics mine). In many of the Psalms the people of God share heartfelt experiences with God—heartfelt cries of joy, anguish, fear, terror, anger, and dismay. These heartfelt cries weren't shared once and forgotten; as part of corporate worship they continue to echo through the centuries. But God doesn't gain insight or understanding from the Psalms or our personal cries to him, so why pray?

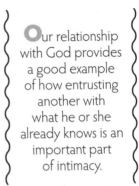

Our relationship with God provides a good example of how entrusting another with what he or she already knows is an important part of intimacy.

I remember my son's first year of school. After a half day of kindergarten he would jump off the bus, enter the house, and be ushered into the kitchen for a debriefing with his mother. As he sipped a cup of juice and downed a few crackers, Kim covered familiar ground. "So what did you do today? What did your teacher say? Did anything funny happen? Did you hear a story? What did you learn?" From day to day, Gresham's answers didn't change much more than the questions did. He did what most kids do in kindergarten: finger paint, learn a new letter, learn a new word, glue beans to construction paper in the shape of the day's number—and repeat. Gresham's answers didn't amaze me, but Kim's response did. Her enthusiasm never waned, her questions were always earnest, and every so often tears would even form in her eyes as he showed her his latest stick figure masterpiece in crayon. In one sense, Kim was not really learning anything from Gresham. She mastered the alphabet, colors, and shapes long ago. And yet she and Gresham were building a relationship, becoming intimate.

What was happening in those kindergarten debriefings?

The answer is in Psalm 62:8, "Trust in him . . . pour out your hearts to him . . . God is our refuge." Our relationship with God isn't about telling God something new but about entrusting him with what's important to us, finding that he cares and even delights in it.

225

Often in marriage, especially as children come into the picture, our communication becomes focused on the logistical needs of the moment. Who's going to pick up the kids from soccer practice? How is Bobby doing in math? How much are Erin's new glasses? Our hearts— and our relationship—can get lost in the details. We become household managers rather than friends and lovers. As we discovered in exploring the importance of honesty, what you think and feel about the details of your life is critical to really knowing and being intimate with your spouse. Realize, too, that more than listening for something new, intimacy means being interested in and expressing concern for what you've heard countless times before, remembering that it has been repeated because it's important to your spouse. So before you roll your eyes and remind your spouse that he or she is telling you the same thing you heard yesterday, remind yourself that (unless he or she is just forgetful) your spouse is entrusting you with something he or she finds important. Delight in the fact that you're being entrusted with the important matters of your spouse's heart.

Acceptance

In the chapter on honesty we learned that it isn't safe to be open and vulnerable to a sinner. To have the courage to reveal yourselves to each other, your marriage needs to be rooted in God's love and purposes.

Sometimes we try to make intimacy safer by making our spouses more like us. We do this instinctively as children. We form cliques based on musical taste, clothing, grades, and neighborhood, and shun those who don't fit in. People can carry that immaturity with them into adulthood and even into marriage. The differences that initially attracted you to your spouse, even dazzled you, can eventually irritate or threaten you. You become critical and judgmental and try to manipulate your spouse into becoming more like you.

As we explored attitudes of honoring versus attitudes of manipulation in chapter 6, we learned that honoring requires an awareness that your spouse doesn't ultimately belong to you but to God. Paul says that you need to regard your spouse as "someone else's servant" (Romans 14:4).

Paul also describes this attitude as acceptance. In Romans 15:7 he writes, "Accept one another, then, just as Christ accepted you, in order to bring praise to God." Husband and wife can both be faithfully following Christ and yet think and do things in radically different ways. For instance, Kim is extroverted. She loves being around others as much as possible. I, on the other hand, am more introverted. I enjoy people, too, but can only take social interaction in much smaller doses and then I need some time alone to recharge my batteries. If we were threatened by this difference, we each could attack the other's personality as less spiritual. I could accuse her of needing people more than she needs God, and she could accuse me of avoiding loving my neighbor. But, in truth, our individual differences are a strength in some situations and a weakness in others. When we learn to accept and even value these differences, we help one another to grow. I'm much more outgoing than I used to be, and Kim has learned the importance of slowing down a bit.

When we learn to accept and even value our individual differences, we help one another to grow.

But what about sin? Should we accept it when our spouses sin against us? As we learned from what the Bible teaches about conflict and forgiveness, you have an obligation in love to graciously, compassionately, and wisely speak to the sin in your spouse's life—and to forgive it. But at the same time, realize that you and your spouse both will continue to battle with your weaknesses and sin until Christ returns and completes his work in you. You can't lead sinless, perfect lives in the here and now; both of you continue to need daily, even moment-to-moment, doses of God's mercy and grace. Live with your spouses with that understanding. You can't and shouldn't make an issue of every sin and annoyance. No one can bear to live under the constant critical gaze of another who's bent on finding fault.

Shared Meaning and Purpose

C. S. Lewis once wrote, "Friendship must be about something. Even if it were an enthusiasm for white mice or dominoes . . . those going nowhere can have no fellow travelers."[16] This holds true for intimacy, too; intimacy must be *about* something. Trying to create intimacy out of your desire for intimacy doesn't work anymore than trying to create friendship out of an enthusiasm for friendship.

When Kim and I first started dating we did all the things young couples do. We went to dinner, saw a movie, went to a concert, and so forth. But our relationship went to a new level when we began to share a few loves with each other. One, in particular, that we share to this day is our love for books and good fiction. One evening as we sat on the sofa together I asked her if I could read a portion of a good book to her. She listened, enjoyed what I shared, and asked for more. Before we knew it I'd spent an hour reading out loud to her. We began a journey that continues to this day, visiting imaginary worlds together, delighting in exciting stories, and making acquaintance with interesting characters. Our love for stories and the process of sharing them with each other gave us a foundation, at least a brick or two of one, with which to build friendship and intimacy.

What interests or enthusiasms do you enjoy with your spouse? If you can't think of any go back to when you first met. What brought you together, what did you enjoy doing together? Often, those initial joys are crowded out by the pressing details of life, especially after children arrive, but they are never past resurrecting. Plus, you can always invent new ones. Brainstorm together to compile a list of things that you might enjoy doing together. During the brainstorming process don't be critical, just write down as many as you can as soon as they come to mind. Keep it simple at first: walking the dog, grocery shopping, playing cards, backgammon—or even reading together. Find simple things to enjoy together and build from there. Once you find them, make them a priority. Not a luxury, intimacy is an important part of worshipping God through your marriage—loving him by loving each other as he loves you.

The most important foundation of all, if you're both Christians, is your common relationship with Christ. The intimacy we have with Christ isn't just about sharing an interest or a joy with another. Being one with him means that we have a purpose and direction in our lives of incredible importance. There can be no higher purpose, no more delightful pursuit than knowing God through Jesus and growing to become more and more like him. Even if your marriage seems devoid of common interests, if you have Christ together, you have a foundation to build upon.

Common Questions about Sex

Are Sexual Problems Always Rooted in Marital Problems?

No. There are physical conditions that can create or contribute to difficulty with sexual intimacy. Hormonal imbalances, conditions that affect blood flow (cardiovascular diseases and diabetes), conditions that affect nerve functioning (neurological disorders), and chronic problems such as kidney or liver diseases can all affect your sex life. For women, menopause can cause a change in sexual functioning. Certain medications (particularly antidepressants), the abuse of medications and drugs, as well as alcohol abuse can affect sexual functioning. If you're experiencing sexual difficulties in your marriage, especially if they seem unrelated to the quality of your relationship, then get checked out by a doctor to diagnose any physical problems.

But sometimes couples simply need more education in how to please their spouse. If you were raised in a home that didn't discuss sex openly, you may lack the knowledge and skill to please your spouse. Or you may have been given a negative view of sex, which makes it difficult for you to enjoy sexual intimacy with your spouse. There are many resources available, even from a Christian perspective, that can help you have a healthy, positive view of sex as well as help you develop skill.

Keep in mind, though, that everything you do, even in handling physical problems, is an expression of your heart. As you experience and deal with physical issues you can be compassionate, caring, faithful, and loving, or you can be impatient, selfish, and mean. Even as you work to address physical or medical problems you must do so worshipfully, both living in dependence on God's love and giving it to your spouse.

Is It Ever Okay to Withhold Sex from Your Spouse?

For one spouse to refuse to be sexually intimate with the other is a serious matter. In the same way that sex is intended to reflect and reinforce the powerful messages of God's love for us, withholding sex from one's spouse sends equally powerful, and potentially damaging, messages as well. But there are many reasons that a spouse may not want to be sexually intimate, and I believe that there are situations in which it's legitimate and appropriate to abstain from sex for the sake of the marriage.

First Corinthians 7:3–5 is the passage that speaks most directly to this question. Paul writes,

> The husband should fulfill his marital duty to his wife, and likewise the wife to her husband. The wife's body does not belong to her alone but also to her husband. In the same way, the husband's body does not belong to him alone but also to his wife. Do not deprive each other except by mutual consent and for a time, so that you may devote yourselves to prayer. Then come together again that Satan will not tempt you because of your lack of self-control.

Unfortunately, this passage has been misused by many husbands to demand sex from their wives. Even the most elementary reading of the passage, however, makes it clear that sexual intimacy is founded on mutuality and care. The passage teaches that we're, in fact, in possession of our own bodies and responsible for how we use them, but that they aren't ours alone. Because husband and wife have become one, the way we use our bodies affects the other. So we must use our bodies carefully, in a way that strengthens the marriage, not selfishly, capriciously demanding or withholding sex.

Notice, too, that Paul isn't prohibiting a season of abstinence. Rather, he's instructing us that abstinence should be mutual (agreed upon by both), for the purposes of prayer (seeking God's help, wisdom, or care), and that the period of abstinence should be limited in order to avoid damaging the marriage by temptation (presumably sexual

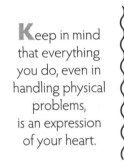

Keep in mind that everything you do, even in handling physical problems, is an expression of your heart.

temptation). The flavor of the passage is that sex is good and appropriate in marriage, and that husband and wife should express care for each other sexually, but that there are reasons that for a period of time a couple may abstain for their spiritual welfare.

So when might a couple decide to abstain from sex? It could simply be a form of fasting. Just as some Christians go without food for a day or two to focus on their relationship with God, a couple may choose to do the same sexually. I know that some men who have struggled with an addiction to pornography will often, as part of a recovery program, abstain from sex with their wives (sometimes up to ninety days) so that they can gain perspective over how sex functions in their lives and regain mastery over it. The reasons, as long as they're guided by love for God and spouse, may vary, but the picture of marital sexuality that Paul presents isn't one of one spouse demanding sex from the other but a thoughtful, spiritual, and mutual exercise of sexuality.

The disruptions of marital sex that are the most painful are unilateral. One spouse determines that they won't or can't have sex with the other and the other is hurt and/or angry about it. Is it ever a good idea to unilaterally decide to abstain from sex? In certain situations, yes. The most obvious situation is one in which a spouse is physically or sexually abused. There's behavior that's so destructive to a marriage that sexual intimacy is inappropriate. When a spouse is physically destroying the marriage with words and fists or has turned sexual intimacy into a degrading expression of anger and control, it may not be wise to make oneself physically vulnerable or to participate in behavior that will only weaken a marriage that's already on the brink of destruction. You shouldn't be navigating these dangerous waters alone. Find good counsel in a wise pastor, a trusted friend, or a biblical counselor—preferably all three—to chart loving courses of action that empower you to do what you can in faith to protect your marriage without jeopardizing you or your family's welfare.

> The love that God has given us in Jesus is something to celebrate.

What about less severe situations? What if there's simply low-grade anger or bitterness that regularly disrupts sexual intimacy? In such situations I urge both spouses to do what they can to address the underlying, aggravating issue, cautioning them against engaging in a power struggle. This is the most common and dangerous temptation. Withholding sex or pressuring for sex communicates powerful messages that, more often than not, aren't messages of love. Do what you can to translate the action of withholding into words that invite honest and gracious dialogue about the hurts and problems that are robbing you of your desire to be physically intimate.

Is It Okay to View Pornography with Your Spouse?

We've established that sex is intended to communicate the messages of intimacy, the kind of intimacy and love that Jesus has for us. What messages does pornography communicate? Most often pornography suggests that the most exciting and enjoyable sex is anonymous, without commitment and without consequences. People aren't portrayed as persons who are to be honored and loved but as objects that only exist to fill the appetites of others. Pornography is, literally, a picture of manipulation.

You won't solve problems of intimacy by feeding messages of manipulation into your hearts and your bedroom. It may be exciting for a season, but you'll find that the selfish and impersonal messages of pornography won't stay safely contained on the screen but will infect your marriage and your attitude toward others.

If you feel that your sex life lacks excitement, stoke that excitement in other areas of your relationship. Become passionate about your spouse as a person and you'll find that it feeds your sexual passion. Consider spicing up your lovemaking in other ways. It's easy for marital sex to become routine. Find playful, wholesome ways to make things more interesting. It can be as simple as making love during the day instead of at night, or in a different room of the house.

Celebrate

Another way to describe marital intimacy is with the word *celebration*. The love that God has given us in Jesus is something to celebrate. It's a love so powerful that when we're in tune with it, it has to find physical expression. In the Bible the return of Jesus is portrayed as a wedding feast. The book of Revelation gives us this image:

> Then I heard what sounded like a great multitude, like
> the roar of rushing waters and like loud peals of thunder,
> shouting: "Hallelujah! For our Lord God Almighty reigns. Let
> us rejoice and be glad and give him glory! For the wedding of
> the Lamb has come, and his bride has made herself ready. Fine
> linen, bright and clean, was given her to wear." (Fine linen
> stands for the righteous acts of the saints.) (Revelation 19:6–8)

As God's people, we're like a bride thrilled to be with our groom at last! Words can hardly capture the joy.

Sex is designed to give us a glimpse of that joy, a physical way to experience and reinforce that kind of love. Sex isn't dirty, though our culture tries to make it that way. Don't give in to that cheap knock-off. Sin isn't what makes sex exciting. If you build an intimacy into your marriage that reflects God's love, then you have every reason to believe that it will show up in the bedroom as a wonderful celebration.

A final word of caution: Don't think that you have to get intimacy "right" at the level of the heart before your sex life improves. Heart-level intimacy is foundational, yes, but thoughtful and caring sexual intimacy can be an important assurance and encouragement in difficult times. Sometimes caring and sincere sexual affection speak the messages of affirmation, acceptance, belonging, and a host of other messages of love in a way that we find difficult to put into words. The inner intimacy of the heart and the outer intimacy of sex form a mutually reinforcing feedback loop. Allow sex to celebrate what's right without insisting on perfection. It can communicate the messages that are important building blocks to growth and lay a foundation for making progress in other areas. Sex can be a wonderful and worshipful experience.

Think about It

- Recall a recent time when you felt intimate with your spouse. Can you identify things that were said or done that made you feel understood and safe? Were there other factors that helped?
- What words come to mind when you think about Jesus' love for you? Are there some aspects of Jesus' love that are more important to you than others?

- Would you say you have more of a positive or a negative view of sex? Why?
- Are there ways that you don't fully accept your spouse? What can you do to express more acceptance? Are there ways that you don't feel accepted? Can you think of a way of constructively sharing your feelings with your spouse?

SECTION THREE

Staying on the Path

Learning to love in the details of your marriage doesn't lead to overnight results in either you or your spouse. Be patient and learn endurance. Learn how to stay on the path. Fortunately, God offers us encouragement and refreshment along the way.

Chapter 16 offers training in the highest form of love, grace. Even when sinned against, grace knows and shares God's love. Grace forgives and has hope. Jesus teaches us to love this way.

In chapter 17, learn how to avoid a common trap of the ordinary moment, the trap of believing that your actions no longer make a difference. This chapter describes why your actions always make a difference and helps you to keep your eyes on the prize.

We all come to marriage with baggage. Marriage is just one more leg in our journey, one more chapter to our story. Chapter 18 helps you to understand the story of your own life, not just the story of your marriage, and how the way God has authored the story of his love for us gives us hope and points us forward along the path.

sixteen

Growing in Grace

What You'll Learn in This Chapter:

- Grace is more than a helping hand from God. Grace is God's love given to us though we don't deserve it and have no hope of rescuing ourselves.
- We need God's grace every moment of every day.
- Grace should find active expression in our marriages. Grace empowers us to love as God has loved us, learning to move toward our spouses in love even when we've been sinned against.
- Grace means that God is bigger than our mistakes and that the repaired is more beautiful than the new. This gives us hope that grace can make our marriages whole.

Grace: An Extreme Makeover

FOR A WHILE my family developed a Sunday evening ritual of watching *Extreme Makeover: Home Edition* as we ate dinner. Though we'd generally held to a no-TV-at-meals policy, my kids' impassioned pleas for an exception were so sincere I caved in just to see what all of the fuss was about.

Every week the show featured a family in a desperate living situation in need of a new, or at least significantly renovated, home. The show documented the progress and challenges of remaking the home in the space of only one week. My children have no interest in learning how to remodel homes. I can't even interest them in cleaning their own rooms. So I was eager to figure out the hook.

There's some tension and excitement as the work crew struggles to meet its self-imposed deadline, but you don't have to watch for long before you realize that the show isn't at all about renovating homes but about *grace*.

One story line features a family with more than a dozen special needs foster children who may have to be taken away because the family can't afford to remove toxic levels of lead found in their home.

In another episode, an Iraqi War veteran with a prosthetic leg tries to raise two daughters single-handedly in a home not equipped for someone with disabilities.

Yet another portrays a single father with a heart condition as he struggles to keep his five children safe in a crime- and drug-infested area in a home that's falling apart.

Every family chosen to appear on the show is in dire straits and living in substandard housing. They are all people in desperate situations with no way out. The family is whisked away on a dream vacation for a week. While they're away, an army of workers demolishes their old house and erects a new one in its place.

In the final segment of the show, the family returns and stands in front of their home, their view blocked by a large bus. As the bus pulls away the family screams, weeps, and leaps with joy as a crowd of a hundred or more workers and neighbors roar their approval and share in their joy. The ending is always the same, but so is our response. We all smile, laugh, and fight back tears.

Because grace is an essential feature of God's love, our understanding and appreciation of it should grow as long as we live.

Grace: unexpected help arrives to rescue those who could never deliver themselves. Grace brings love that you didn't earn and help that you could never provide for yourself. When the world glimpses it on TV it weeps at the hope that such love exists. Who doesn't want to be loved that way? Who wouldn't want to be a part of sharing that love with another?

Jesus offers something more than a radical home makeover. He invites you to be loved and remade. Marriage gives you a chance to share it with your spouse. If you're going to stay on the path of loving your spouse, you're going to need a deep and growing understanding of what grace is, how to live out of it, and how to extend it to your spouse.

Grace: Bookends, a Helping Hand, or a Caterpillar in a Ring of Fire

Because grace is an essential feature of God's love, our understanding and appreciation of it should grow as long as we live. Jerry Bridges summarizes grace this way: "*Grace* is God's free and unmerited favor shown to guilty sinners who deserve only judgment. It is the love of God shown to the unlovely. It is God reaching downward to people who are in rebellion against Him."[17] When we think about grace our starting point should be the undeserved love that God gives us.

Christians often tend to have a narrow understanding of grace. When we first enter into relationship with God we acknowledge our inability to rescue ourselves from the brokenness and rebellion of sin, and we accept his love as an undeserved gift in Jesus. We understand that we're saved, at least initially, by God's grace. This is the grace that will get us into heaven when we die. In the meantime, however, we turn from depending on grace alone and buckle down to earn God's approval on our own. In that sense, we live with grace as the spiritual bookends of our lives. It's what brings us into relationship with God; it's what gets us across the finish line. In between, we live as if our holiness were all up to us.[18]

In her book, *From Fear to Freedom*, Rose Marie Miller refutes the notion that we can at any point in our lives do anything to save ourselves. Quite correctly, she insists that we need the grace of God every moment of every day. She describes an illustration that she heard her husband give during a lecture.

> Two seventeenth-century theologians were debating on the nature of grace. One said that grace is like one parent guiding a toddler across the room to the other parent, who has an apple for the child. The nearby parent watches the youngster; if he almost falls, this parent will hold him for a moment so that he can still cross the room under his own power. But the other theologian had a different view. For him grace comes to us only in the discovery of our total helplessness. In his concept, we are like a caterpillar in a ring of fire. Deliverance can only come from above.[19]

If we're toddlers being steadied by a loving parent, then grace is a little more than a helping hand, but we're still largely left to our own devices, relying on our own abilities. Let the second image sink in: a caterpillar in a ring of fire. It's a much better picture of grace. A caterpillar only crawls; its best efforts at salvation could only be dragging itself across consuming flames. A shove in the right direction only reinforces its own useless efforts and pushes it more quickly into the flames. It doesn't need help getting started; nor does it do any good to meet the caterpillar on the other side with a fire extinguisher. If the caterpillar is to escape the flames, deliverance must be total, and it must come from beyond the caterpillar.

What Grace Means

I Need Jesus Every Moment of Every Day

Jesus likened his relationship with his disciples to that of a vine and its branches.

> Remain in me, and I will remain in you. No branch can bear fruit by itself; it must remain in the vine. Neither can you bear fruit unless you remain in me. I am the vine; you are the branches. If a man remains in me and I in him, he will bear much fruit; apart from me you can do nothing. (John 15:4–5)

Picture a grapevine with its branches. Every ounce of water, every nutrient essential to life has one way of reaching the branch. It must flow from the vine into the branch. Sever the connection with the vine, and the branch immediately begins to die. The image of the vine and branches is an image of continual dependence and need. Grace is a way of describing God's response to our continual need. We aren't automobiles that need our tank filled up once a week but branches that must be supported and nourished every moment. The moment we aren't nurtured by God's love we begin to die spiritually.

Too often we cut ourselves off from the vine by looking to ourselves when we're struggling. Instead of turning to God we try to work out problems on our own. This response separates us from grace, and we become like a severed branch trying to draw life out of thin air. Why not turn to him instead? Living in God's grace means embracing the truth that Jesus alone can solve our problems and that we need him every day.

Moving toward My Spouse Even When It Hurts

In the context of our relationship with God, grace is essentially passive. God has done and is doing something for us that we can't possibly do ourselves. Grace requires utter dependence on Christ as a branch depends on a vine.

Grace, however, as an aspect of love must be reflected in our relationships with others, especially our spouses. In marriage, grace is more of an action word; it's something that we must actively *do* or practice toward others. Relationship with God by his grace will always result in love expressed as grace toward our neighbors.

Earlier, in chapter 4, we began to venture into the realm of grace when we observed that God's love isn't about giving to get. We looked at Matthew 5, in which Jesus tells us that we shouldn't just love those who love us—everyone does that—but we should also love our enemies as God does. Jesus points out that we're surrounded every moment of every day with God's gracious love for his enemies. He blesses the evil as well as the good with the benefits of sunshine and rain. But loving your enemy is more than choosing to love when you aren't getting what you want; it means loving even when the other person is actively sinning against you.

Learning from Jesus

If we want to understand how to love this way, we must look to and worship Jesus. In providing a window into Christ's own mind-set as he chooses to bless those who sin against him, Isaiah 50 offers unique insight into the mind-set of grace. Although written centuries before Jesus' birth, the book of Isaiah is recognized as containing one of the more illuminating prophecies about the Messiah.

Unlike other passages in Isaiah, chapter 50 talks about the Messiah from a first-person perspective: the Messiah himself describes what he's thinking and doing. In that sense, it's a unique perspective.

The Mind-set of a Servant

The Sovereign LORD has given me an instructed tongue,
to know the word that sustains the weary. He wakens me
morning by morning, wakens my ear to listen like one being
taught. (Isaiah 50:4)

Jesus has the mind-set of a servant. He lives to serve his heavenly
Father and others. To offer gracious love to your spouse you have to be
willing to see your role as that of a servant. Being a servant isn't about
giving your spouse what he or she wants but what he or she needs—
and letting God define what that is. Notice that Jesus focuses on how
God instructs and directs him. Often we're so focused on what our
spouses are doing, especially when they're disappointing or hurting us,
that we respond more to them than to God. Focusing on God and his
goals enables you to serve your spouse and not be controlled by him
or her.

Confidence that God Is Present and Active

The Sovereign LORD has opened my ears, and I have not
been rebellious; I have not drawn back. I offered my back to
those who beat me, my cheeks to those who pulled out my
beard; I did not hide my face from mocking and spitting.
Because the Sovereign LORD helps me, I will not be disgraced.
Therefore have I set my face like flint, and I know I will not
be put to shame. He who vindicates me is near. Who then
will bring charges against me? Let us face each other! Who is
my accuser? Let him confront me! It is the Sovereign LORD
who helps me. Who is he that will condemn me? (Isaiah
50:5–9a)

Here we have, in agonizing detail, what it meant for Jesus to move
toward those who were sinning against him. It's brutal both physically

and spiritually. When we suffer at another's hands, we're most vulnerable to defeat, either by withdrawing or by attacking, returning evil for evil. How did Jesus endure and resist temptation?

Shame, or disgrace, is often our greatest enemy in extending grace. Jesus' words here are especially striking. In the moment of being horrifically sinned against, how can he say that he won't be disgraced or shamed? It's shameful to have your beard plucked out and to be spat upon. Jesus isn't denying the pain or even the emotional torment of his suffering, but clearly he is focusing on something that keeps him grounded in his identity and purpose.

> To persevere through the difficulties of marriage, you must have faith that God is present and active even when you can't see what he's up to.

Jesus' focus is his confidence in God's presence and purpose. He knows that God will vindicate him; he will be proven right. God won't allow Jesus' suffering to be pointless; Jesus is convinced that it will accomplish God's purposes. The shame that would be intolerable would be for sin to have the last word, for God's gracious purposes to be thwarted, and for Jesus to bear this suffering only for it to be proven that his confidence in God was for nothing. But God will vindicate him and accomplish his good purposes: His people will be saved.

To overcome in the most difficult moments, when your spouse's sinful behavior tempts you either to despair or to strike back, you need to know that trusting in God and doing good isn't pointless. Even in the midst of suffering and being sinned against, Jesus knows that God is present and active—he has faith. To persevere through the difficulties of marriage, you must have faith that God is present and active even when you can't see what he's up to. When you believe that, you believe that your actions make a difference. There's no guarantee that your spouse will respond to God's love, but you'll be spared slavery to bitterness, fear, and hopelessness. You'll experience the victory of knowing that the sins of others can't separate you from God's presence, love, and power.

An important note about spousal abuse: Although Jesus physically suffered out of his love for us, no one should passively accept abuse from a spouse.

Recognize that there were many times that Jesus' enemies tried to physically harm, even kill him, and he avoided and evaded their plans. A basic element of wisdom is to see trouble coming and avoid it when possible (Luke 4:28–30; John 8:59; 10:39; 11:53–54).

But also understand that Jesus was not a victim of his suffering but part of a plan. He made a decision to suffer at the time and place of God's choosing with God's purposes clearly in mind. Jesus said,

> The reason my Father loves me is that I lay down my life—
> only to take it up again. No one takes it from me, but I lay it
> down of my own accord. I have authority to lay it down and
> authority to take it up again. This command I received from
> my Father. (John 10:17–18)

Jesus was not cowed into submission and suffering by a bully to avoid being abandoned or losing a relationship. He chose his course of action according to God's plan to remake the relationship. His suffering was not submission to a destructive and perverse version of marriage.

The point is, Jesus' suffering and sacrifice was a choice that he freely made out of love—out of God's plan and Jesus' decision to minister to us. On many other occasions Jesus said no to the plans of wicked men to harm him. If you're in an abusive marriage, don't consider Jesus' example or my words as instruction to endure abuse. You need wisdom to know how to carefully and wisely address the abuse with the goal of stopping it. You shouldn't be traveling this path alone. Seek the help of a wise pastor or counselor with experience in counseling victims of spousal abuse.

Understanding that Grace Is the Only Way

Who among you fears the LORD and obeys the word of his servant? Let him who walks in the dark, who has no light, trust in the name of the LORD and rely on his God. But now, all you who light fires and provide yourselves with flaming torches, go, walk in the light of your fires and of the torches you have set ablaze. This is what you shall receive from my hand: You will lie down in torment. (Isaiah 50:10–11)

At this point in the passage it's as if Jesus turns directly to us and speaks. We've marveled at his faith and love; now he wants us to wrestle with his words. Do you honor and respect his actions for you? Are you willing to obey and follow him? You're faced with a decision: you can try to find our own way through the dark moments of being sinned against, follow the wisdom of the world, or create your own "light" if you choose. You can try to hide from the pain of being sinned against, launch your own first strike, or find some other compromise. The choice is yours. But Jesus makes it clear: when you reject his path and choose your own, you're, in effect, rejecting him. When you reject Jesus, love incarnate, you can't expect him to bless your efforts. There are consequences to rejecting Jesus. You can only expect suffering to be added to suffering.

God Is Bigger Than My Mistakes

Next to shame and fear, regret is one of the greatest enemies of grace. Feeling bad about sin is a critical ingredient to repentance, but after that, a lingering, gnawing regret—a sense that you can never recover from what's happened—can sap you of the energy and faith to persevere in marriage. I've sat with couples who shared that they believed their marriage was a mistake. Continuing with counseling, they believed, was pointless because anything they could do to make things better would just be building on a monumental mistake, like trying to build a house on quicksand.

But grace itself is the antidote to regret. Without denying that we sin and make mistakes or foolish decisions, grace argues that God is bigger than them all and will use them both to glorify himself and bless us. Grace isn't God adding something to our best efforts but working through our worst efforts and redeeming us. God doesn't need our wisdom, our good decisions, or wholesome motives to accomplish his purposes for us.

Grace isn't God adding something to our best efforts but working through our worst efforts and redeeming us.

Every one of us can look back on our lives and find examples of doing the wrong things for the wrong reasons. In all honesty, I'm very glad that I married Kim, but at twenty-three, my ideas about what marriage was and how to choose a spouse were idiotic. I consider my marriage to Kim a credit to God's grace, not my wisdom or virtue.

Consider Jesus' sacrifice on the cross. God accomplished the greatest good of all time through the actions of wicked and indifferent people. Pontius Pilate, Roman governor at the time, had no love for Christ or God's plan, but turned Jesus over to an angry Jewish mob so as not to jeopardize his cushy position. Jewish religious leaders were not crucifying Jesus to make atonement for sins but trying to secure their power base. Roman soldiers were just doing their job nailing one more criminal to a tree. No one was there to accomplish God's good purposes. But God's love, power, and grace bent the most wicked motives and deeds to his loving plan (Acts 2:23).

The Repaired Is More Beautiful than the New

Many of us think that once something has been broken it can never be as good as it once was. After all, we don't expect used cars to be as nice as new ones. And once the elastic has been stretched out of our clothes, they never quite fit right again. But not only is God bigger than our mistakes; he actually works through our sin, folly, and weaknesses to make our lives and marriages more beautiful than ever.

That doesn't mean bringing us to the point of forgetting past mistakes and hurts but learning to see them through the lens of God's love and activity in our lives.

At one point in their history, Israel's relationship with God was so bad that God decided to send them into exile. First he brought the Assyrians who destroyed Israel's ten northern tribes, and then a few hundred years later he brought the Babylonians to destroy the remaining two tribes. When the capital city of Jerusalem was conquered, most of its inhabitants were deported as servants and slaves, and the temple itself was demolished. Though God had warned them of what he would do if they didn't repent, Israel couldn't conceive of being sent away from the Promised Land. Nor could they imagine God's own temple, the symbol of his very presence with his people, being destroyed.

> No matter why you married, no matter what sins damaged your marriage, God's restoration will make it beautiful.

After seventy years God released Israel from captivity and miraculously provided the wealth of surrounding nations to rebuild his temple. Despite Israel's best efforts, however, the new temple paled in comparison with the first. The people were crestfallen, and they wondered whether the days of God's blessing had been irrevocably lost. Was there no way to get back to what was or what was meant to be?

God told his prophet Haggai to say to the people,

> "Who of you is left who saw this house in its former glory? How does it look to you now? Does it not seem to you like nothing? . . . Be strong, all you people of the land," declares the LORD, "and work. For I am with you, declares the LORD Almighty. . . . This is what the LORD Almighty says: "In a little while I will once more shake the heavens and the earth, the sea and the dry land. I will shake all nations, and the desired of all nations will come, and I will fill this house with glory,"

says the LORD Almighty. . . . "The glory of this present house will be greater than the glory of the former house," says the LORD Almighty. "And in this place I will grant peace," declares the LORD Almighty. (Haggai 2:3, 4b, 6–7, 9)

God encourages his people, not by denying the beauty and grandeur of the previous temple but by pointing them to how he intends to use the one they just built. What makes the new temple glorious is how he will use it to draw all nations to himself. Their wealth and devotion will flow to the new temple, and in that, God will be glorified. Though not explicitly stated, this temple was certainly more beautiful than the last because it was a sign of God's redemptive love. It was a temple built by the hands of a people humbled and repentant and brought back home by God.

No matter why you married, no matter what sins damaged your marriage, God's restoration will make it beautiful, not by hiding the past or camouflaging the scars but by helping you to see God's faithfulness and love in it and even using it to draw others to himself.

Think about It

- Where do you turn when you need help? How, specifically, can you turn to God rather than to yourself when you feel hurt, sinned against, or know that you've blown it?
- Recall an instance when you received love when you least expected it or deserved it. Can you think of someone who needs love that they might not expect or deserve?
- What are some ways that you understand love better or love your spouse more because you've persevered through tough times?

seventeen
Your Actions Make a Difference

What You'll Learn in This Chapter:

- To combat hopelessness and stay on track remember that your actions make a difference. Your actions, regardless of their effect on others, always change you, either leading you to become a more loving person or a more hardened, manipulative one.
- When words seem to have no effect on your spouse, remember that actions speak louder than words.
- To stay on track in marriage, instead of just focusing on your spouse, place your hope in Christ himself, finding joy and meaning in him.
- Faith means believing that God is active even when we can't see it. Through Jesus, God is active and calls us to action.

Learned Helplessness

"WHY SHOULD I be nice to him? He'll never be nice to me."

"Why should I listen to her? She'll never listen to me."

"This is never going to work. What's the use?"

These are messages of hopelessness. The most dangerous moments in marriage, and life, occur when you believe that nothing you do will make a difference. Once you believe that love is pointless and step onto the threshold of indifference and despair, you not only lose your connection to your spouse but to God as well.

Psychologists have observed the connection between depression and the belief that there's nothing you can do to change your circumstances. Sometimes this idea is described as "learned helplessness." In the late 1960s psychologist Martin Seligman and others conducted experiments with three different groups of dogs giving each group various levels of control over unpleasant shocks by pressing levers.[20] The first group had complete control, the second group had variable control, and the third group had no ability to control the shocks at all. Later all three groups were placed in a situation in which they could escape shocks by jumping over a low barrier. Dogs from the first two groups quickly learned to jump the wall to improve their situation, but most dogs from the third group simply laid down and whined.

We aren't dogs, but the analogy fits: If you believe that your choices make no difference and there's nothing you can do to "escape the shocks," you're in grave danger of lying down and giving up.

Let's Not Become Weary in Doing Good

God knows and understands how hard it is to continue doing what's right when, by all appearances, it seems to have no effect. In Paul's letter to the Galatians he writes to those of us who would lie down and whine,

Do not be deceived: God cannot be mocked. A man reaps what he sows. The one who sows to please his sinful nature, from that nature will reap destruction; the one who sows to please the Spirit, from the Spirit will reap eternal life. Let us not become weary in doing good, for at the proper time we will reap a harvest if we do not give up. (Galatians 6:7–9)

Planting and harvesting a crop is a process that takes time and effort. Farming requires hard work and patience. Crops don't spring up overnight; they require weeks and months of careful watering, weeding, and tending. Love requires patience too. Your actions do make a difference, but the difference isn't always obvious at first.

> If you're sowing the seeds of his Spirit, the seeds of love, those seeds are guaranteed to produce a result.

Paul reminds us that God is overseeing this farming process, guaranteeing the outcome. If you're sowing the seeds of his Spirit, the seeds of love, those seeds are guaranteed to produce a result. God won't be made a fool; the gospel of Jesus will accomplish his good goals for your life. But we must understand this guarantee accurately. God isn't promising that your spouse will change for the better, though when you act in love you certainly make this kind of change more likely. God promises to complete the work he's begun in *you*. Don't look for changes in your spouse; look for them in yourself.

When you're discouraged, you need to remember that the greatest treasure of all is yours to be had, the treasure of knowing and growing in the love of Jesus. Your actions always make a difference whether or not your spouse ever changes. When you live in love, worshipping and imitating Jesus in the hard moments of marriage, you're changing; you're becoming more like your Savior and the person God has created you to become.

You may be thinking, "Wait a minute, this all feels like a bait and switch. I want to know how to change my marriage, and you're just telling me to forget about that and focus on Jesus." Not at all. I'm asking you to make sure you have your priorities in order. Too often, Christians treat Jesus as a means to an end. We include Jesus in our lives to make sure we get the things that we want, a happy marriage among them. The framework of our lives is our personal wants and desires. Jesus is a welcome part of the picture as long as he fits into that framework.

> Your actions will always change you for good or ill, so choose carefully.

The Bible, however, offers a radically different picture: Jesus is the framework. He determines what fits in the picture and what doesn't. His framework is the only one that makes sense out of love. Learning to love well by worshipping Jesus gives us our best hope for having a thriving, happy marriage, but we must accept that Jesus intends to work through our marriages in many ways to shape and change us, and that won't always feel good or produce the results we want.

These same words of Paul serve as a warning too: God won't be mocked. Unloving actions change you as well. If you plant seeds of bitterness, manipulation, and selfishness, then you'll produce a harvest of misery. When we address the sins of others, be especially careful not to sow the wrong kinds of seed. A few verses earlier, Paul encourages us to do what we can to help each other overcome sin and warns us of danger:

> Brothers, if someone is caught in a sin, you who are spiritual should restore him gently. *But watch yourself, or you also may be tempted.* Carry each other's burdens, and in this way you will fulfill the law of Christ. If anyone thinks he is something when he is nothing, he deceives himself. *Each one should test his own actions.* (Galatians 6:1–4a, italics mine)

Living with a sinful spouse is dangerous even when you're trying in love to help him or her. Obviously, one danger is that you become entangled in the same sort of sin. Becoming angry is easy when you're married to an angry person, or becoming fearful when you're married to a fearful person, or becoming greedy when you're married to a greedy person. But the danger at the root of all of these is pride—the danger of thinking that you're something when you're nothing. The temptation is to focus on the sins of your spouse and lose sight of yourself as someone who's tempted to sin by serving your own desires, fears, and idols. You can fool yourself into thinking that you're saying and doing loving things when, in reality, you're just serving yourself. That's why you must stay connected to the ultimate reasons that you choose to love, no matter what your spouse is doing. You love because you love and worship Jesus, who is love.

I once counseled a woman whose husband had been generally neglectful and done some awful things. She was right to challenge his sinful behavior, but on one occasion her method was to pick up a knife and chase him around the house! Clearly, she was not acting in love. She was sowing the wrong kind of seed. That's an easy one to spot, but how do you know what kind of seed you're sowing? Again, Paul gives us guidance as he writes, "But the fruit of the Spirit is love, joy, peace, patience, kindness, goodness, faithfulness, gentleness and self-control" (Galatians 5:22–23a). If you want to know what kind of seed you're planting, examine the fruit that your attitudes and efforts are producing by asking a few questions: What am I becoming? Does my response to my spouse fit the list in verses 22 and 23? Your actions will *always change you* for good or ill, so choose carefully.

Actions Are More Powerful Than Words

If you're like me, you're never at a loss for words, especially when you're angry or feel you've been wronged. And as we've learned, speaking carefully and honestly with our spouses is an important part of love, especially in the midst of conflict. But we need to pay attention not only to what we say but also to what we do because it's well known that actions speak louder than words.

Silenced Spouses Whose Lives Speak Volumes

In his first epistle, Peter addressing wives writes,

> Wives, in the same way be submissive to your husbands so that, if any of them do not believe the word, they may be won over without words by the behavior of their wives, when they see the purity and reverence of your lives. (1 Peter 3:1–2)

In Peter's day, a wife was totally dependent on her husband for survival. Without independent legal standing or other means of supporting herself, a wife could be in grave danger if she displeased her husband. She could find herself placed outside of the home, divorced; and that could be a social, financial, and personal disaster. But Peter offers wives hope. He reminds them that the power of the gospel isn't dependent on words. Even if these women are absolutely silenced by their husbands, forbidden to speak to them about Jesus, through their Christlike behavior they have a powerful way of addressing their husbands. By living lives of love and imitating Jesus, these wives are proclaiming the gospel to their husbands all day long.

Peter is pointing the women to Jesus, who in the most crucial moments of his ministry was essentially silent. He uttered no lies, no threats, and no words of self-justification. In this passage, Peter quotes from Isaiah 53, which foretells the suffering of the Messiah.

> He was oppressed and afflicted, yet he did not open his mouth; he was led like a lamb to the slaughter, and as a sheep before her shearers is silent, so he did not open his mouth. (Isaiah 53:7)

Even without words, Jesus was able to rescue us from sin. His loving and gracious actions were effective, and they echo throughout history and into the lives of his followers. Even a silenced wife, who in every other way may appear powerless, takes powerful and effective action every time she chooses to love rather than retaliate in anger or cower in fear.

The Light of the World

But this isn't just encouragement to silenced spouses. Jesus instructs all of us to make his love visible through our actions. He says,

> You are the light of the world. A city on a hill cannot be hidden. Neither do people light a lamp and put it under a bowl. Instead they put it on its stand, and it gives light to everyone in the house. In the same way, let your light shine before men, that they may see your good deeds and praise your Father in heaven. (Matthew 5:14–16)

Jesus tells us about the power that our actions have to influence others for good. When words fail, remember that a life of love directs your spouse to Jesus. Let your light shine, even when words seem pointless.

Remember what we've learned about worship; our love for God is expressed by our love for those around us. Loving others makes God's love visible to them.

Keep Your Eyes on the Prize

Practicing Hope

It's important to make a daily decision about what you're hoping for. That may sound strange because we usually think of hope as a feeling, not an action. But make no mistake, hope is something you do.[21] Jesus explains the importance of practicing hope this way:

> Do not store up for yourselves treasures on earth, where
> moth and rust destroy, and where thieves break in and steal.
> But store up for yourselves treasures in heaven, where moth
> and rust do not destroy, and where thieves do not break in
> and steal. For where your treasure is, your heart will be also.
> (Matthew 6:19–21)

Jesus makes two simple observations. First, your happiness and well-being have everything to do with what you value or treasure—where you place your hope. Jesus is addressing one of our biggest temptations, the temptation to trust in our possessions and wealth. The lesson is simple. If your whole life is given over to acquiring and enjoying wealth, what will happen when you lose the very things you've based your life upon? What happens when an identity thief ruins your credit, your house is destroyed in a flood, or the stock market collapses? If you've given your whole heart to those things, they've become your treasure. You'll suffer the same fate as your possessions. The flood that wipes out your home will wipe out your heart. The thief that makes off with your wealth makes off with your heart.

Jesus' second point is simply to encourage you to make a better choice. Invest your heart in something that lasts, something that's secure and won't disappoint you. He speaks of "treasure in heaven." When you think of treasure in heaven, don't envision angels floating on clouds or streets paved with gold. Remember, God has given his people the greatest gift imaginable, Jesus. Whatever wonders await us in heaven, the focus of our existence there will be our relationship with God through Jesus. When you think of treasure that way, you realize that you already have received something like a down payment on it. Today you have an intimate relationship with Jesus, and his Spirit lives inside of you. You're connected to him at all times and can seek encouragement or share your thoughts, desires, and fears anytime you choose.

When you place your hope in Jesus you've taken wise action. No robber, no moth, no amount of rust, and no spouse can steal Jesus from you. A spouse's failures, sins, ignorance, and weakness can't prevent God from giving you the greatest gifts and joys that he has for you through his Son.

Hidden Treasure

Jesus tells a simple parable that gives us several reasons to act even when we're tempted to believe it makes no difference. Jesus said,

> The kingdom of heaven is like treasure hidden in a field. When a man found it, he hid it again, and then in his joy went and sold all he had and bought that field. (Matthew 13:44)

Jesus acknowledges that sometimes his kingdom is hard to see. The phrase "kingdom of heaven" refers to Jesus' power, rule, and presence in our lives. He's our King, carefully ruling and guiding us. Sometimes we wonder what he's up to because it doesn't seem like he's doing anything at all. Sometimes Jesus' kingdom seems hidden from view like buried treasure.

Just like the man in the parable, you might step over it without noticing it a thousand times before you stub your toe on it and realize you've hit the lottery. Even those of us who know that Jesus is our treasure get discouraged because he doesn't do things the way that we do. We want dramatic, instantaneous, and lasting change. Jesus' work, however, is often subtle, working change in and through us over time, and allowing for many ups and downs.

Notice, that when the man found the treasure there were still sacrifices to be made. Apparently the treasure couldn't be moved, so he had to sell all he had to buy the field that concealed the treasure. Imagine the precious things he had to sell to raise the money required to buy that field. Did he spend time trying to devise a scheme that would allow him to keep his prized possessions and lay hold of the treasure? Can you imagine the drubbing his public image took? Can't you hear the hecklers? "Bob must have lost his mind! He sold his half-million-dollar home to buy the abandoned lot out by the gas station!"

The most powerful phrase in this parable is "in his joy": the sacrifices are real, but so is the joy. Because the man knew the real value of the treasure, he was able to do what was necessary without being defeated or living in despair. Notice the implicit promise in Jesus' words: As you follow me you'll have hard days and face disappointment, but the treasure is real and is worth having at any cost.

Keeping your eyes on the prize means that in moments when your actions don't seem to matter, you choose to place your hope in Jesus rather than your spouse. You choose to believe the truth that having Jesus as your treasure is worth the sacrifices because you're receiving a joy that no spouse or challenging marriage can take away. You choose to live for eternity but savor today the sweet relationship you have with Jesus.

Have Faith

In a difficult marriage, keeping to the path requires faith. *Faith,* like hope, is one of those religious words that's so often used (and misused) that we've almost forgotten what it means. Faith is more than a good feeling that everything is going to be all right. Faith doesn't mean working up certain feelings or keeping a stiff upper lip. So how does the Bible define faith?

More Than a Feeling

Hebrews 11 begins with this definition, "Now faith is being sure of what we hope for and certain of what we do not see. This is what the ancients were commended for" (Hebrews 11:1–2).

Hebrews contrasts what is seen with what is hoped for. Faith focuses on hope even in the face of disappointment or frustration. Even when experience doesn't seem to align with them, faith lives out of the certainty of God's promises and purposes.

Faith isn't an emotion. Whenever your experience falls short of what you want, you're going to feel bad. Faith is focusing on what God says is true even when your experiences and emotions and God's promises don't seem to add up. You'll feel bad in the difficult moments of marriage. Being called to faith isn't a rebuke for negative emotions or an exhortation to work up positive ones but a call to maintain your focus on God's promises, love, and faithfulness even when they aren't visible in your marriage.

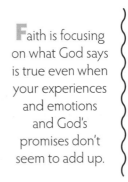

Faith is focusing on what God says is true even when your experiences and emotions and God's promises don't seem to add up.

True faith is most obvious when it empowers you to action that's *opposite* to your emotions. Doing what you feel like doing doesn't take faith. Faith, being focused on the unseen person and activity of God, often calls you to move against your fears, doubts, disappointment, and anger. That doesn't mean that you have to deny those feelings. On the contrary, you have the freedom to acknowledge and confess them because you aren't allowing yourself to be defined by them. In your marriage, you choose to act not just because you feel things but because you're moved by another relationship that's more powerful, your relationship with God. The power of that relationship becomes most obvious when it moves you to do what God wants, rather than what you want.

Active, Not Passive

"This is what the ancients were commended for" (Hebrews 11:2). To learn faith we need examples, and Hebrews 11 is full of them, from the well-known heroes of faith like Noah, Abraham, and Moses to the lesser known like Abel, Enoch, and Rahab. In all of them, what jumps out is that they were people of action. So often we think of faith as passive. (Not only do we think of it as an emotion but an emotion that, more or less, happens *to* you.) But in each of the examples in Hebrews 11, God's people are engaged in taking action. Noah builds a boat on dry land in a world that's never seen rain. Abraham and his family leave civilization and comfort to take a journey to a new home they've never seen. Rahab turns her back on everything she's ever known in Jericho to throw in her lot with the Israelites. The list goes on. These are men and women who took action, and the Bible helps us see how their actions made a difference.

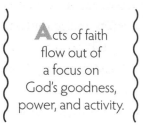

Acts of faith flow out of a focus on God's goodness, power, and activity.

Not panicked reactions, rash grabs at control, or prideful attempts to be heroic, these people's actions were responses to God's promises. Hebrews 11:6 states, "And without faith it is impossible to please God, because anyone who comes to him must believe that he exists and that he rewards those who earnestly seek him."

Faith rests on this most basic of beliefs: the belief that God is real, he takes action, and he rewards those who seek him. Everyone named in Hebrews 11 trusted in a God they couldn't see who acted in ways they didn't expect. Nevertheless, they believed that the invisible God would bless them if they sought and trusted him.

Acts of faith flow out of a focus on God's goodness, power, and activity. Why would you respond to your spouse's harshness with gentleness? Why would you choose to speak truth when it would be easier to remain silent? Why would you undertake an act of kindness when kindness won't be returned? Because you believe there's another actor on the scene. Though you can't see him, you know that he's good and rewards those who seek him.

Faith Means Knowing That God Is Active

Exodus 17 provides an interesting picture of how faith in God's activity empowers our actions. God has just freed the Israelites from their captivity in Egypt. They've seen amazing displays of God's power: plagues of frogs and flies, the Nile River turned to blood, the Red Sea parted, food and water miraculously provided. God has been visibly active and has proven his love. In chapter 17, however, for the first time, God asks the Israelites to do more than observe his activity and power. He asks them to take up arms and fight a fierce enemy, the Amalekites.

Fighting men were chosen and sent out to battle. Moses took up a position on a nearby hill, and just as he did at the shore of the Red Sea, he raised his staff in the air calling on God's blessing and power. At first all was well, but as the battle raged on and on, Moses' arms tired and began to sag. As long as Moses' arms were raised the Israelites were winning, but whenever Moses' arms fell the Israelites began to lose. Finally, Moses was given a stone to sit on, while a man on either side of him held his arms up for him.

An old man sitting on a stone with a staff in his hands and two other men holding up his arms for him. What an odd picture. What does it mean? The most obvious meaning is that God was the one who was ultimately fighting the Amalekites and determining the outcome of the battle. As long as Moses held up his staff, the symbol of God's presence and power in Moses, God was active in the battle. But remember, there were real people in the field of battle shouting, wielding weapons, sweating, and bleeding. God was in the battle, but he was acting in and through his people. Israel was called to action with the understanding that God would work through them to determine the outcome.

Faith Means Looking to the Savior Whose Arms Never Grow Tired

Exodus 17 also reminds us that we need a Savior whose arms don't get tired. I don't know if the Israelites could see Moses up on the hill with his arms raised, but I can imagine either being a warrior in the field or a loved one nervously watching the pitched battle with one eye on the battle and the other on Moses. I wouldn't be afraid that God was not for us but that our mediator, the man who stood as our representative, wasn't up to the task. Wouldn't it be terrifying to think that your life rested on the muscle tone of a man in his eighties!

Thankfully, Hebrews takes us further even than Moses. The list of Hebrews 11 reaches a crescendo in chapter 12 as we're reminded of our great Savior, Jesus.

> Let us fix our eyes on Jesus, the author and perfecter of our faith, who for the joy set before him endured the cross, scorning its shame, and sat down at the right hand of the throne of God. (Hebrews 12:2)

In Jesus we have a Savior who has known and lived through all of our battles without faltering or failing. Jesus stretched out his arms—in a very different way—on our behalf.

Think about It

- If you've ever experienced it, how does it feel to think that your actions make no difference? How did you get out of that frame of mind?
- Can you think of examples when your spouse's actions, not his or her words, really impacted you? Over the next week take special note of how you're acting around your spouse. Notice how your spouse responds. Make a special effort to enact a small kindness.
- Make Jesus your treasure so you aren't ruled by disappointments in your marriage. Can you think of things that Jesus has said or done that are especially powerful to you? If so, write them down and spend time meditating on them and thanking him for them. In what other ways do you connect to Jesus' love?
- Choose an example from Hebrews 11, or elsewhere in the Bible, or in your own experience of someone who lived out of faith. (Remember, faith isn't about feeling confident but about taking right and loving action in the face of negative emotions.) How do you live differently than this person? Pray and ask God to show you what right and loving actions you need to take to live by faith this week.

eighteen
Knowing Your Story

What You'll Learn in This Chapter:

- Our marriages are unfolding stories, not just a series of random events or a collection of facts. The way we understand and retell the story of our marriages to ourselves and others shapes the way we live in our marriages.
- The Bible is the story of God's marriage with his people. Though his people often understood it differently in the moment, it was always a story of his faithfulness in the midst of their brokenness and sin. God regularly warns his people to be careful how they remember things and to practice getting the story right, for their own sakes.
- Just like Israel, we need to be able to spot and feed on the manna, the daily bread that God provides for us.

What's the Story?

My Parents' Story

One Saturday morning when I was a young boy my father stepped out of the house with tools in hand and a look of determination on his face. For weeks my mother had been asking him to repair a hole (apparently created by squirrels) far up on the side of our house, and he had decided that it was time to take care of the problem. I don't remember seeing my mother's face, but I'm sure she was smiling to herself as she heard the ladder clank up against the side of the house and the sound of hammer and nails. Within minutes my father was back in the house, having apparently made quick work of the problem. My mother, eager to behold the sight of her home without a hole in it, stepped around the side of the house and stared dumbfounded at my father's handiwork. He had taken an old, weather-beaten license plate and nailed it over the hole. In my father's defense, I suspect he considered this a temporary patch, but nonetheless, my mother was not happy to see a license plate, no matter how temporary, emblazoned on the side of the house.

> Couples who have a positive view of their story are able to maintain a positive view of each other and their marriage.

I was too young to be privy to the conversations that followed, but I'm fairly certain that both had that ordinary moment feeling I described in the first chapter of the book—that awful frustrating feeling of having lived through this marital moment far too many times. I'm sure it was not the first time my mother felt like my father didn't care about something important to her, and it was not the first time my father felt unfairly criticized. But as frustrating as that moment was for them, they're able to laugh about it now because they've worked on their marriage for forty-five years, and many problems that once seemed maddening and impenetrable now seem almost silly. This small episode, once marked by frustration, has become part of a bigger story of continuing growth and joy in the Lord Jesus.

Knowing Where You've Been Has Everything to Do with Where You're Going

John Gottman, PhD, a well-known researcher and author on the subject of marriage, argues that one measure of the strength of a marriage is how husbands and wives view their past—how they tell their story. Couples who have a positive view of their story are able to maintain a positive view of each other and their marriage. In fact, reflecting on the positives of their history becomes a resource for handling present challenges.[22]

If you don't have a positive view of your marriage, Gottman's findings probably aren't that encouraging to you. But perhaps there's more to appreciate about your story than you realize. Understand that your history isn't just a collection of dates and facts. It is a *story*. When you reflect on your history, you actively interpret it, highlighting some parts, downplaying others, and choosing words and images that provide a framework of meaning, purpose, and direction. Unhappy couples often remember their story in a way that highlights the pain and struggle and edit out the positive parts, even God himself. Having a positive sense of the story of your marriage isn't just a matter of getting your facts straight but of letting God provide an interpretive framework of meaning and purpose that provides hope and connects you to Jesus.

God Tells His People Their Story

The Bible itself is the story of a marriage—God's marriage to his people. Throughout his relationship with them, in the most discouraging moments, God challenges them to revisit and reinterpret their story. The question is: Does the story strengthen the marriage or weaken it? It often depends on who's telling the story, God or his people. The

Israelites' deliverance from Israel and their journey through the wilderness provides a good example.

Rescued or Abandoned?

After four hundred years of slavery, in a miraculous and powerful display of his love, God delivers his people. Like a husband rescuing his bride from a villain, God demands and secures her freedom with displays of power that shake Egypt to its core. God unleashes plagues of flies, boils, locusts, and hail. The Nile River turns to blood, for three days darkness covers the land, and finally, every firstborn son of the Egyptians is killed (Exodus 7—11).

God's purpose in it all is that Israel love and worship only him. After their dramatic and bold rescue, Israel spends forty years on a slow walk through the desert on their way to the land God has promised them. When Israel encounters hardships and problems, they utter ordinary complaints that display a faulty memory.

Having barely begun their journey, Israel begins to doubt God's goodness. Trapped by Pharaoh's army, just before God parts the Red Sea, Israel cries out to Moses,

> Was it because there were no graves in Egypt that you brought us to the desert to die? What have you done to us by bringing us out of Egypt? Didn't we say to you in Egypt, "Leave us alone; let us serve the Egyptians"? It would have been better for us to serve the Egyptians than to die in the desert! (Exodus 14:11–12)

And soon after,

> In the desert the whole community grumbled against Moses and Aaron. The Israelites said to them, "If only we had died by the LORD's hand in Egypt! There we sat around pots of meat and ate all the food we wanted, but you have brought

us out into this desert to starve this entire assembly to death."
(Exodus 16:2–3)

Israel even complained about the manna, the bread that miraculously appeared every morning saying, "If only we had meat to eat! We remember the fish we ate in Egypt at no cost—also the cucumbers, melons, leeks, onions and garlic. But now we have lost our appetite; we never see anything but this manna!" (Numbers 11:4b–6).

Already Israel is telling herself the story in a way that can only lead to unhappiness and failure. They remember Egypt as a land of plenty, as if they'd been well fed and happy, and they think of God as a thief who snatched them from their home and abused them. They have the story all wrong. As the book of Exodus opens, they're miserable slaves crying out to God for deliverance:

> The Israelites groaned in their slavery and cried out, and
> their cry for help because of their slavery went up to God.
> God heard their groaning and he remembered his covenant
> with Abraham, with Isaac and with Jacob. So God looked
> on the Israelites and was concerned about them. (Exodus
> 2:23–25)

God Teaches Us How to Remember

At the end of their long journey, just as Israel is poised to enter her new home, God shares his perspective on their decades in the wilderness. Not surprisingly, it's a very different version of events:

> Remember how the LORD your God led you all the way in
> the desert these forty years, to humble you and to test you in
> order to know what was in your heart, whether or not you
> would keep his commands. He humbled you, causing you to
> hunger and then feeding you with manna, which neither you
> nor your fathers had known, to teach you that man does not

live on bread alone but on every word that comes from the mouth of the LORD. Your clothes did not wear out and your feet did not swell during these forty years. Know then in your heart that as a man disciplines his son, so the LORD your God disciplines you. (Deuteronomy 8:2–5)

There's a lot to appreciate in this passage and to apply to our own lives and marriages.

Remember

God commands us to remember how he's been active in our hardships. Our remembering flows out of worship and reflects faith and love, or idolatry and self.

To Know What Was in Your Heart

Israel's hardship was a test that God used to reveal their hearts. We associate tests with students sitting down with paper and pencil prepared to pass or fail. Most often, however, the Bible uses "test" the way a goldsmith or silversmith would use it. The metallurgist heats or otherwise tries and tests a metal to reveal and remove impurities, leaving a richer, stronger, purer metal. God knew the impurities that lay in the hearts of his people before he led them out of Egypt, but those impurities needed to be exposed so that the people could see them and God could remove them. In the wilderness there were no Egyptians to blame and no distractions that might allow them to avoid the subject. It was just Israel, God, and the desert crucible. Our histories serve the same purpose, showing us what we're really like and giving us an accurate understanding of ourselves and our real needs.

To Teach You

What does God's testing of Israel reveal? The hardships provoke grumbling and hopelessness and reveal hearts that crave safety and comfort—hearts that want to trust self, not God.

How does God go about teaching Israel to trust and turn to him? He *causes* hunger. God intentionally leads them to where they experience their need—along with their inability to meet their need on their own. Then he *feeds* them manna, a miraculous food that requires the one eating it to trust God (but more about manna later).

Hardship may reveal your own mistakes and foolishness but by no means indicates God's absence. On the contrary, he asks you to experience all the ways that you need him, and then he asks you to turn to him as your Savior.

> God's motives in the journey are the same as a parent who wants what's best for his child.

His Faithfulness

God reminds Israel that he's been with them and met their needs every step of the way. They were clothed, fed, cared for, and strengthened to complete their journey. He never left or abandoned them. Elsewhere in the Bible, God's relationship with Israel is described as that of a husband to a wife; here, however, the relationship is described as that of a father who disciplines his children. God's motives in the journey are the same as a parent who wants what's best for his child. God doesn't lead Israel into hardship because he's callous, indifferent, or mean-spirited, but because he loves his people and wants to see them mature and become the sons and daughters they were created to become.

When we recall our stories, we need to remember that we've been accompanied by God, our loving Father, who leads us through trials, but only out of love so that we can mature as his children and learn to depend on him rather than ourselves. Your marriage isn't a sign of God's wrath or abandonment. Even in the hardest moments, your loving Father has been there to reveal and meet your deepest needs.

Dangers of Forgetting

God's command to remember precedes a warning about the consequences of forgetting. Picturing their satisfaction and happiness living in the Promised Land, God warns, "You may say to yourself, 'My power and the strength of my hands have produced this wealth for me'" (Deuteronomy 8:17). When that happens, he adds, they're surely on the path to idolatry—on the path to destruction. The danger of a faulty memory isn't merely unhappiness; a faulty memory sets you on a course of pride, rebellion, and destruction.

Like every aspect of our lives, our memories are shaped by the condition of our worshipping hearts. Apart from God we're inclined to interpret our lives, including our past, as evidence that God doesn't care for us. Whatever our ills, they're his fault; whatever our blessings, they're a testament to our virtue or ability. An important part of worshipping God and protecting our hearts and our marriages is remembering by faith. As you revisit your history, look for the ways it reveals your need for Jesus and the ways that God has been drawing you to himself.

Daily Bread

If you're a follower of Jesus, Israel's story is your story. If you're connected to Jesus, then your history stretches back to the very first people of faith. Referring to Israel's trials in the wilderness, the apostle Paul writes, "Now these things occurred as examples to keep us from setting our hearts on evil things as they did" (1 Corinthians 10:6). In other words, knowing how your story is like theirs can keep you on track in the present. We may be separated by thousands of years of history and culture, but in our hearts we're more like Israel than we're different from them. We can use their story to make sense of our own.

An important part of the wilderness story is God's provision of daily bread for his people—a picture of his daily presence and love.

Early on, God begins to supply Israel with manna, a breadlike substance that appears on the ground every morning. The Bible describes it this way:

> The manna was like coriander seed and looked like resin.
> The people went around gathering it, and then ground it in
> a handmill or crushed it in a mortar. They cooked it in a pot
> or made it into cakes. And it tasted like something made
> with olive oil. When the dew settled on the camp at night, the
> manna also came down. (Numbers 11:7–9)

The manna has peculiar qualities that are meant to be instructional. It appears every day, and there's as much as is needed for that day and no more; once the sun grows hot it melts away (Exodus 16:17–18, 21). If the Israelites gather more than they need, the next day the leftovers will smell and be infested with maggots (Exodus 16:19–20). Also, no manna appears on the Sabbath, the mandated day of rest and worship. Instead, the Israelites gather twice as much as they need the day before so that they'll not break the Sabbath. What are we to learn from this miraculous bread?

Learning to Trust God One Day at a Time

As God's warning about forgetting teaches, our own sinful nature will always steer us away from God, toward self-reliance. It's like driving a car that needs an alignment. If you let go of the wheel even for a second, you drift toward the ditch. So, in his wisdom, God takes that into account in the way he loves us. It would have been a disaster if God had sent Israel on her way from Egypt to the Promised Land with everything she needed and met her on the other side. Even with his daily presence Israel doubted his goodness and trusted in herself. How much more so if he had given her everything she needed. The manna, God's provision given in daily increments, shows exactly how we need to be loved and how we ought to calibrate our expectations of him.

Wouldn't it be nice if God waved a magic wand and gave us perfect marriages this instant? But if this happened, instead of having to trust God day to day, wouldn't you take the credit for your success? Rather than becoming angry and disappointed with God for what's lacking in your marriage, expect him to walk with you as he did with Israel, and watch for his faithfulness day by day.

God Works in the Ordinary Details of Life

Bread is a basic food. Sure, God could have provided lobster bisque, but there's a message in the fact that he provided bread. God wants us to humbly accept what we need, and he does not feed our lusts by providing us with everything we want. God recognizes that he loves sinners with idolatrous cravings and fears. It isn't love to give us everything we want. Anyone with children already knows this. Sometimes God surprises us with something spectacular that we asked for, but we must be willing to humbly accept what we need from God and trust him to decide what that is.

Jesus, Our Daily Bread

Jesus said to them, "I tell you the truth, it is not Moses who has given you the bread from heaven, but is my Father who gives you the true bread from heaven. For the bread of God is he who comes down from heaven and gives life to the world." "Sir," they said, "from now on give us this bread." Then Jesus declared, "I am the bread of life. He who comes to me will never go hungry, and he who believes in me will never be thirsty." (John 6:32–35)

Obviously, what we need in our marriages isn't physical bread but spiritual. Physical bread is important when you're in danger of physical starvation; spiritual bread is important when you're in danger of starving in your marriage.

We started this journey together appreciating that ultimately marriage and everything else points us to Jesus. As you live through the details of day-to-day marriage, there are encouraging signs of God's activity, love, and concern. But every day, whatever the circumstances, Jesus himself, the gift of God's love, is always with you and will never leave you. Whatever your aches and longings, remember that marriage was ever only intended to draw you closer to him.

> But every day, whatever the circumstances, Jesus himself, the gift of God's love, is always with you and will never leave you.

I counseled a woman once whose husband seemed withdrawn and indifferent to her. There was a lot of unspoken hurt and anger on her part. She had believed that love meant holding her tongue and overlooking it all. Meanwhile, she was dying on the inside, and her marriage was becoming colder and colder. I encouraged her to begin speaking the truth in love by sharing her thoughts and feelings, including her anger and hurt, with her husband, inviting him to open up.

She came back to counseling disheartened. She'd started speaking up, and they'd had several arguments that week. Her husband seemed as angry as she. She felt discouraged and questioned the wisdom of my advice. Rather than seeing this as a defeat I encouraged her to see it as God's provision—as manna. Even in his anger, her husband was beginning to engage with her. It was uncomfortable, but compared with the relational coldness of the week before, angry engagement was a step in the right direction. As she took courage in God's involvement, she was able to engage her husband with greater faith and love.

The Rest of the Story

My faith and my own marriage have been strengthened because of the highs and the lows in my parents' marriage. I've seen God cause my parents to hunger and then feed them the manna of his grace and love. As I've watched their marriage change and grow over the years, I've seen the story of Jesus himself emerging.

Let me put the license plate story in context:

My father was not trying to be funny when he nailed that license plate to the side of the house. He was raised on a working farm in a large family. And in the world he grew up in, functionality always took place over form. It didn't matter what it looked like as long as the job was done. That's life on a farm. But even more important to him was the safety, belonging, and acceptance that was abundant there. He and his siblings functioned as their own tribe, working, playing, laughing, and crying side by side. They loved the farm, but it was only a container for the joy of family they shared. The farm only had to function; it only had to be a place for them to be family; it didn't have to look good.

> God uses the mundane to show his love in Christ to you and the world around you.

My mother was not being vain when she was horrified to see that license plate up on the side of the house. She was raised in an upper-middle-class family. Her father owned and her mother helped operate a successful business in a town where image mattered. In her family, success and appearances shaped relationships and one's standing in the community. Taking care of things was just part of making good use of your resources and being successful with them.

Both families were onto something: acceptance and belonging are important as is hard work and taking care of what you have. But sometimes, in ordinary moments, my mother's sense of responsibility and stewardship collided with my father's sense of belonging. Frustrating? Yes. Painful? Yes. A mistake? No. Over the years God has schooled them both in the strengths and weaknesses that they brought to marriage. My father has learned that belonging isn't the whole story of love, and that loving his wife means paying attention to details that seem unimportant even when it takes more time. My mother, on the other hand, has learned that sometimes it's important to sacrifice the appearance or care of things for the sake of others; that being patient and gentle in God's eyes is more important than how we might appear to anyone else. Through it all they've learned to lean more and more upon the love of Jesus. If they'd made their love for each other conditional upon getting what they wanted, they'd have been lost in the wilderness for sure. Marriage has been a wonderful classroom for them, and for anyone who has cared to notice them.

Manna

A couple of summers ago I sat on the beach with my father watching the waves roll in as the kids played in the sand.

My father started telling me the story of how when he was a young man he was with a couple of other guys who yelled an ugly racial slur at an elderly black man crossing the street in front of their car. My father didn't yell anything at the man, but he didn't chastise or stop his friends either. He told me on the beach that day that he would never forget the look on that man's face—pain mingled with quiet dignity. He told me that from that time on he's done his utmost to prevent another person from feeling what that man must have felt, determined never again to deserve the weight of that man's gaze.

After a few minutes my father started what, at first, seemed a new topic until I realized the connection. "You know, the other guys in our Bible study rib me about this, but over the last six months or so I've made it a point to wipe down the tiles after I take my shower in the morning," my father started. The significance of this wasn't lost on me. My mother toiled for years living with three men (my father, brother, and me) who never really got the hang of picking up after themselves and taking care of things the way they should—kind of like that hole in the side of the house. My father continued, "I've come to understand that the details count as much as anything. It's in the details that we have the chance to show Jesus how much we love him by loving others." I don't think I could have said it better.

In my father's stories I see the power of love expressed in simple, ordinary moments. The power of an African-American man's penetrating gaze, who probably will never know how his simple response changed my father's life. The love of a husband who thinks to wipe down the shower stall. I'm amazed that the God of the entire universe would make himself visible in those moments and bless me with eyes to see and be encouraged.

What's the Story of Your Marriage?

In *The Fellowship of the Ring* by J. R. R. Tolkien, an unlikely group of characters setting out on a daunting quest receives this bit of encouragement from a wise person:

> The road must be trod, but it will be very hard. And neither strength nor wisdom will carry us far upon it. This quest may be attempted by the weak with as much hope as the strong. Yet such is oft the course of deeds that move the wheels of the world: small hands do them because they must, while the eyes of the great are elsewhere.[23]

The same words can apply to marriage. What we do with our "small hands," the seemingly unimportant everyday tasks of marriage, is of the utmost importance. God uses the mundane to show his love in Christ to you and the world around you. The "eyes of the great" may look elsewhere to find meaning and purpose and joy, but you have an opportunity in the ordinary moments of your marriage to make choices that really matter.

So what's your story? Why did God have you marry the person you married? How do your struggles help you to see yourself and your need for Christ more clearly? How will you make the most of every ordinary moment of your marriage so the amazing story of God's love for us is written in letters as large as your life?

Think about It

- Think about your story, even before you were married. What have the difficulties in your life and relationships taught you about yourself? Do you see any themes or patterns?
- Can you think of an event in your marriage that captures the story of your marriage, the highs and the lows, the beauty and the struggles?
- Can you think of ways that God has met your needs in ways that you couldn't? In particular, how has he taught you to seek and trust him above all else?
- Recall moments in your marriage that show God's faithfulness and care. Did something wonderful happen unexpectedly? Did things turn out better than you thought?
- Where does God offer you daily bread in your marriage? Where do you find tangible evidence of his love and care?

Notes

1. There are different types and forms of love. Obviously, marital love is different in many ways than friendship or the love parents have for children, etc. While love takes different forms depending on the nature of the relationship, all love finds its origin and purpose in God himself. In other words, I'm not denying that there are differences between God's love and ours; I'm simply pointing out that the Bible expects our love in its various forms to be expressions of God's love.

2. Willard F. Harley Jr., *His Needs Her Needs: Building an Affair-Proof Marriage* (Grand Rapids, MI: Fleming H. Revell, 1986), 18–20.

3. C. S. Lewis, *Mere Christianity* (San Francisco: Harpers, 1952), 188.

4. In many translations verse 23 is indented and formatted as a couplet to indicate that it is poetic verse or song. That doesn't necessarily mean that Adam broke out in verse at this moment, but clearly it is portrayed as a very powerful and moving moment.

5. Many commentators have considered God's use of "us" and "our" as references to the Trinity, but there are other ways of interpreting it. Understand, however, that the doctrine of the Trinity and our corresponding relational nature are established in many other

passages in the Bible regardless of how one understands "we" or "us" in this verse.

6. C. S. Lewis, *The Weight of Glory* (New York: The Macmillan Company, 1949), 2.

7. C. John Miller, *The Heart of a Servant Leader: Letters from Jack Miller*, ed. Barbara Miller Juliani (Phillipsburg, NJ: P & R Publishing, 2004), 146.

8. Dan Allender and Tremper Longman III, *Intimate Allies* (Wheaton, IL: Tyndale House Publishers, Inc., 1995), 33–35.

9. Lewis, *The Weight of Glory*, 14–15.

10. These three styles or patterns of relating to others were first observed, to my knowledge, by psychoanalyst Karen Horneye, who in various publications, most notably including *Our Inner Conflicts* (New York: W. W. Norton & Company, Inc., 1945), described these three patterns of relating as "neurotic trends" that were expressions of basic attitudes toward self and others. Much later Michael Bobick independently observed in his doctor of ministry project these same three patterns of relating and explained them as distorted expressions of what have been called the "three offices of man" described in the Bible as prophet, priest, and king. Dr. John Bettler, giving credit to both, shared these observations in counseling courses he taught at Westminster Theological Seminary.

11. This term was first used by anthropologist Gregory Bateson in the 1950s as he studied patterns of communication within families. Bateson and his colleagues' research laid important groundwork for what would become family systems theory.

12. Ken Sande, *The Peacemaker: A Biblical Guide to Resolving Personal Conflict*, 2nd ed. (Grand Rapids, MI: Baker Books, 1991), 17–21.

13. Michael E. McCullough, Kenneth I. Pargament, and Carl E. Thoresen, *Forgiveness: Theory, Research, and Practice* (New York: Guilford Press, 2000), 7.

14. Ibid., 9.

15. Deborah Blum, *Sex on the Brain: The Biological Differences Between Men and Women* (New York: Penguin Group, 1997), 66–68.

16. C. S. Lewis, *The Four Loves* (New York: Harcourt Brace, 1960), 66–67.

17. Jerry Bridges, *Transforming Grace: Living Confidently in God's Unfailing Love* (Colorado Springs, CO: NavPress, 1991), 21–22.

18. Ibid., 20.

19. Rose Marie Miller, *From Fear to Freedom: Living as Sons and Daughters of God* (Wheaton, IL: Harold Shaw Publishers, 1994), 4–5.

20. Martin E. Seligman and Steven F. Maier, "Failure to escape traumatic shock," *Journal of Experimental Psychology: General* 74, no. 1 (1967): 1–9.

21. Edward T. Welch, *Depression: A Stubborn Darkness* (Winston-Salem, NC: Punch Press, 2004), 260.

22. John M. Gottman and Nan Silver, *The Seven Principles for Making Marriage Work* (New York: Three Rivers Press, 1999), 63, 70.

23. J. R. R. Tolkien, *The Fellowship of the Ring* (New York: Houghton Mifflin Company, 1988), 283.

Scripture Index

Genesis

1	64, 65
1:4, 10, 12, 18, 21, 25	58
1:26–28	64
2	64, 65, 66, 95, 220
2:17b	98
2:18	58, 59
2:21–22	59
2:23	60
2:24	60, 63, 66, 95
2:25	97
3	98
3:7	97
3:8	98
3:14–19	140
3:15	140, 141
32	x
32:25	x
32:26	x

Exodus

2:23–25	271
7—11	270
14:11–12	270
16:2–3	271

16:17–18, 21	275
16:19–20	275
17	264, 265
25:10–22	165

Leviticus

16:1–19	165
16:2	165
19	81
19:11, 16b, 18	81
19:17–18	156

Numbers

11:4b–6	271
11:7–9	275

Deuteronomy

6	27
6:4–5	27
8:2–5	272
8:17	274

2 Samuel

11	174

Psalms

13:1–3	209
51:3–4	174
62:8	225
71	28, 29
71:1, 5, 8	28
103:3	66
103:8	66
103:10	66
115	34, 35
115:3–7	34
115:8	34
115:12–13	35
139:1–4	224

Proverbs

9:7–8	134
10:17	189
12:18	123
12:23	123
15:23	133
17:14	138, 156
17:27	123
18:6–7	123
18:13	131
18:19	145
20:3	156
21:9	45

Isaiah

9:6	138
50	244
50:4	245
50:5–9a	245
50:10–11	248
53	258
53:3	110
53:7	258

Jeremiah

2:1–2	221

Ezekiel

16:8–14	221

Haggai

2:3, 4b, 6–7, 9	251

Matthew

5	50, 244
5–7	188
5:14–16	259
5:17	50
5:21–22	188
5:21–22, 27–28	50
5:27–28	188
5:43–45	48
5:43–48	78
5:46–47	47
5:48	50
6:19–21	260
7	82, 134
7:1–5	146
7:3–5	134
7:5	155
7:6	134
7:12	82
12:24	42
13:44	261
18	186
18:22	186
18:32–34	187
19:16–22	17
22:37–40	20
23:23–24	21
27:50–52	165

Mark

3:1–6	110
3:21	42
3:22	42
8:31–33	110
10:21	19
10:31–32	199
10:35–38	198
10:42–45	199
12:30–31	26

Luke

4:28–30	247
11:15	42
12	141, 142, 143
12:49–53	139
17:4–6	190

John

6:32–35	276
8:59	247
10:17–18	247
10:39	247
11:3	43
11:4	43
11:5–6	43
11:11–13	43
11:14b–15	44
11:25–26	44
11:27	44
11:32b	43
11:34–36	110
11:40	44
11:53–54	247
15:4–5	51, 243

Acts

2:23	249

8:1–3	142
9:1, 13, 21	142

Romans

6:16, 21, 23	67
7:18b–20	100
8	69
8:28	69
8:29	70
12:1–8	88
12:9	109
12:10, 14	109
12:15	177
12:15–16a	109
14:4	227
14:4a	83
14:9–10	84
15:7	227

1 Corinthians

1:10–17	157
5:1	157
7	157
7:3–5	230
8:1b	158
8:4	158
8:7	159
8:9–13	159
10:6	274
10:23–24	160
10:25–27	158
11:20–22	157
12	88
12:4–11	212
12:11	212
12:14–31	212
13:1–2	215
14:39–40	157

Galatians

3:26–28	202
5:22–23a	257
5:23	138
6:1–4a	256
6:7–9	255

Ephesians

1:3–6	130
4	105, 128, 130, 132, 143
4:15	105, 123
4:17–24	104
4:25	95, 104, 123
4:29	123
5	63, 143, 220
5:18b–21	204
5:22–24	208
5:22–33	143, 197
5:25–27	61, 202
5:25–29, 33	204
5:31–32	64
5:33	210
6	143
6:1–5	143
6:5–9	143
6:10–12	142
6:14–17	144

Philippians

2:3	83
2:5–7	83
4:5	214
4:8	185

Colossians

3:18–19	197

Hebrews

1:3	68
4:15–16	110
5:7	110
10:19–22	166
11	262, 263, 264, 266
11:1–2	262
11:2	263
11:6	264
12	266
12:2	266
12:14a	138

James

2	82
2:4	79
2:8	82
2:8–9	80
4:1	144
4:2	147

1 Peter

2	215
2:20b–25	62
3:1–2	63, 258
3:1–7	197
3:1, 7	215
3:7	63, 202

1 John

3:1–3	35
4:7–8	9
4:7–12	8
4:9	40
4:9–10	10
4:11–12	12
4:19	81

Revelation

19:6–8	233
19:7–9	221